AF292002

7 REECE MEWS

FRANCIS BACON'S STUDIO

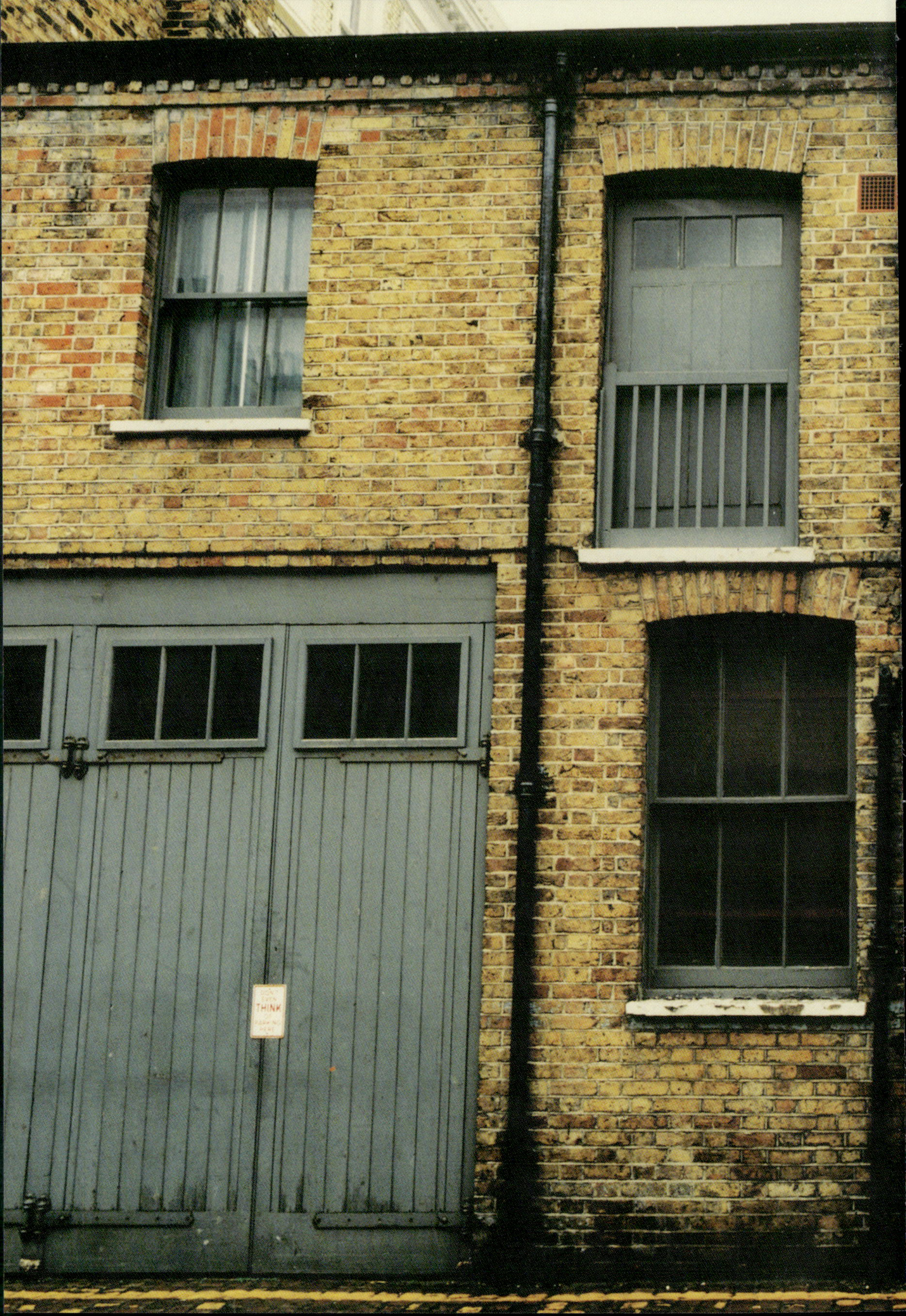
THINK

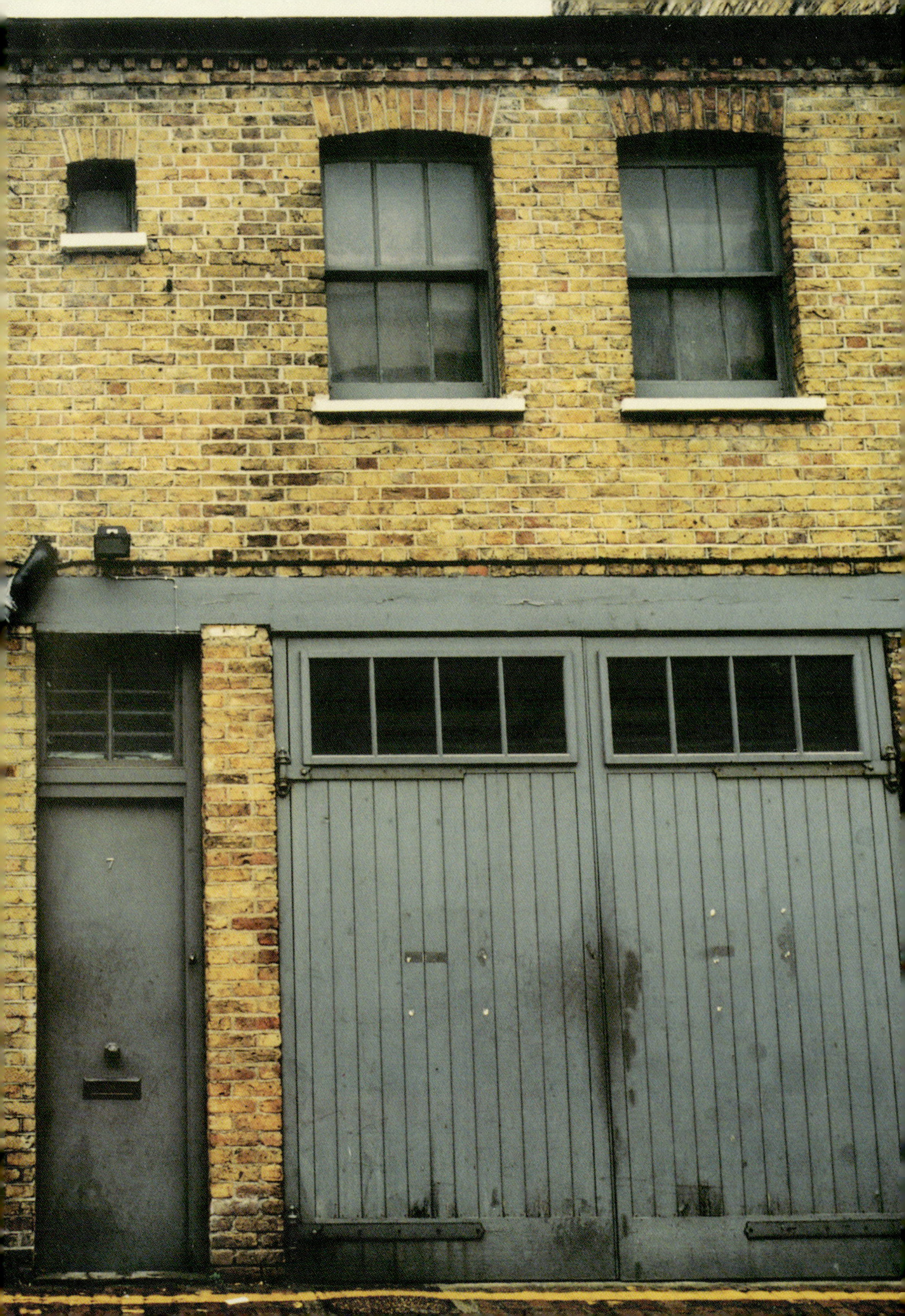

7 REECE MEWS

FRANCIS BACON'S STUDIO

Foreword by John Edwards | Photographs by Perry Ogden

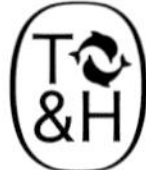

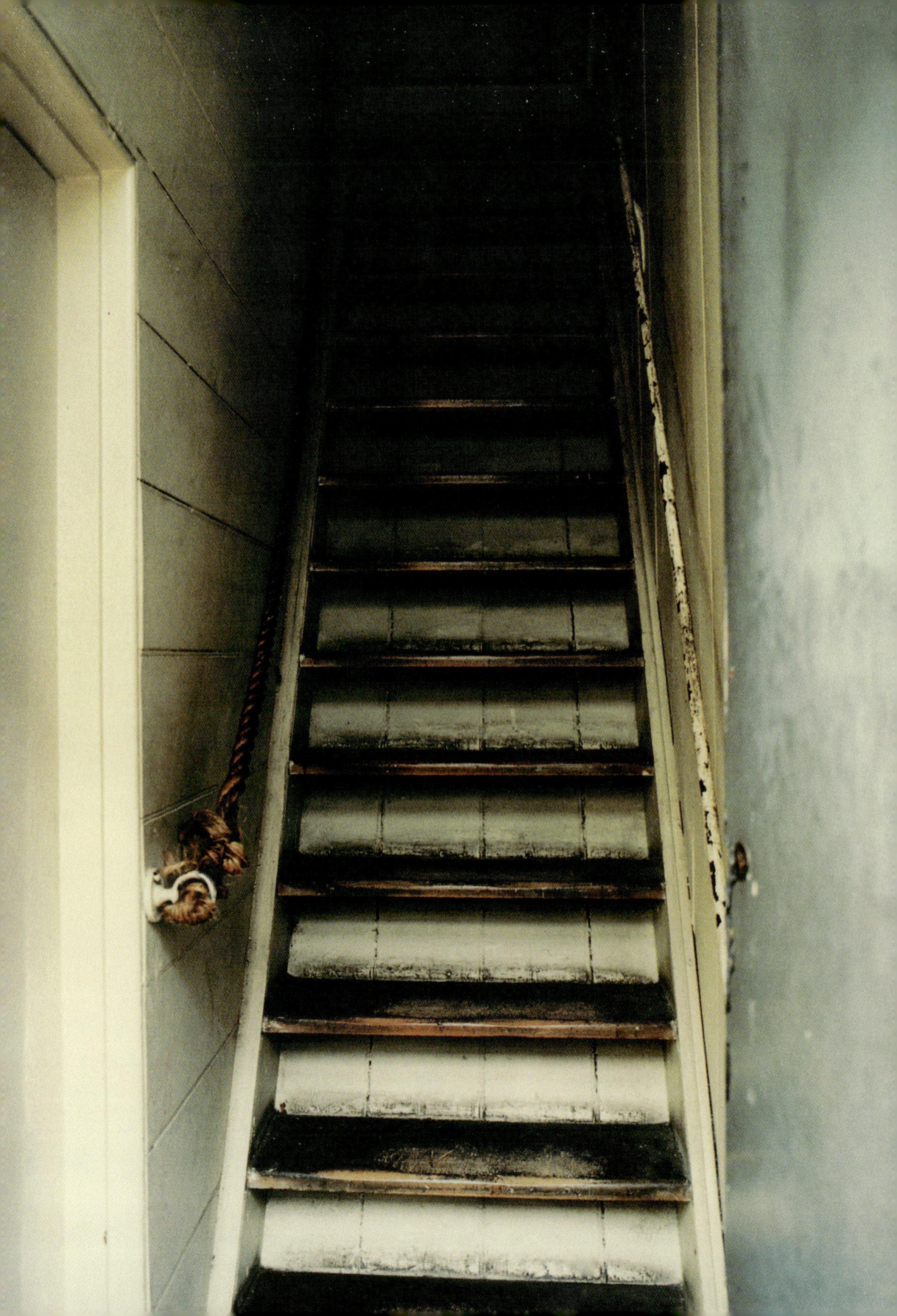

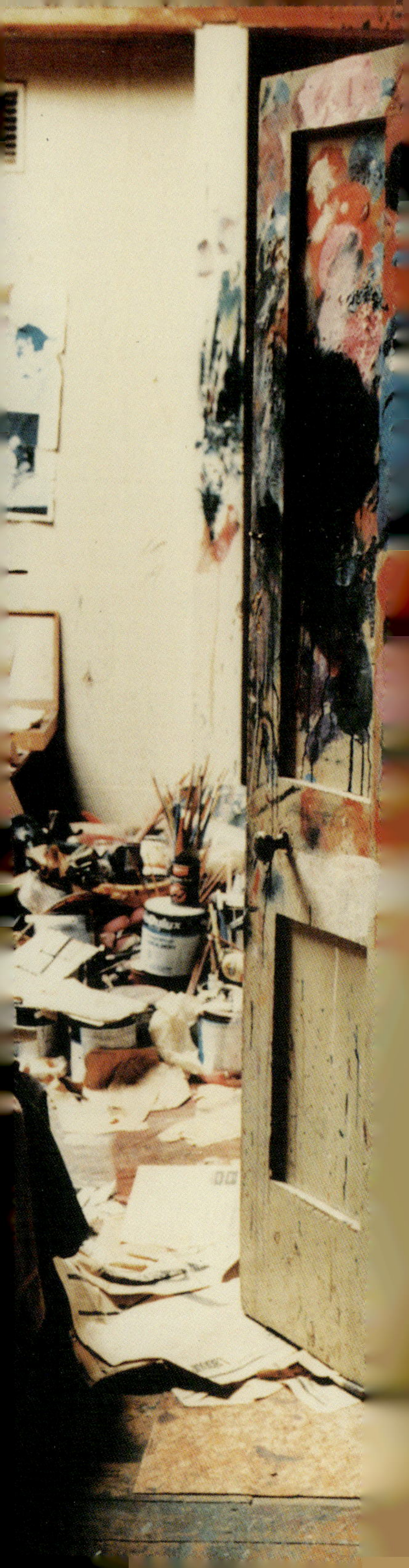

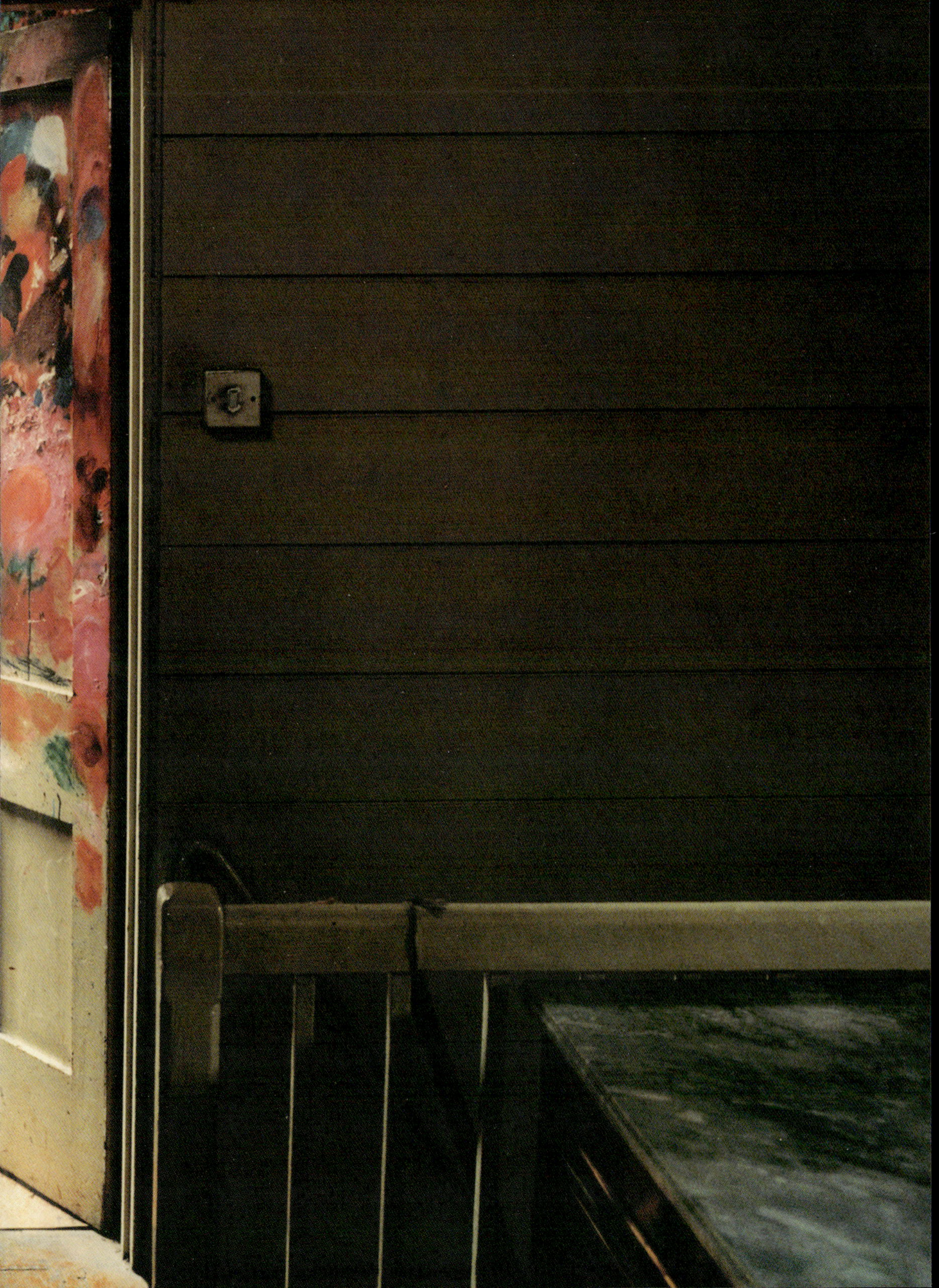

Foreword by John Edwards

Soon after I met Francis Bacon in 1976 he invited me to Reece Mews. 'People think I live grandly you know, but in fact I live in a dump.' By the time I'd climbed up the steep, wooden stairs, guided by the rope banister, I could see he was right. 'You ain't 'alf lamping it* a bit Francis', I thought to myself. I was shocked.

He opened a bottle of champagne – probably vintage Krug – and I stayed the night. He slept on the couch, and I slept on the old circular bed. It was an odd, bottle-green colour, with the headboard spattered with paint. The sofa, too, had paint stains all over it. We called its colour 'Belcher's Green' because it reminded him of his paintings of Muriel Belcher.

As we sat at the dining table in the bedsitting room I noticed the door to his studio was ajar. Through the gap I saw an unbelievable mess. In fact the chaos was much worse in those days than it was later on. I'm naturally tidy so I was puzzled by the sight of dozens of small canvases, all with holes cut into them, all over the floor and mixed up with hundreds of photographs, books and bits of cloth. 'I've been meaning to tidy up in here for a long time', he said, 'but never seem to get round to it.' I volunteered to help. 'Well, if you could, that would be wonderful. I'd gladly pay you.'

A week later, I went in and filled about ten dustbin bags with newspaper cuttings, magazines, old books and tins of old paint hardened by the years and beyond use. Everything was covered with a fine orange and pink dust. I later learned that this was the raw pigment he liked so much, but which, because he was asthmatic, was so damaging to his health.

'Lamping it' – Cockney rhyming slang for living like a tramp.

The studio had become so messy and chaotic that he couldn't move around to paint properly, and he was delighted with the tidy-up as it gave him a new freedom of movement. He seemed genuinely thrilled. He was so pleased that, in order to make even more space, he asked me to continue the process by destroying about twenty large canvases, many of which looked finished to me. I slashed them all into tiny bits with a Stanley knife. He insisted on this because in the past people had stolen discarded bits from the dustbin outside. The smaller canvases, 'postage stamps' as he called them, he destroyed himself. Even with all this editing down, each year he still managed to produce a substantial number of big paintings with which he was satisfied.

There were always hundreds of books in the studio, the kitchen/bathroom and the bedsitting room. Boxes upon boxes of letters and photographs were piled up everywhere. He liked to keep 10" × 8" transparencies of all his old paintings, but those went missing soon after his death.

Every now and then I would clear out obvious rubbish to make extra room for him. Miss Beston from the Marlborough Gallery would also often come round and clean up when he was away, but that always ended up with him not being able to find things. 'Oh! I can't find a thing', he'd shout. His own mess had some kind of order that he understood, and he could generally find what he wanted.

Francis wouldn't allow anyone to smoke in the studio, but I must confess that I sometimes did. He had a fear of fire and was terrified at the prospect of the studio, with all its turpentine, dry paper and wood, going up in smoke. He allowed only his closest friends into the studio. They would often ask him why he didn't clear it out totally or build another floor on top to give himself more space, but he told me that he feared that that would be far too big an interruption to his working days. He never made any attempt to change the building in any way.

During the time I was destroying those canvases, to my great surprise, thick wads of banknotes tied with elastic bands began to fall out from between the canvas and stretcher. Substantial sums of cash he'd hidden there and forgotten about. Probably winnings from the casino. 'I often hide my cash in there but I can't ever remember quite where. I got into the habit to hide it from George Dyer.' Many of these rolls of cash were so old that they were no longer legal currency. When I showed him the wads of dusty pounds and French francs he roared with laughter and said I could keep them. Most of the money was out of date, but there were still a few hundred pounds that were good and I was very glad of it at the time.

On another occasion, a smaller clean-up this time, we had to search for a Patek Philippe watch he had hidden in a sock. No matter how hard or for how long we tried we couldn't find that watch, and even when the archaeologists from the Hugh Lane Gallery dismantled the studio it didn't turn up. Francis used old socks and bits of corduroy trousers to press into wet paint to create a particular texture he liked. The watch must have been thrown out with the hardened socks in one of our many clear-outs over the years.

He loved the mornings, that's when he worked best, and even after very late nights of drinking that floored me – thirty years younger than him – he'd always be in the studio bright and early, painting.

He loved it in that little room and said he could work better in there than in any studio he'd ever had. Even though he was offered grand studio spaces many times, he never considered moving. South Kensington was his favourite part of London, and he loathed the countryside. He liked the routines of South Ken life, taking his bedsheets and towels to be laundered in Harrington Road and his shirts to another little laundry in Glendower Place. He told me proudly that they did everything by hand there. He did all his own cooking, and was a very good cook indeed, often using Château Pétrus to make stocks.

By day, his time was spent between the studio and the kitchen/ bathroom. In the winter months he found it cosy to sit by the gas oven with the door open to keep him warm, especially if he was having a bath later. The bedsitter was for nights and for drinking. The studio was only for work and had a different atmosphere. I would often sit in there talking to him as he painted. He held the brush like a sword and stood far back from the canvas, like he was fencing with an unseen opponent. I never saw him clean his brushes, but he'd occasionally wipe them on his dressing gown or on an old sock or shirt.

He would sometimes draw on tracing paper, slowly mirroring images underneath. He saw no value in these sketches, though, and thoughtlessly discarded them later. He never drank while he painted but when he'd finished he'd come and have a glass of wine with me in the kitchen.

Early in our friendship he told me and his friends that he intended leaving Reece Mews to me in his will, and he often asked what I would do with it when he'd gone. I told him I'd probably leave it as it was because I liked the studio too, but he encouraged me to build up and add another floor. I have now fulfilled that wish, and the studio, which was for so many years the heart of our home, is now in Dublin. A little corner of South Kensington moved to Ireland, his birthplace. The thousands of papers, books, photos, the rotted curtains, the moth-eaten bedspread, the brushes and paints, the discarded canvases – all in Dublin. I think it would have made him roar with laughter, his own special laugh, full of warmth and joy.

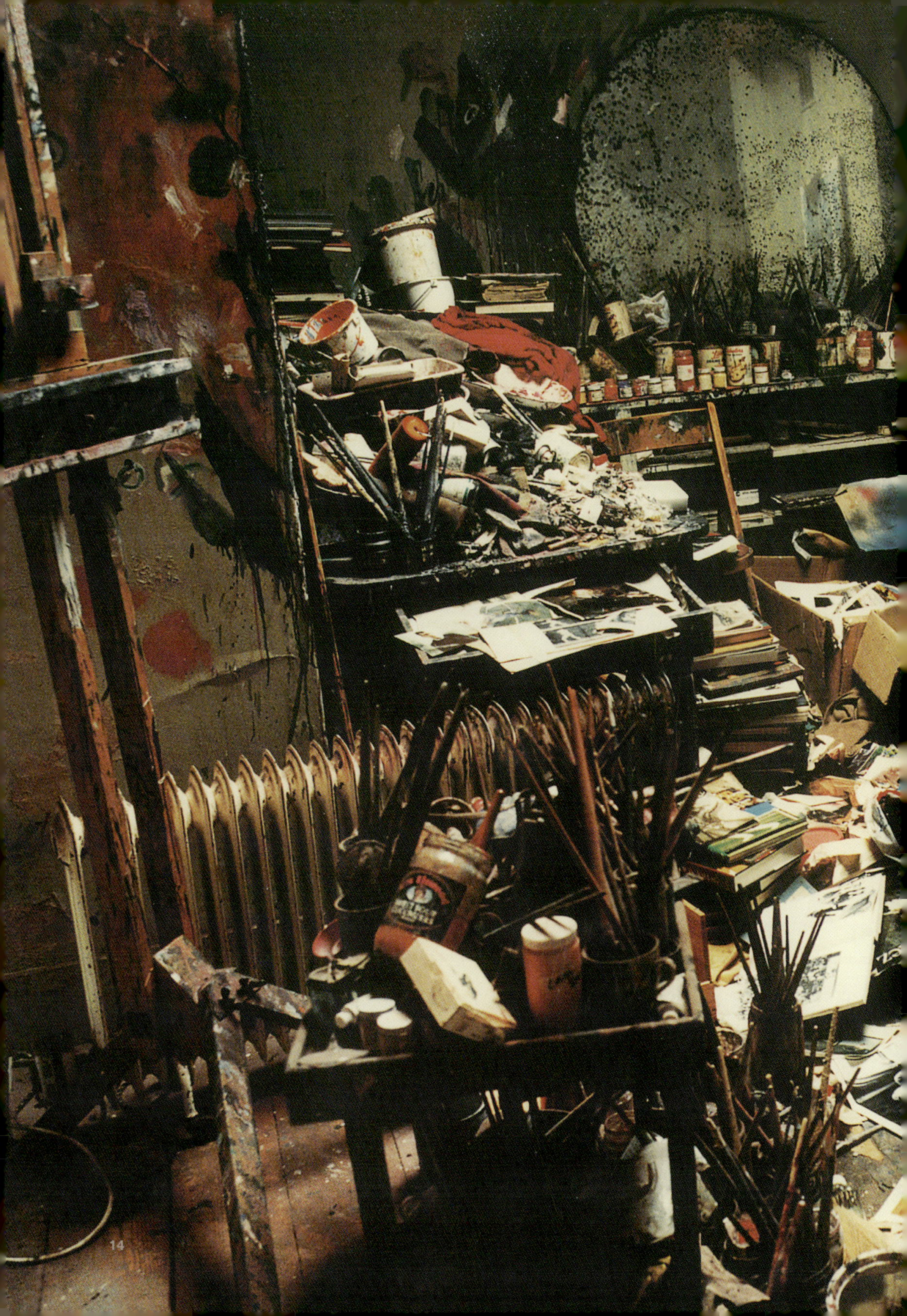

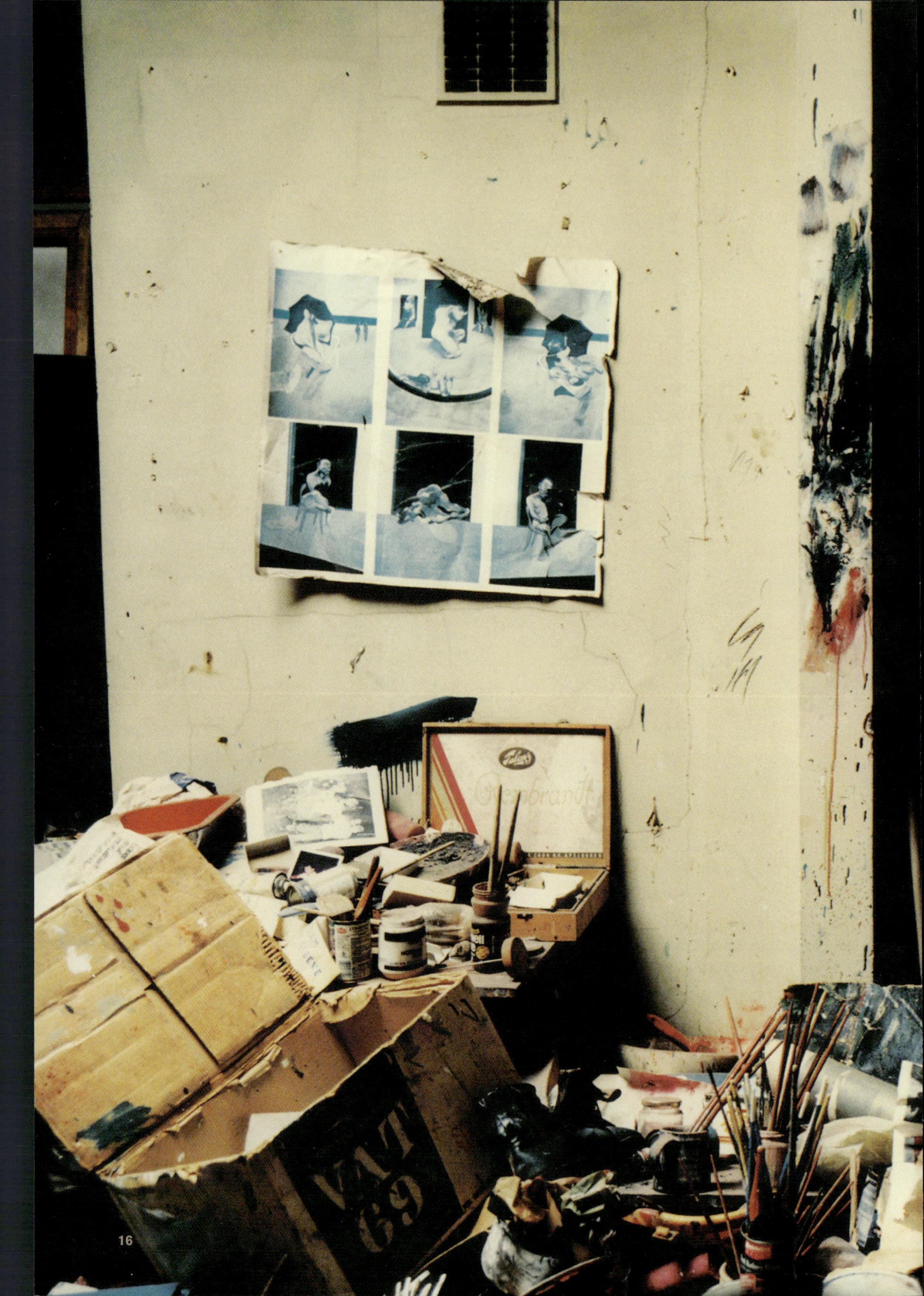

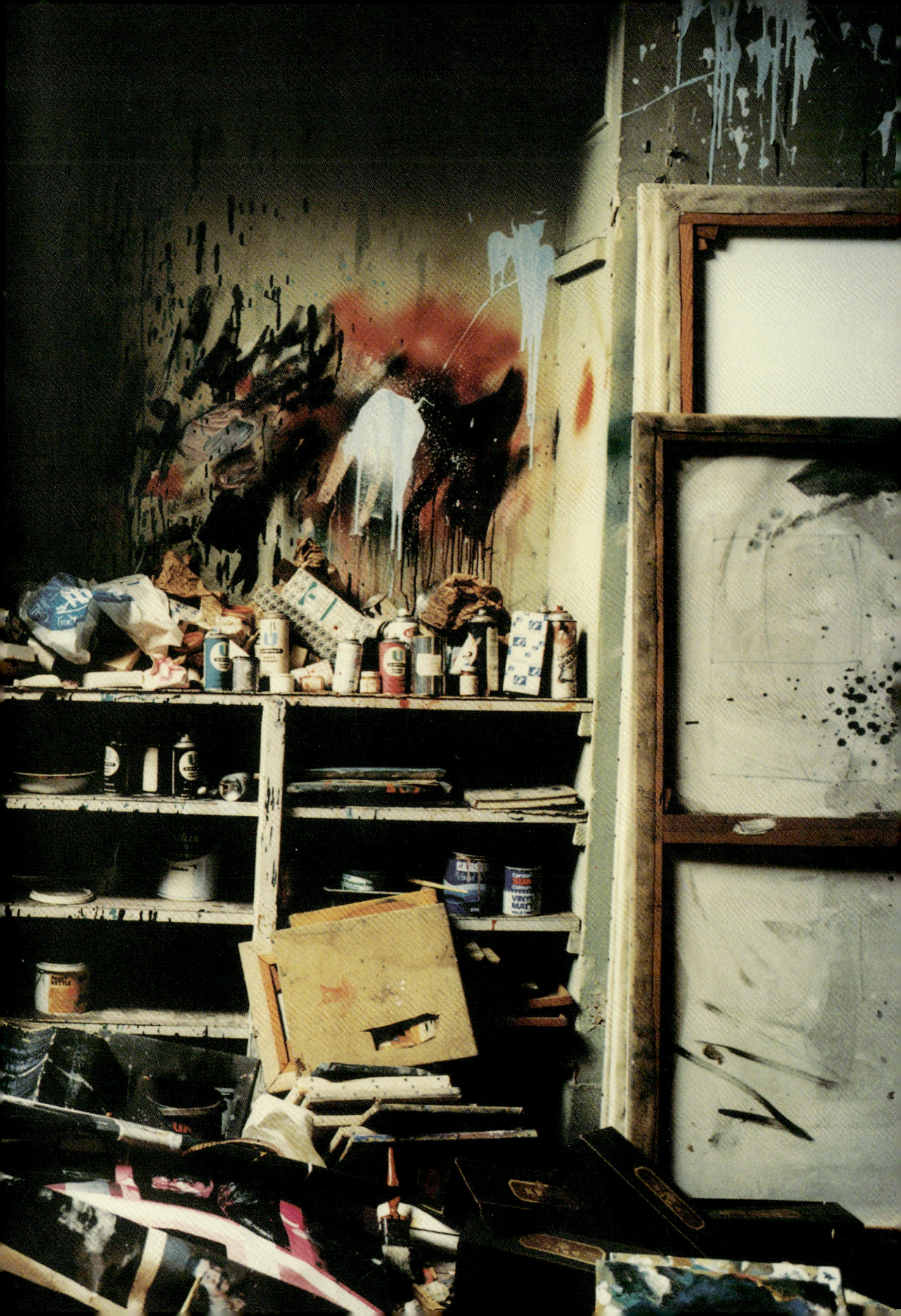

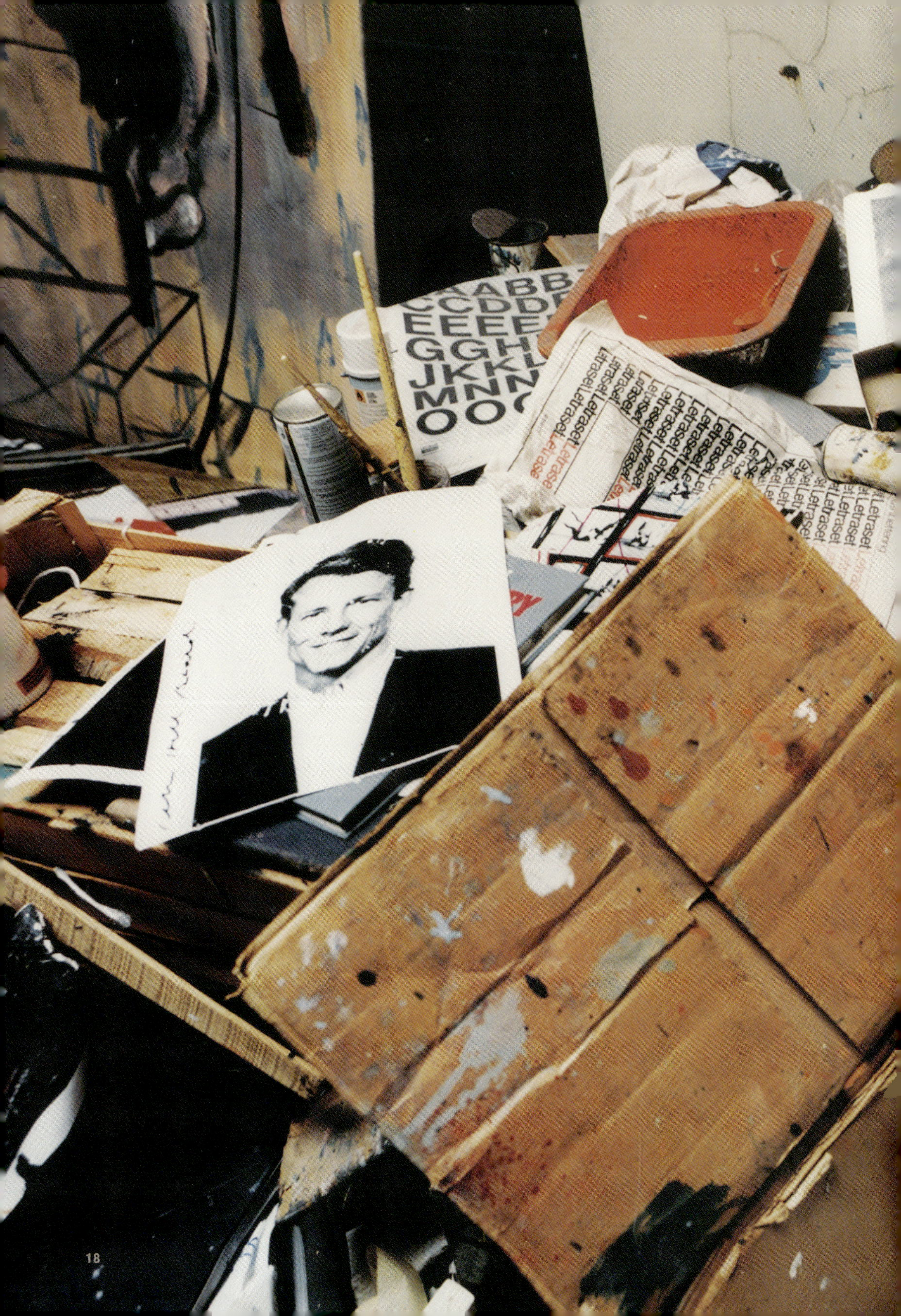

CCDDE
EEEE
GGH
JKKL
MNN
OO
Letraset Letraset Letraset
Letraset
Letrase

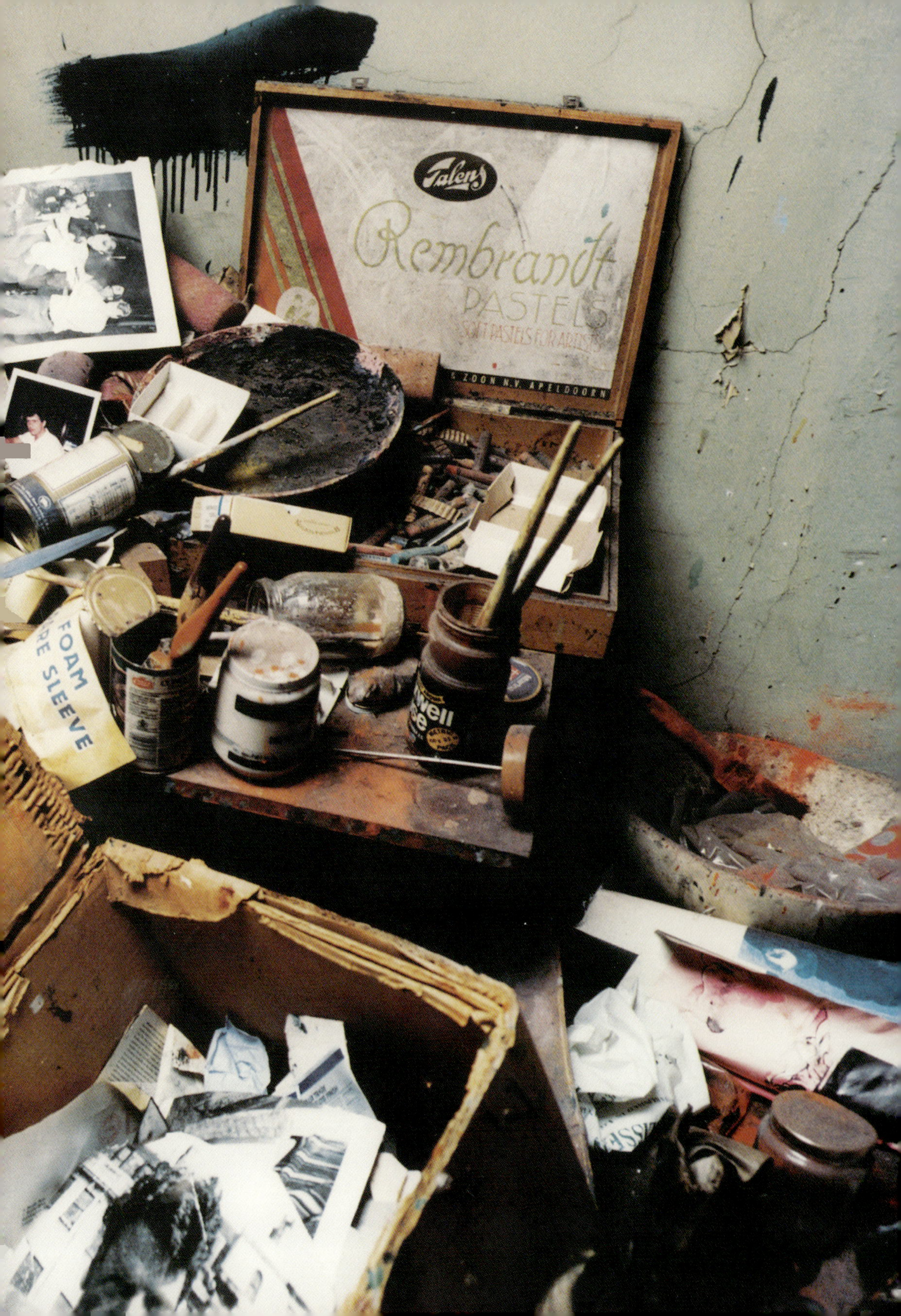

Talens
Rembrandt
PASTELS
SOFT PASTELS FOR ARTISTS
ZOON N.V. APELDOORN
FOAM
DE SLEEVE

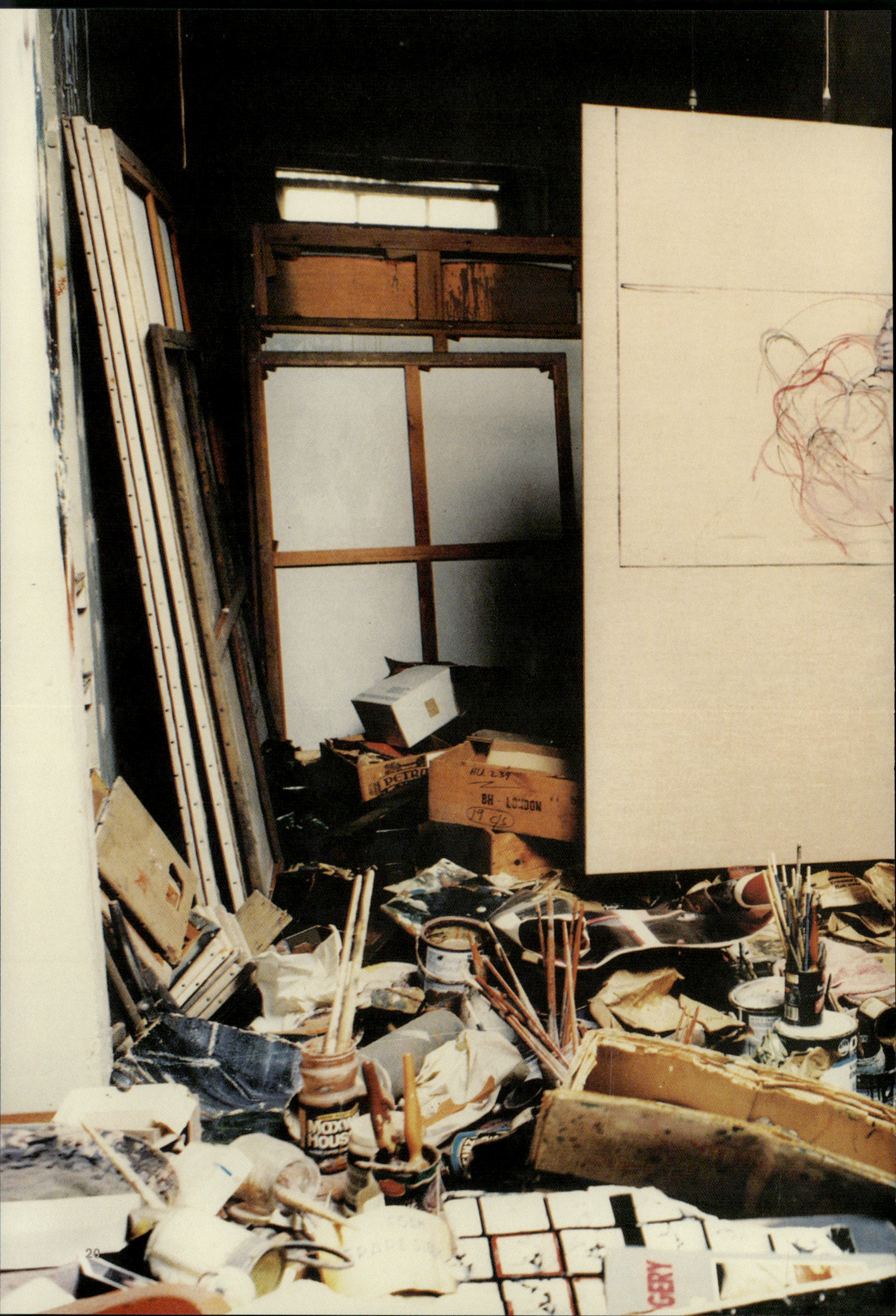

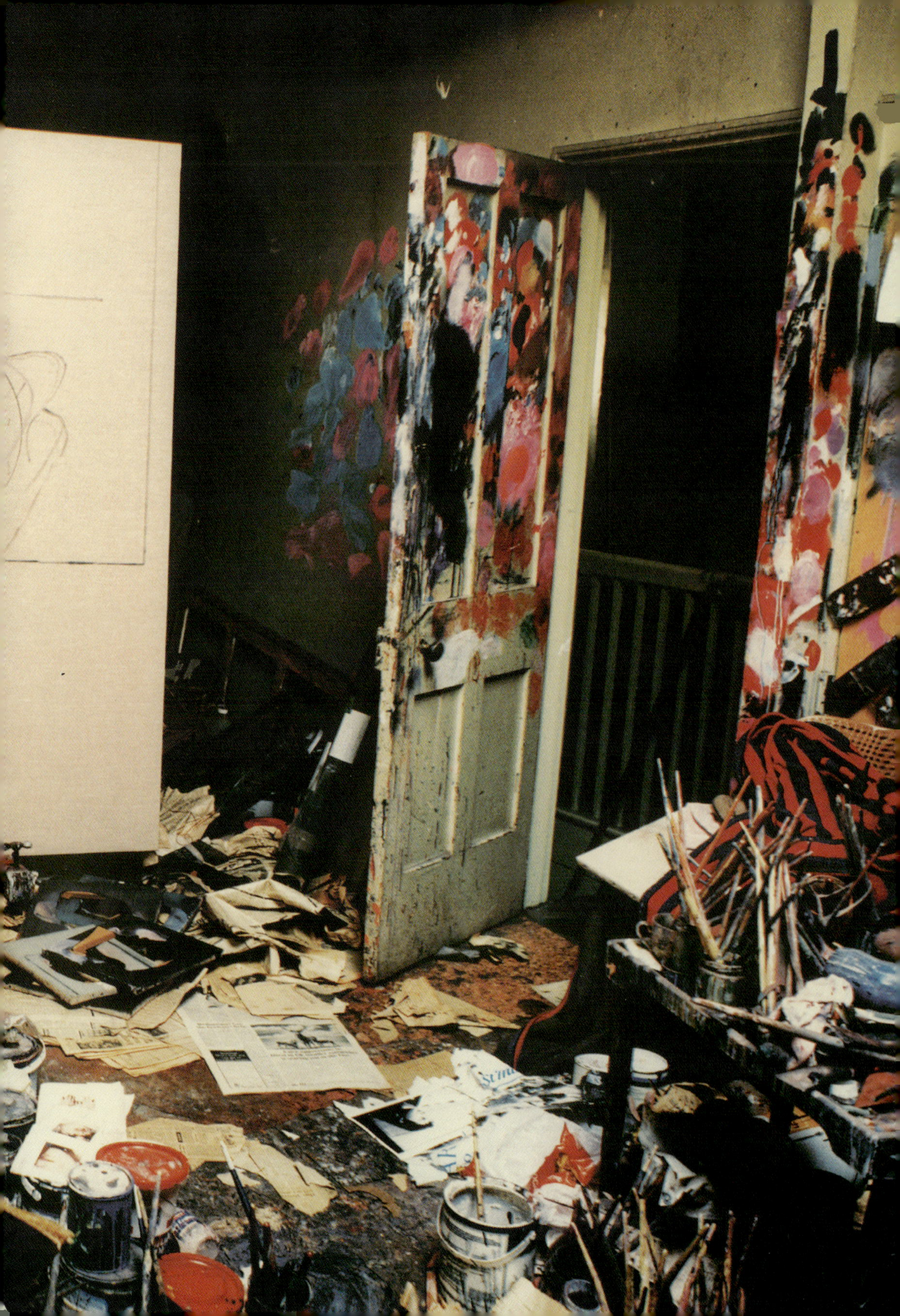

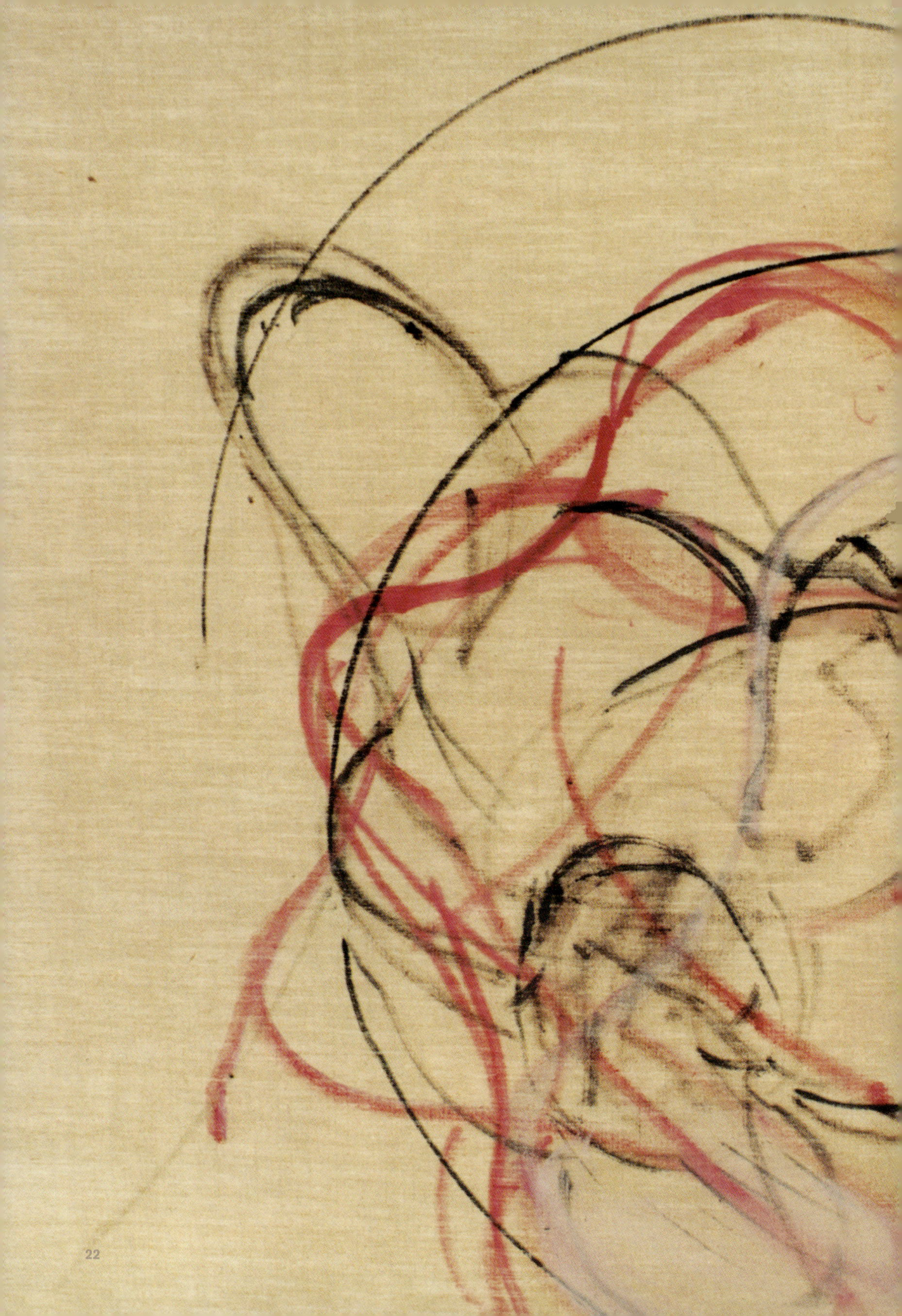

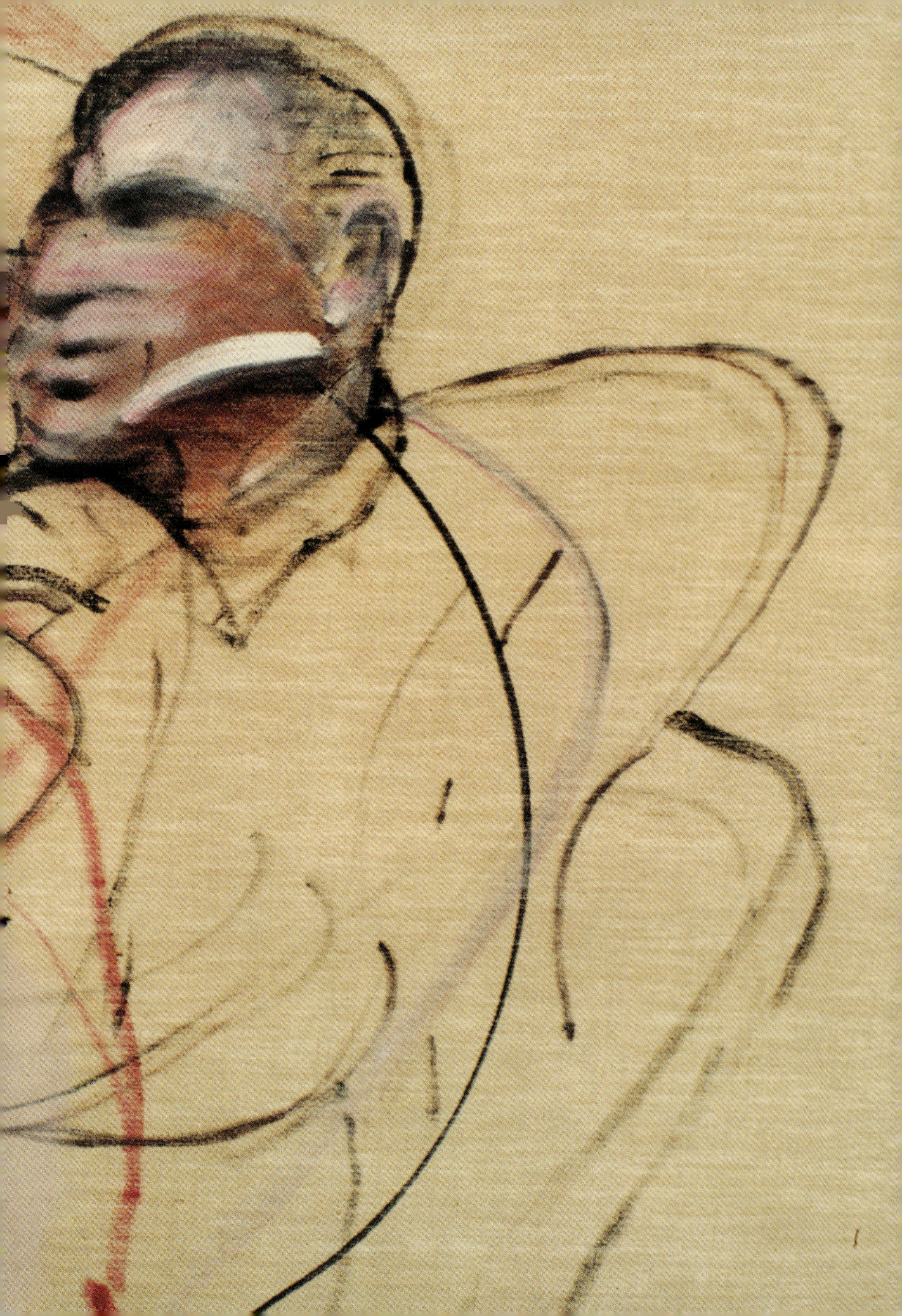

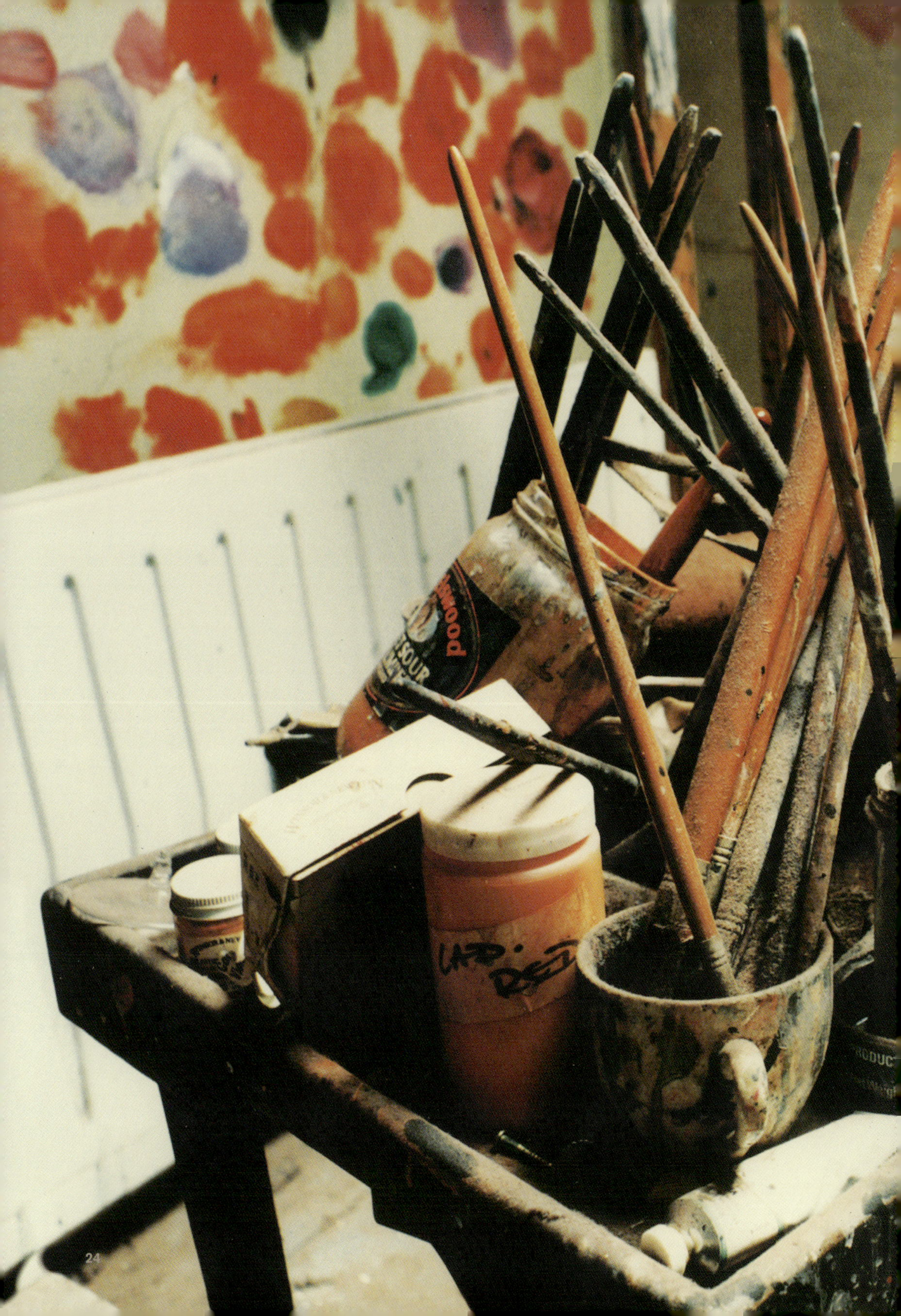

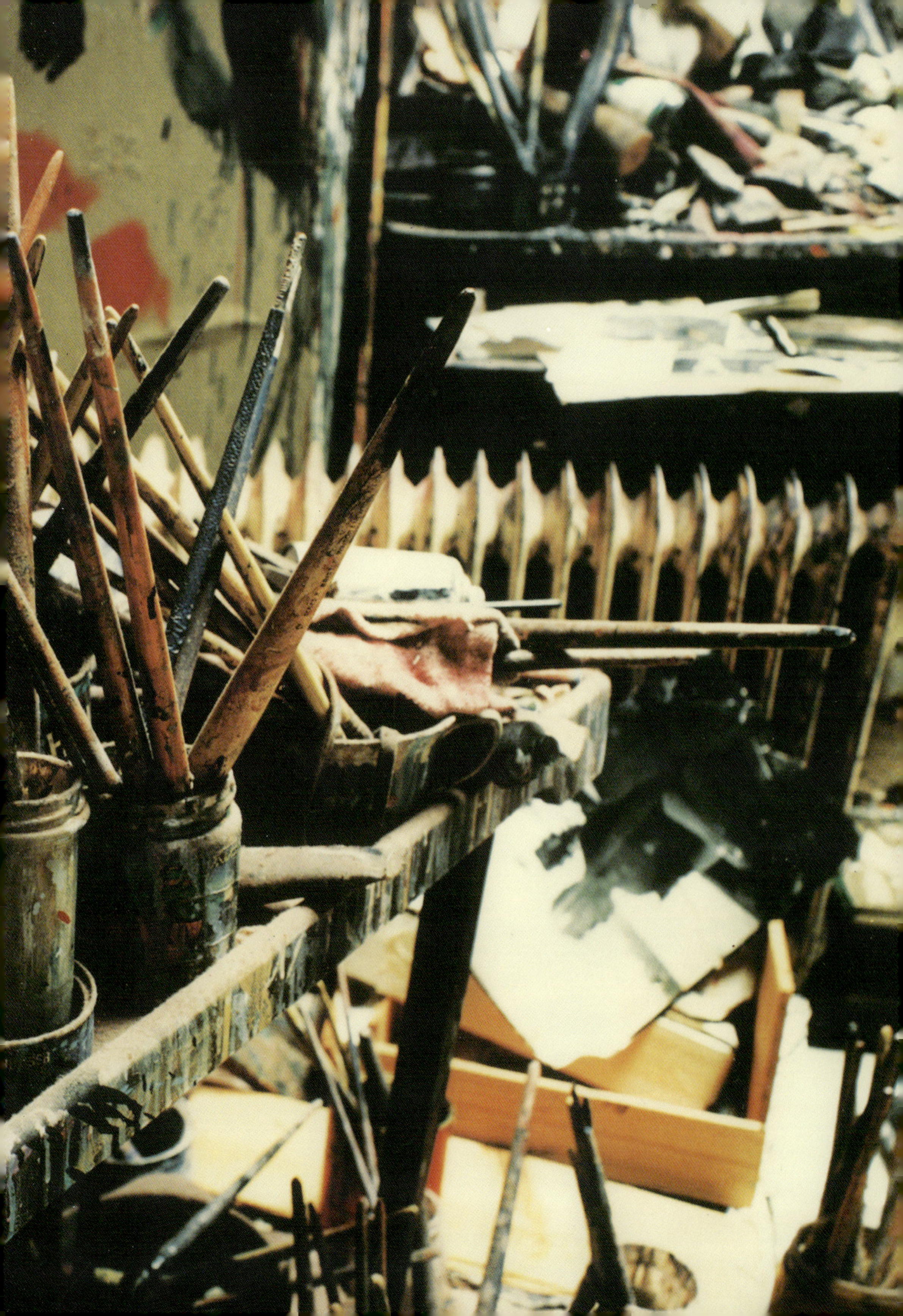

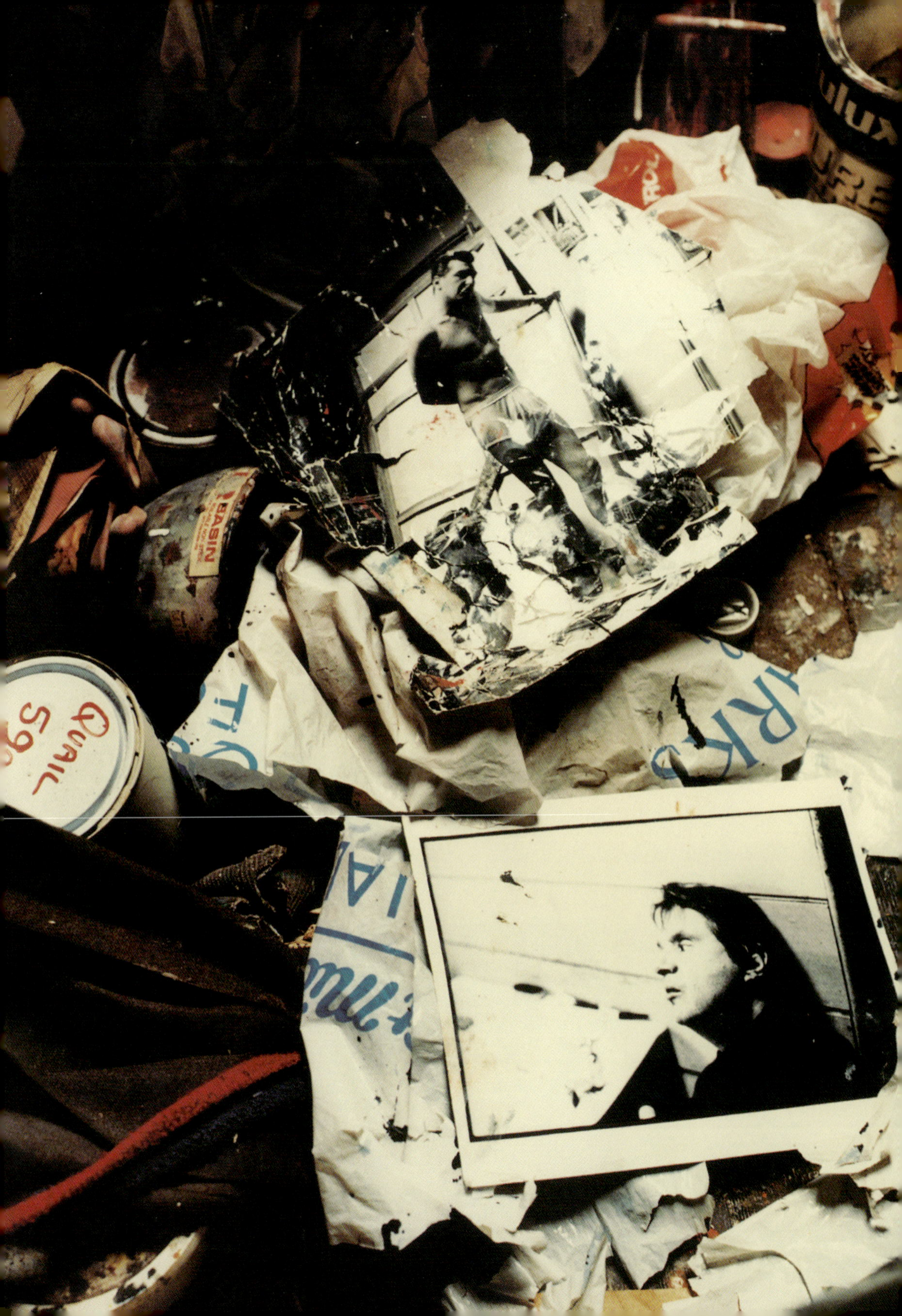

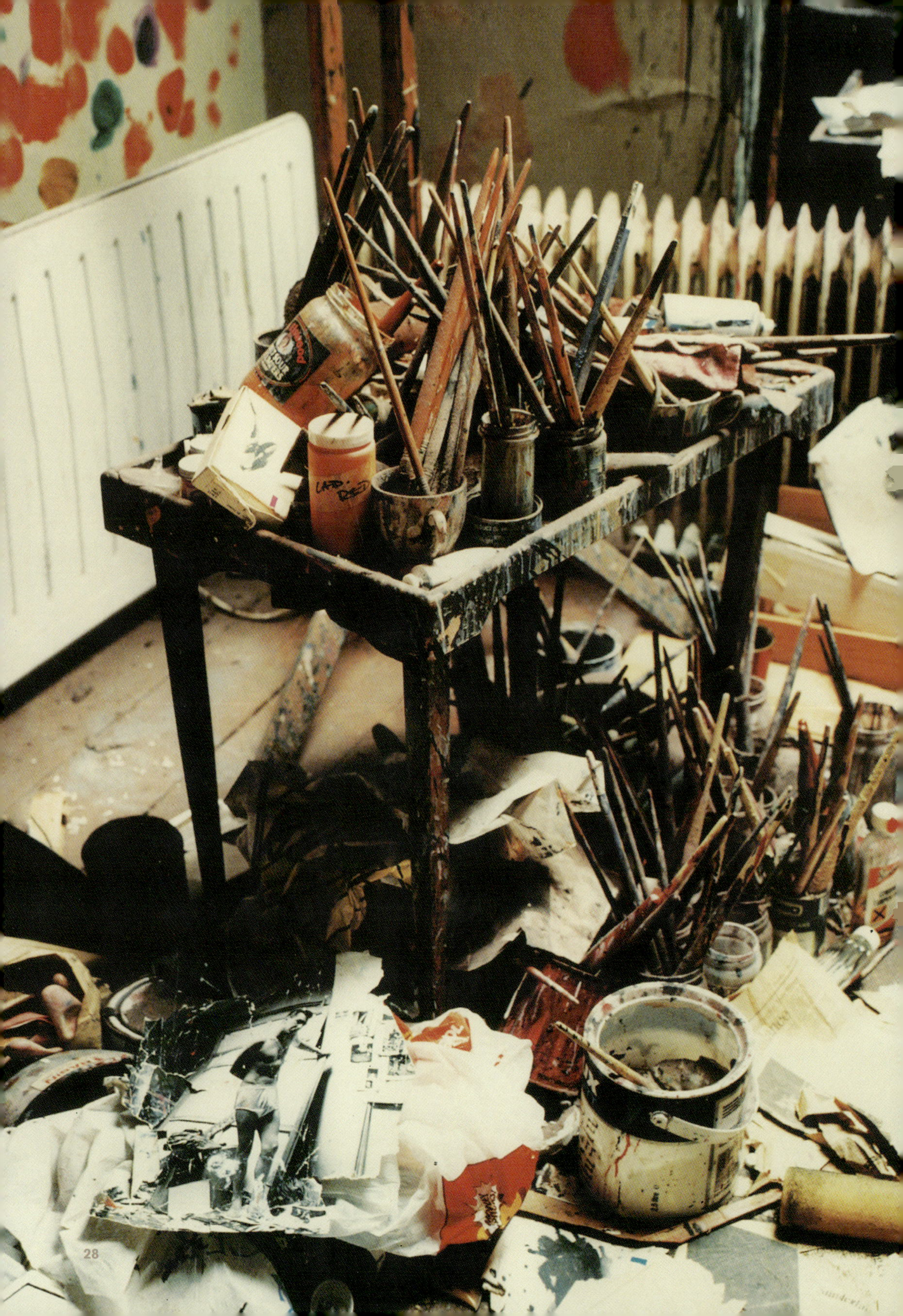

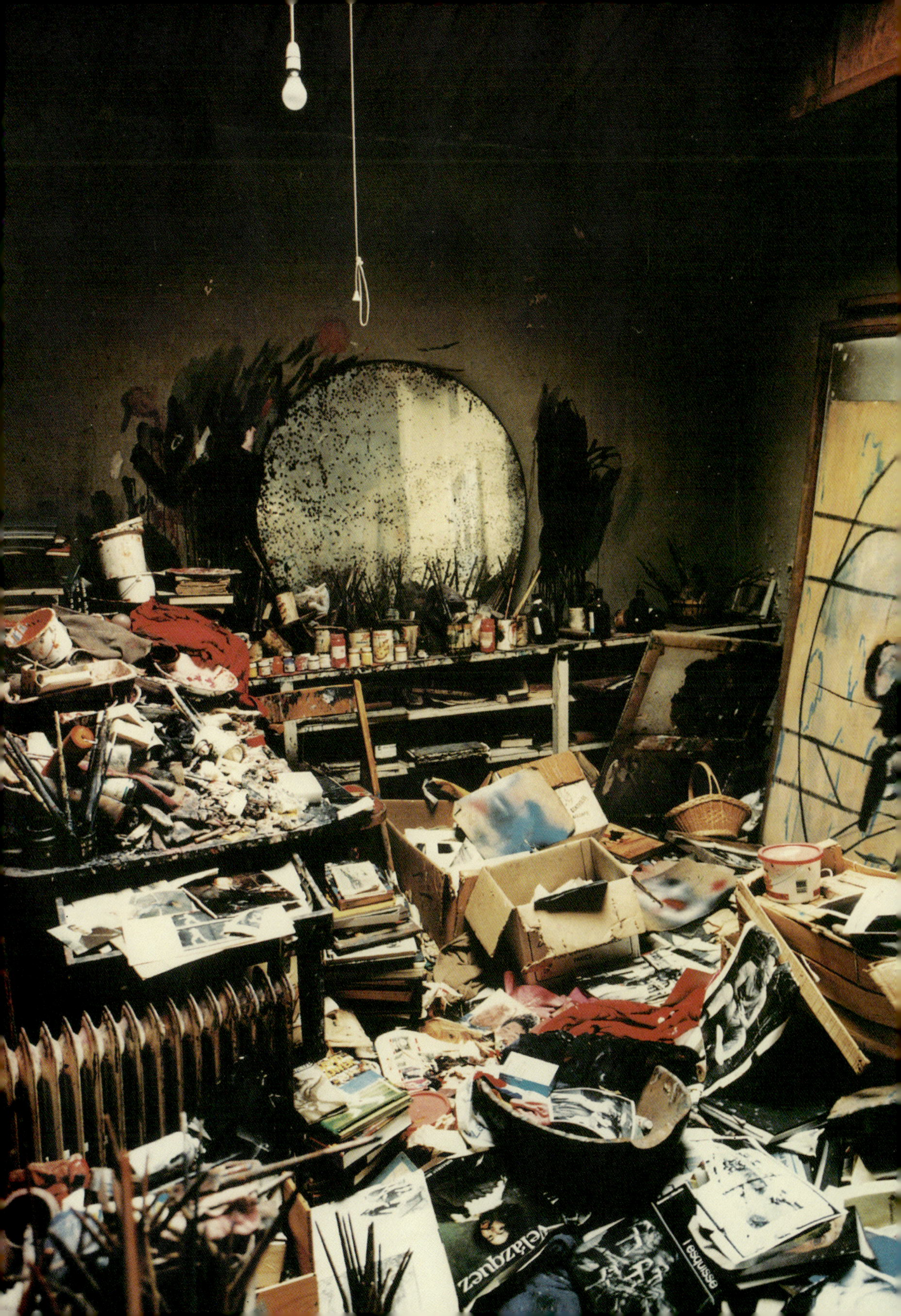

Velázquez

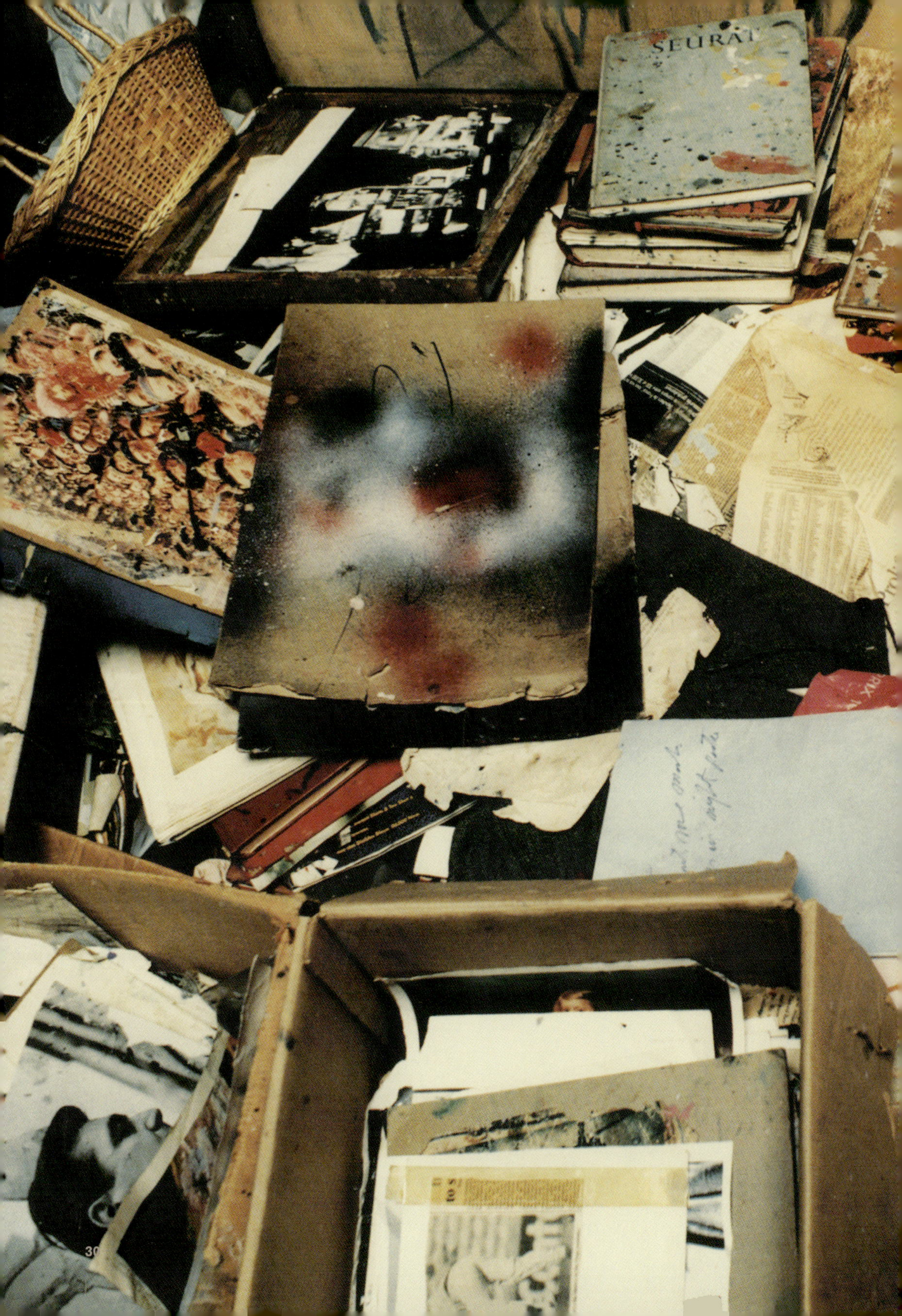

SEURAT

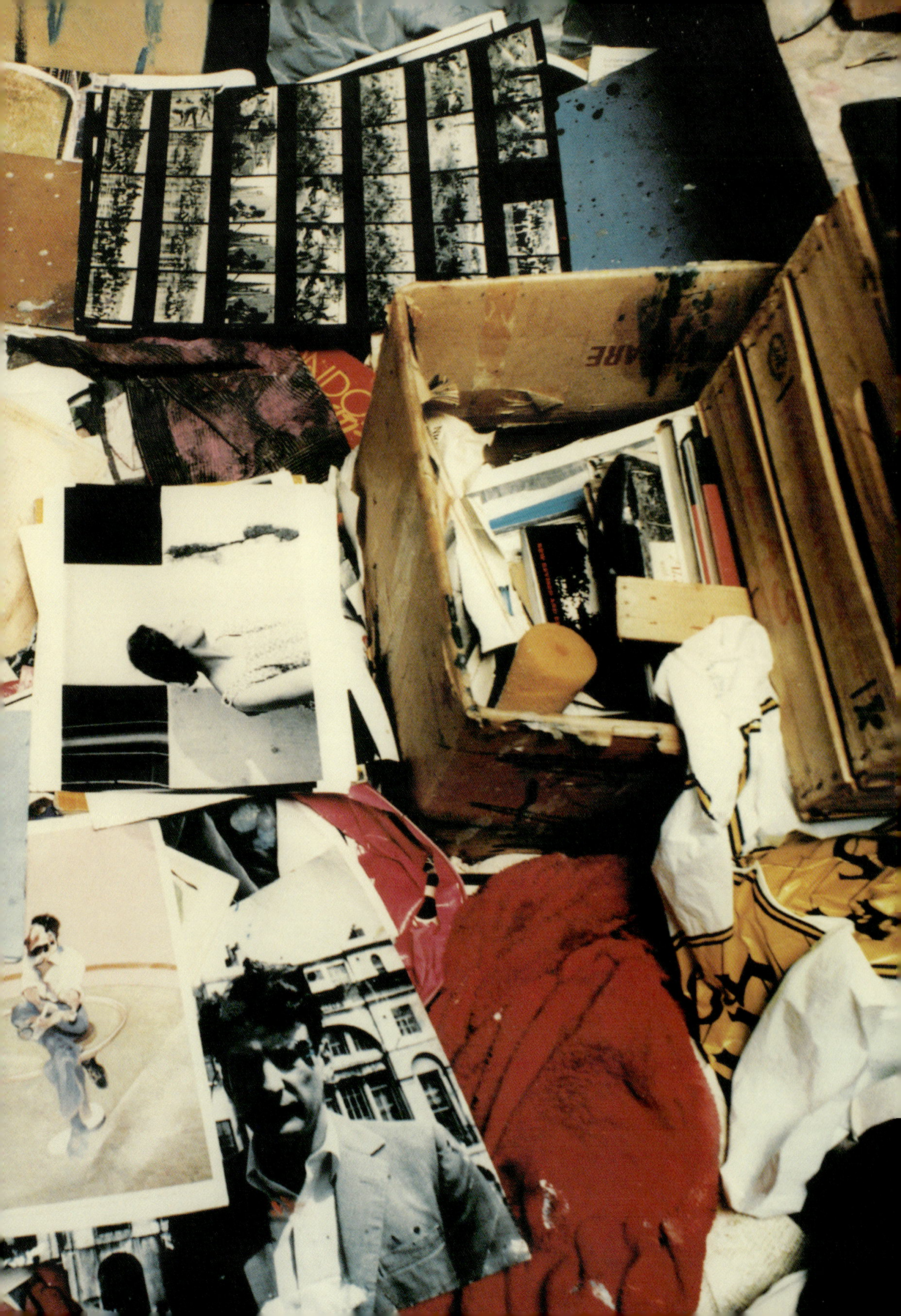

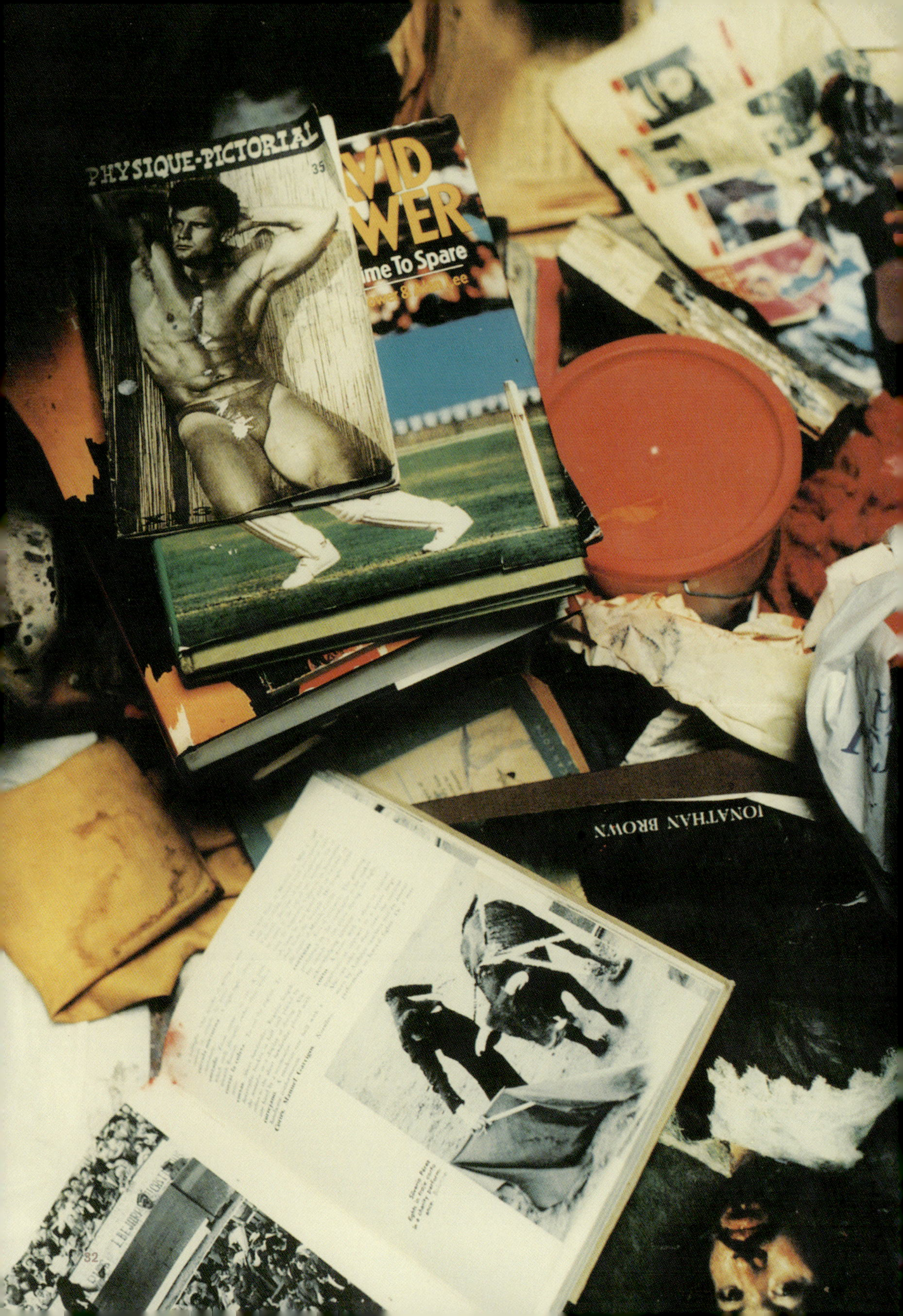
PHYSIQUE·PICTORIAL
35
VID
WER
me To Spare
JONATHAN BROWN

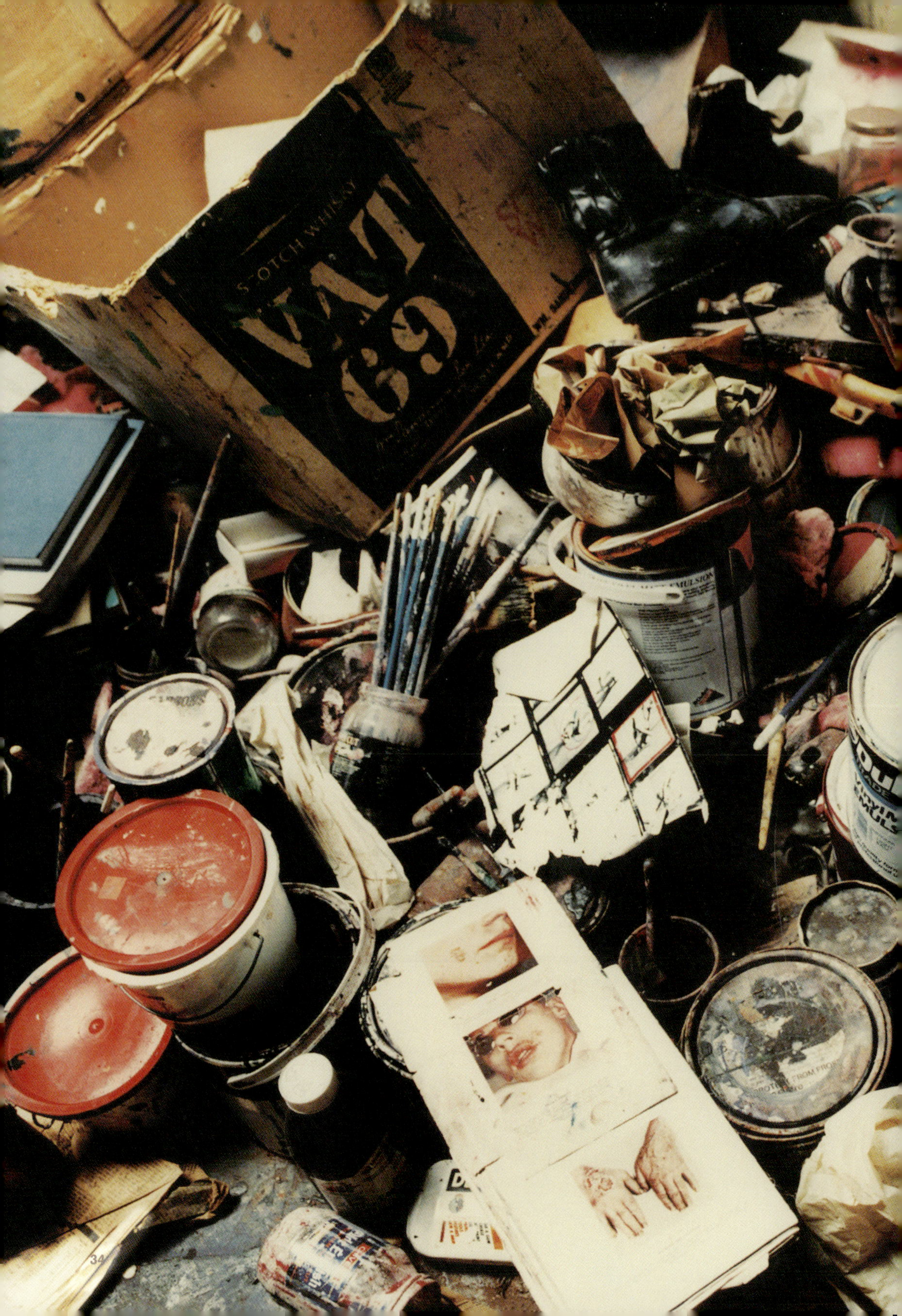

SCOTCH WHISKY
VAT
69

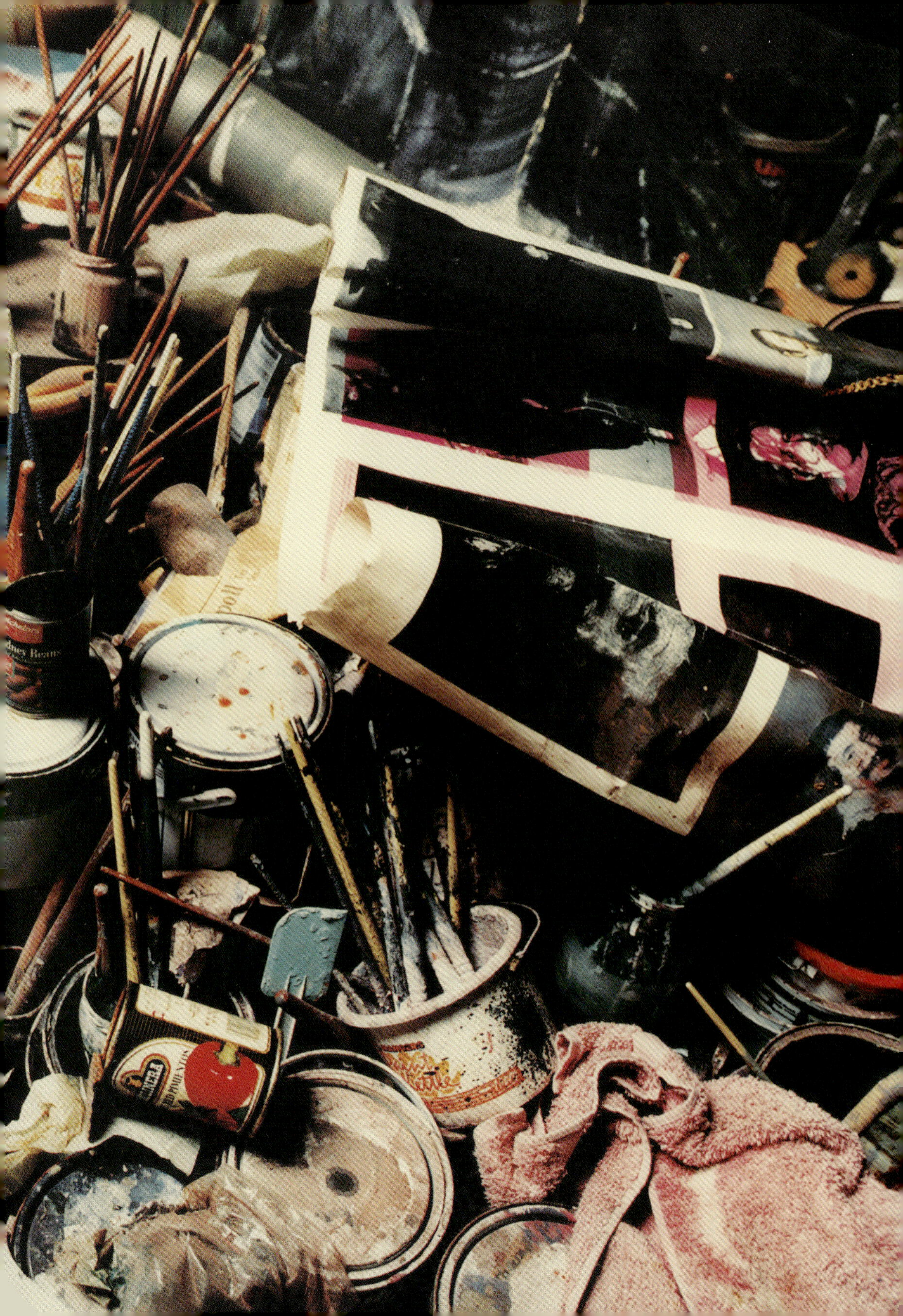

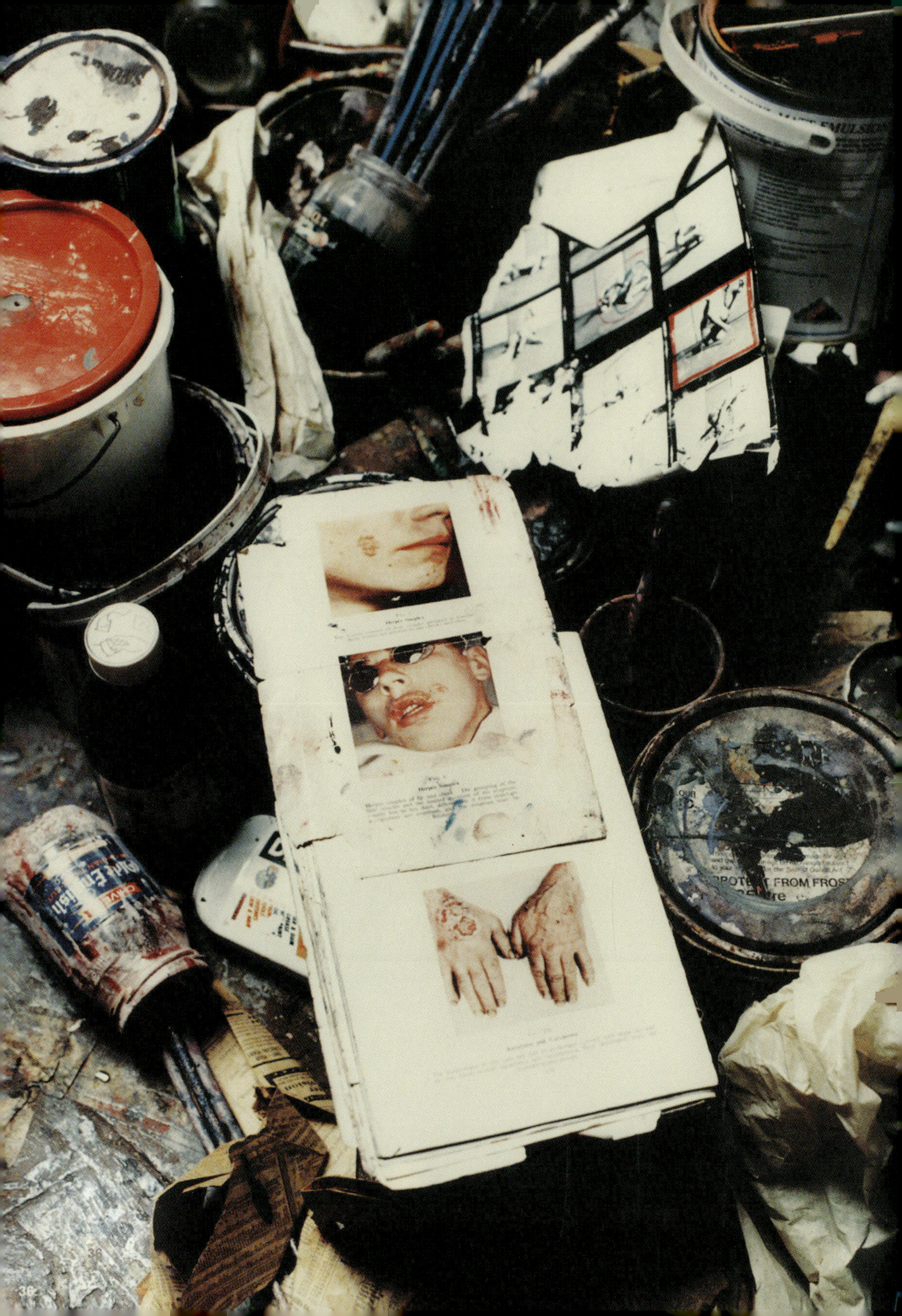

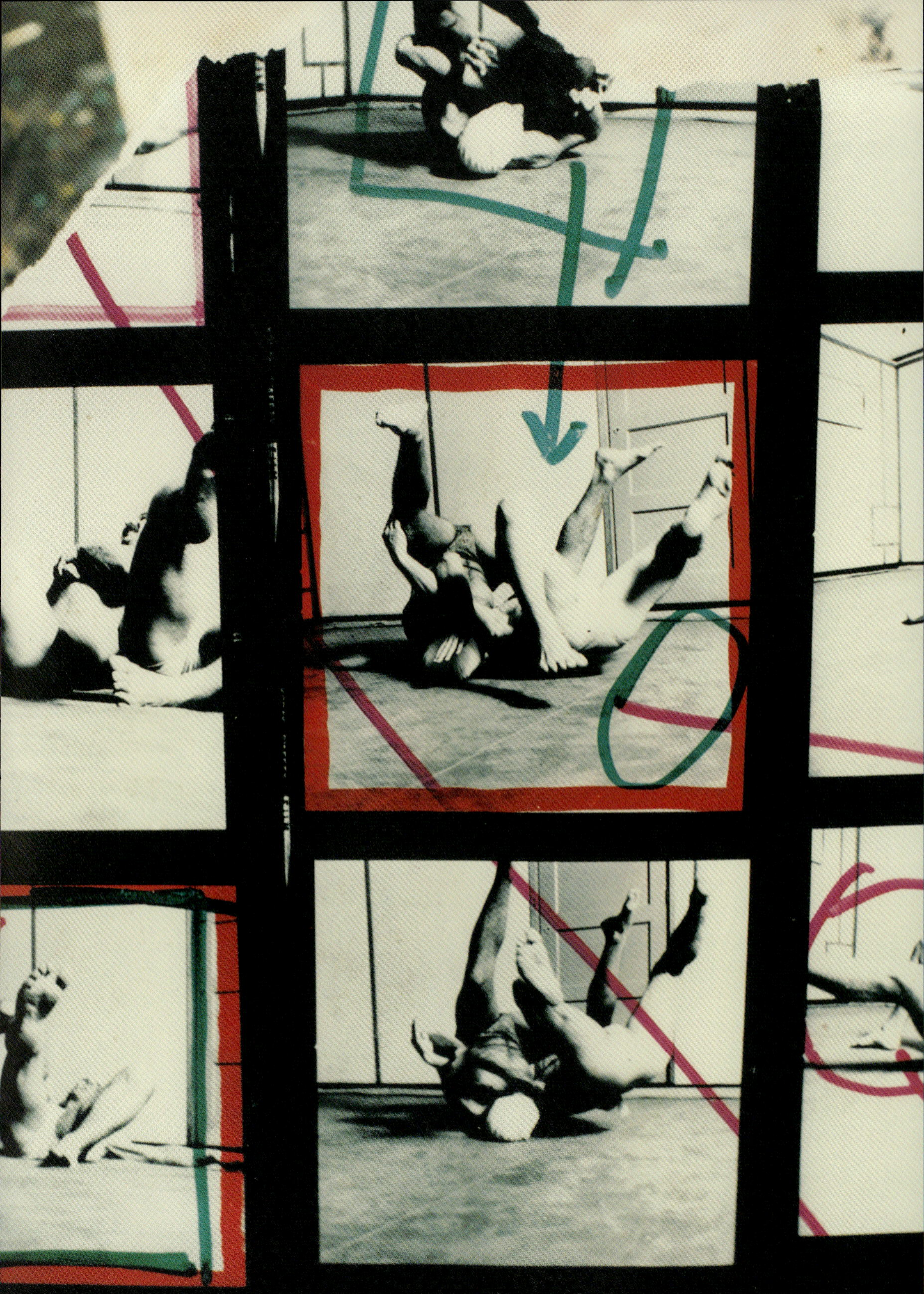

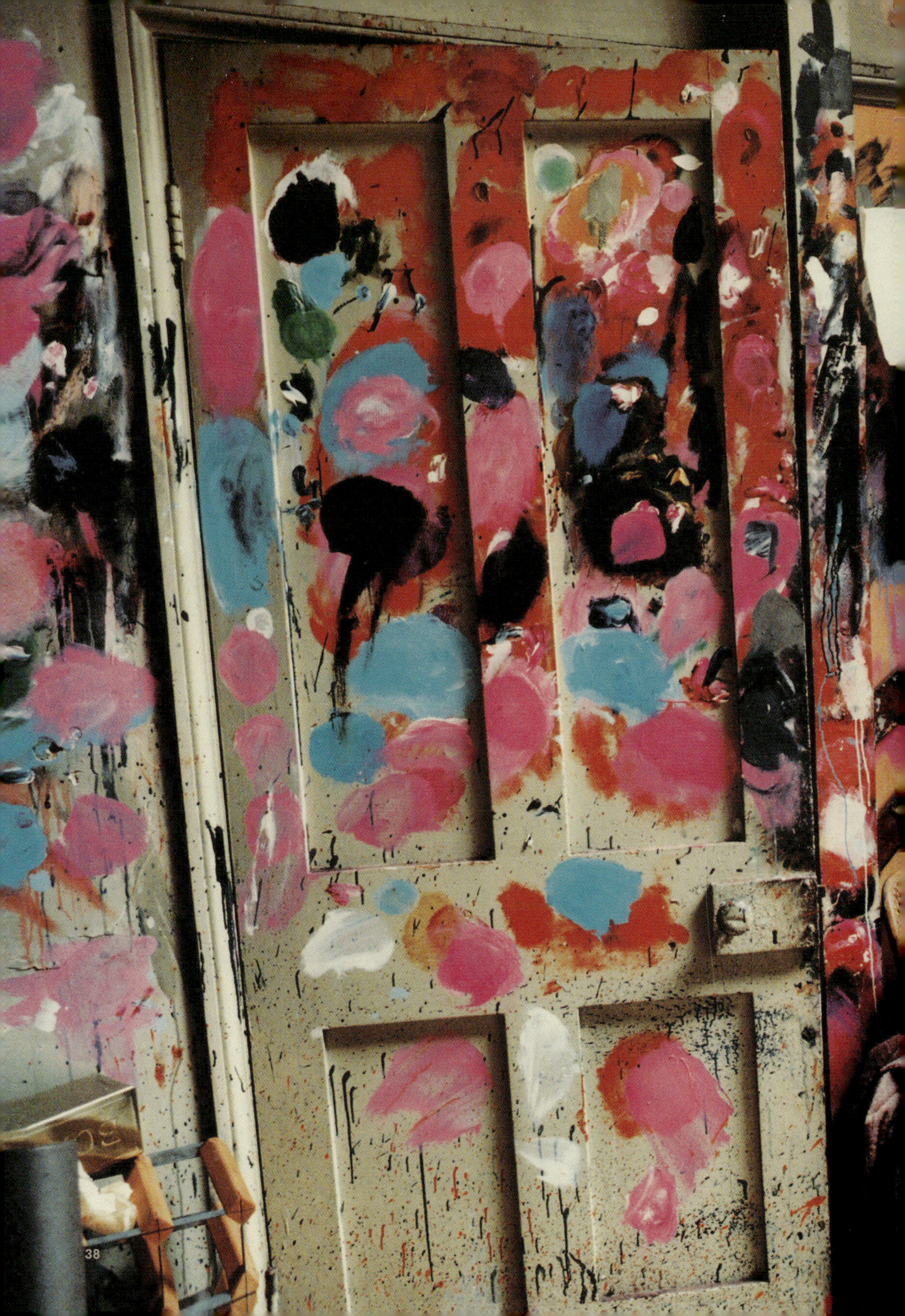

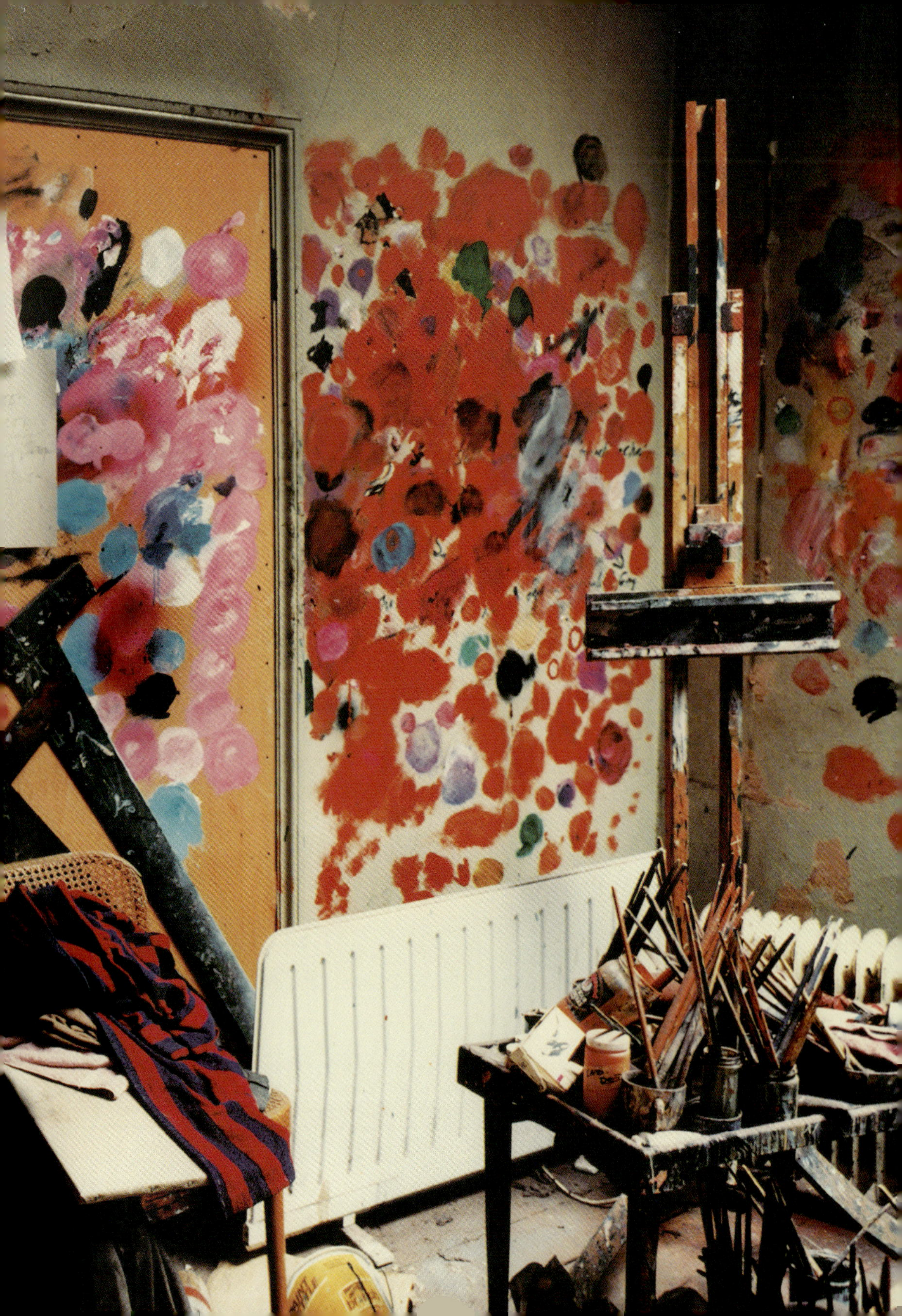

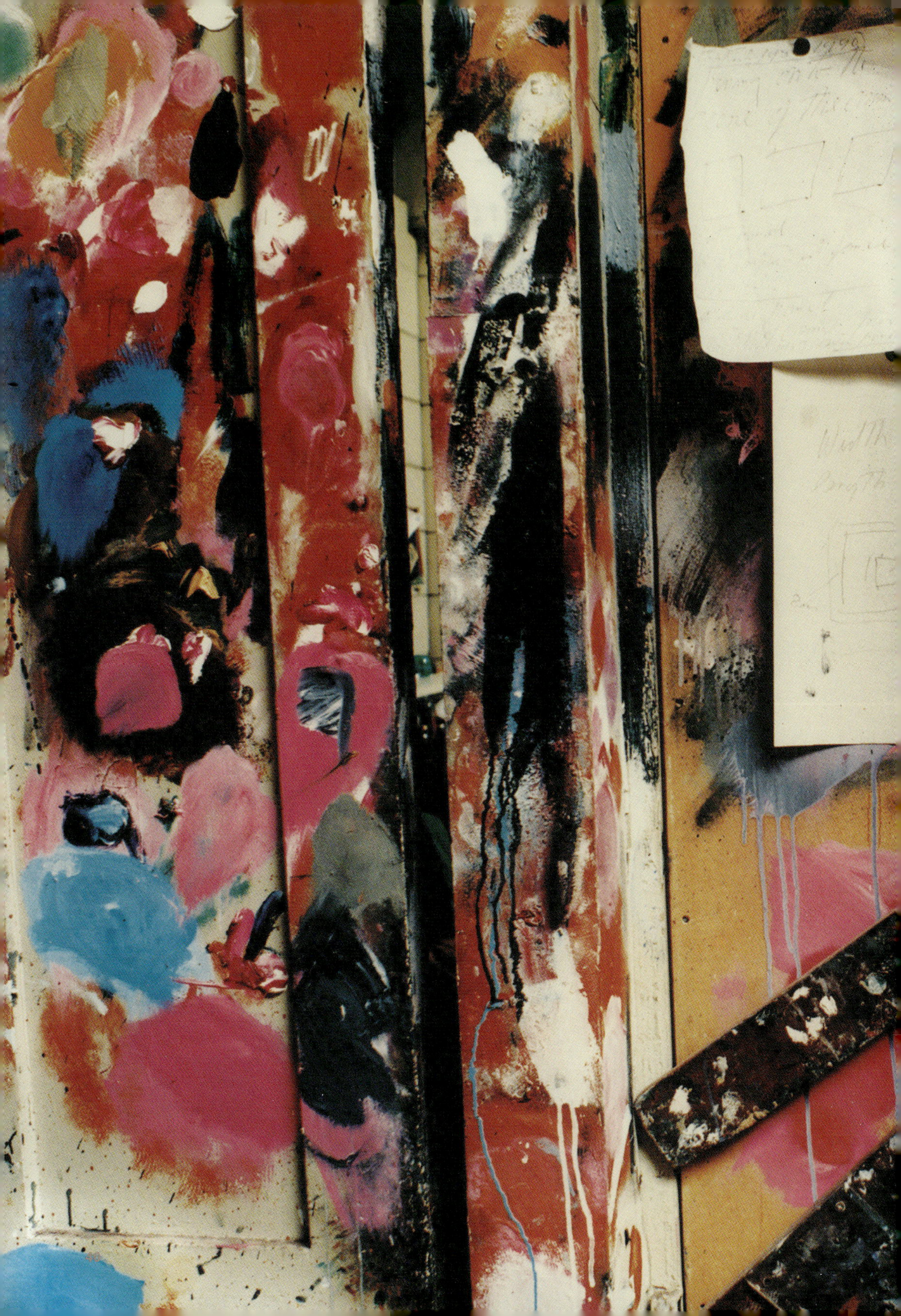

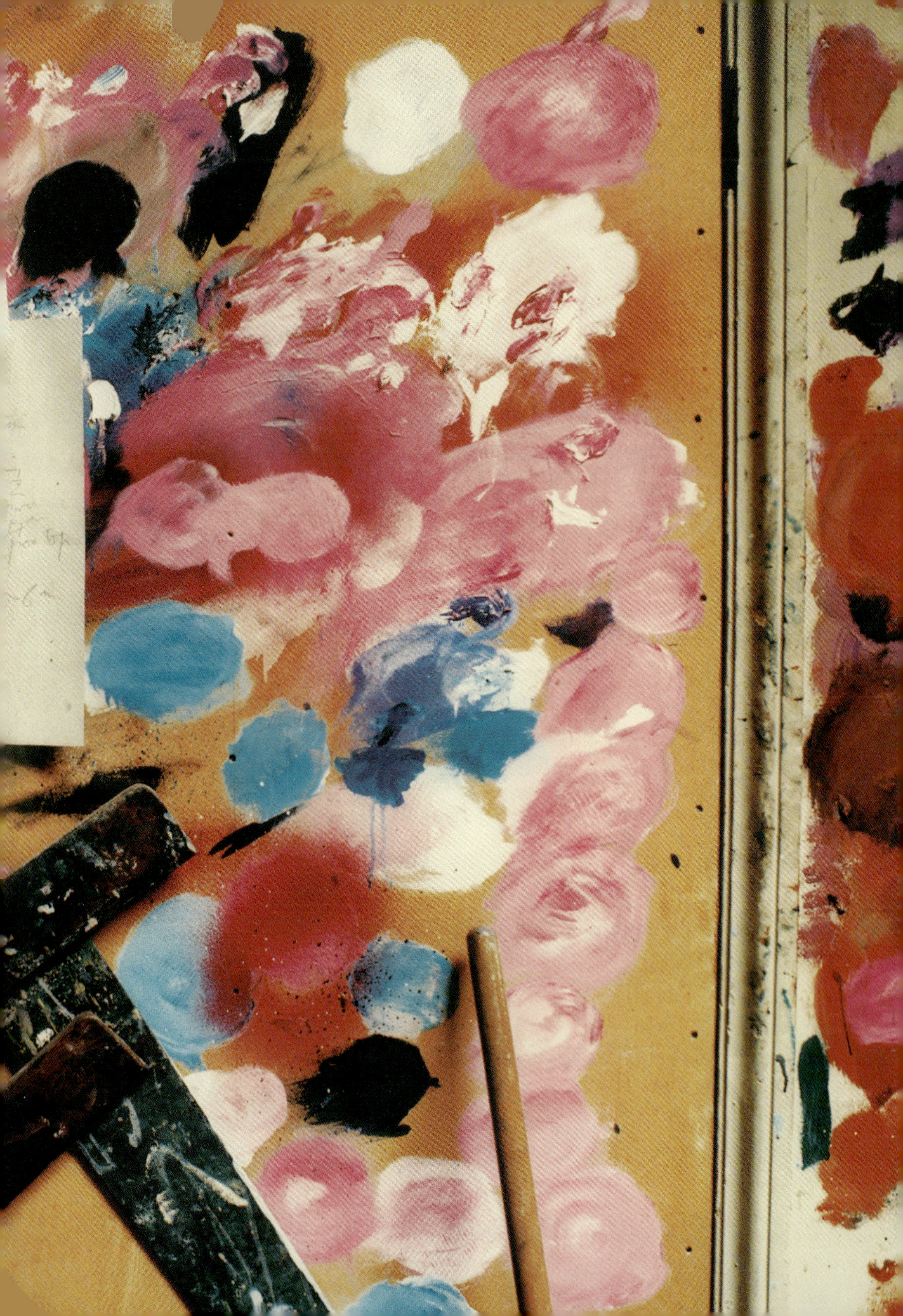

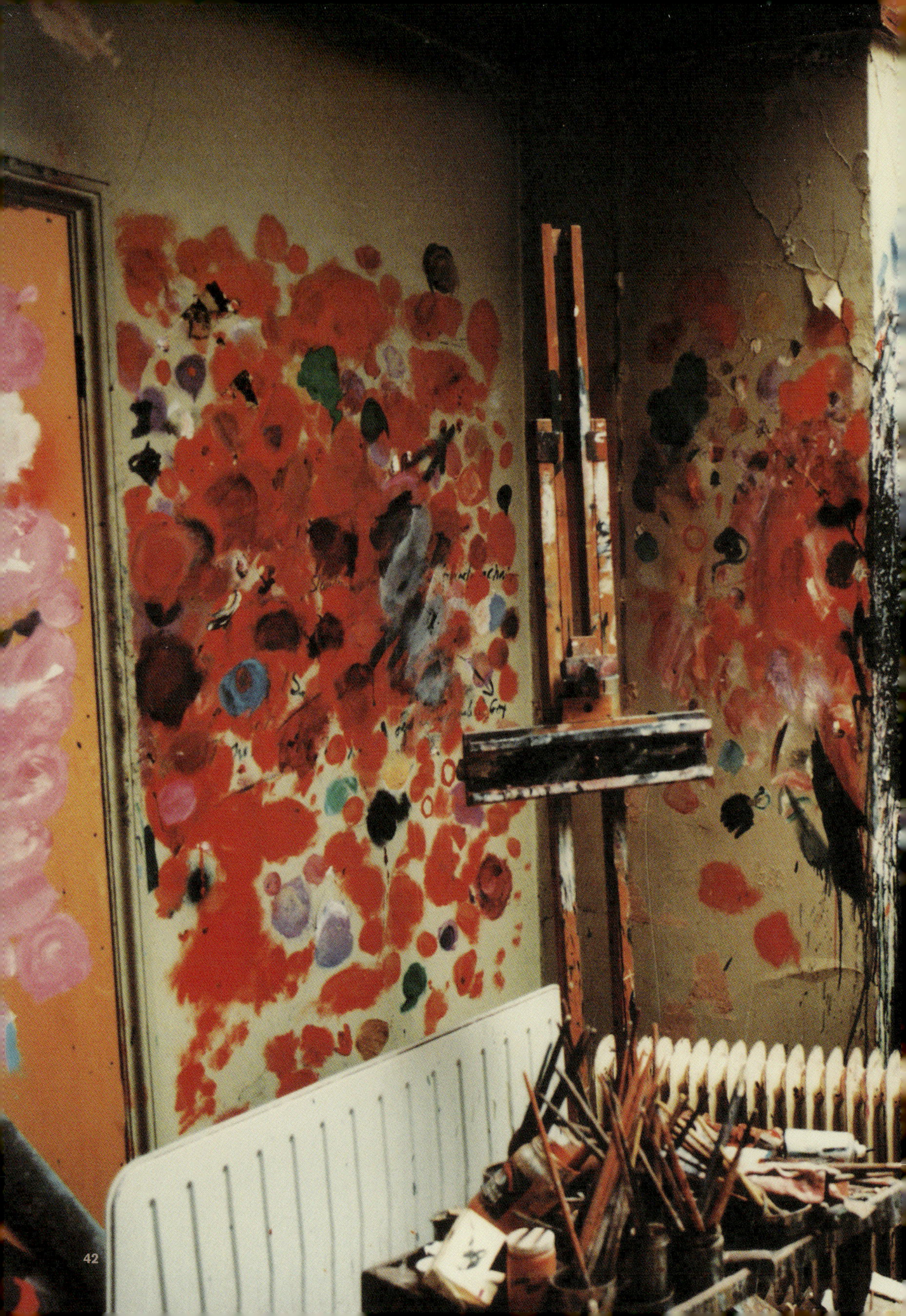

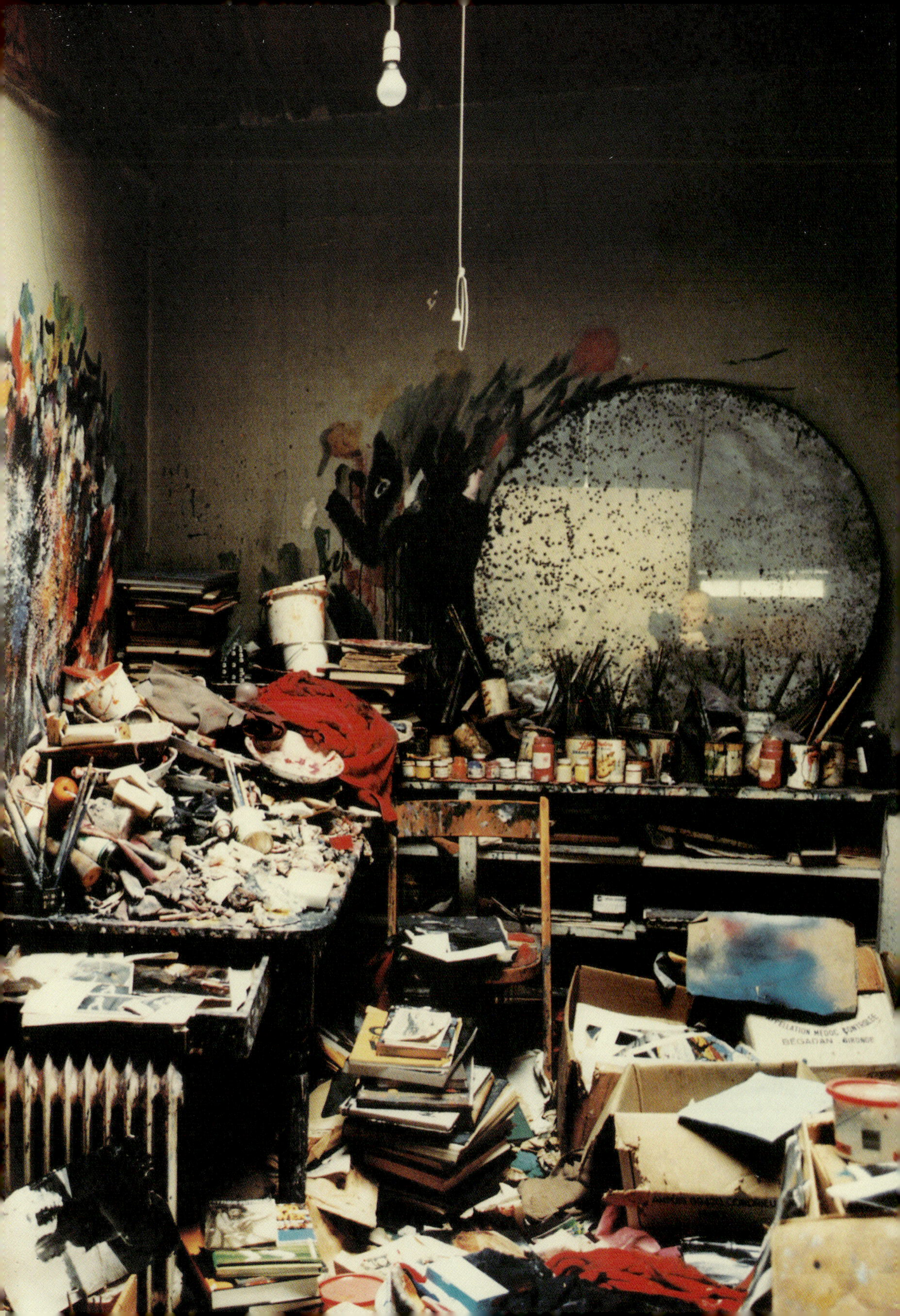

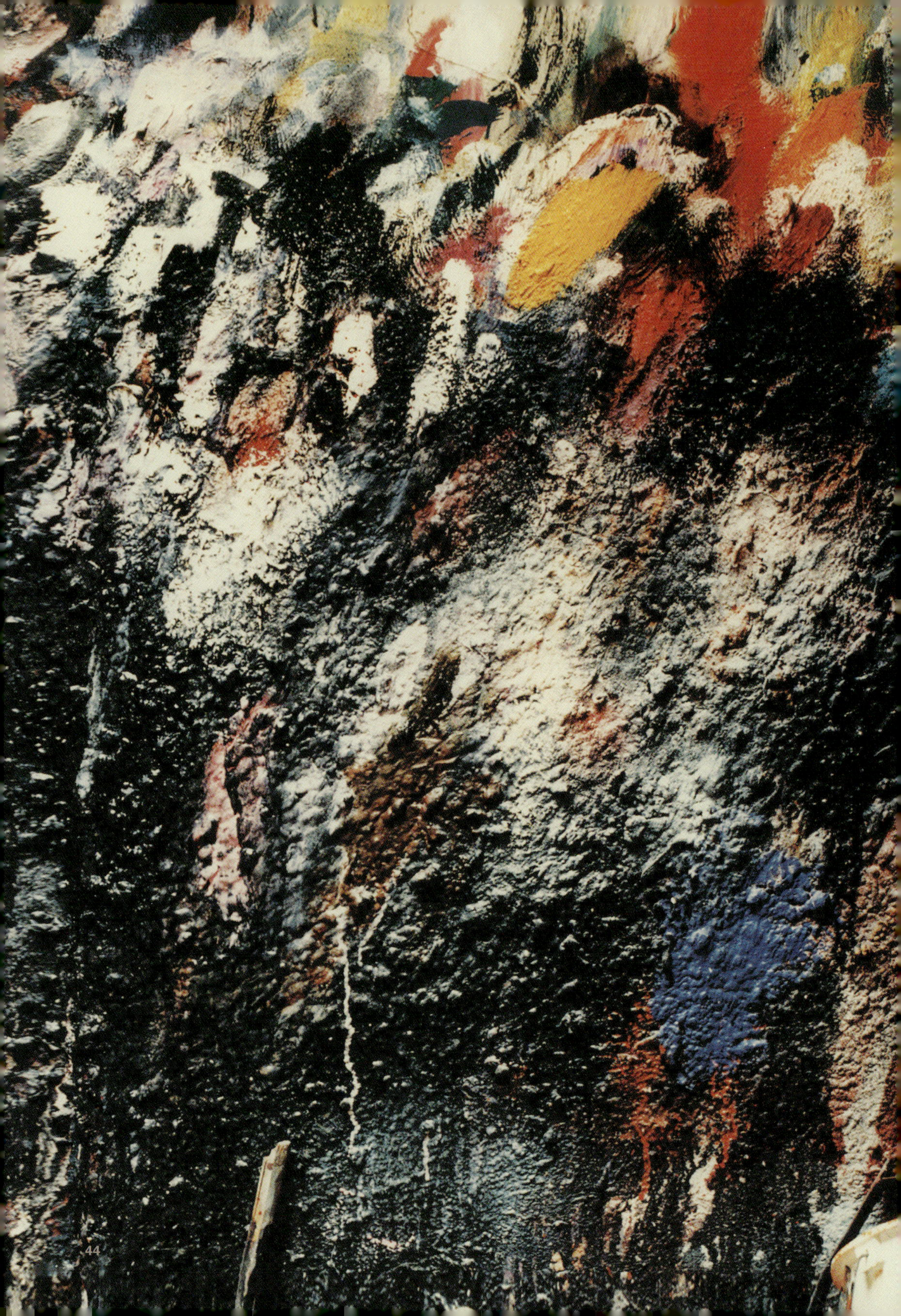

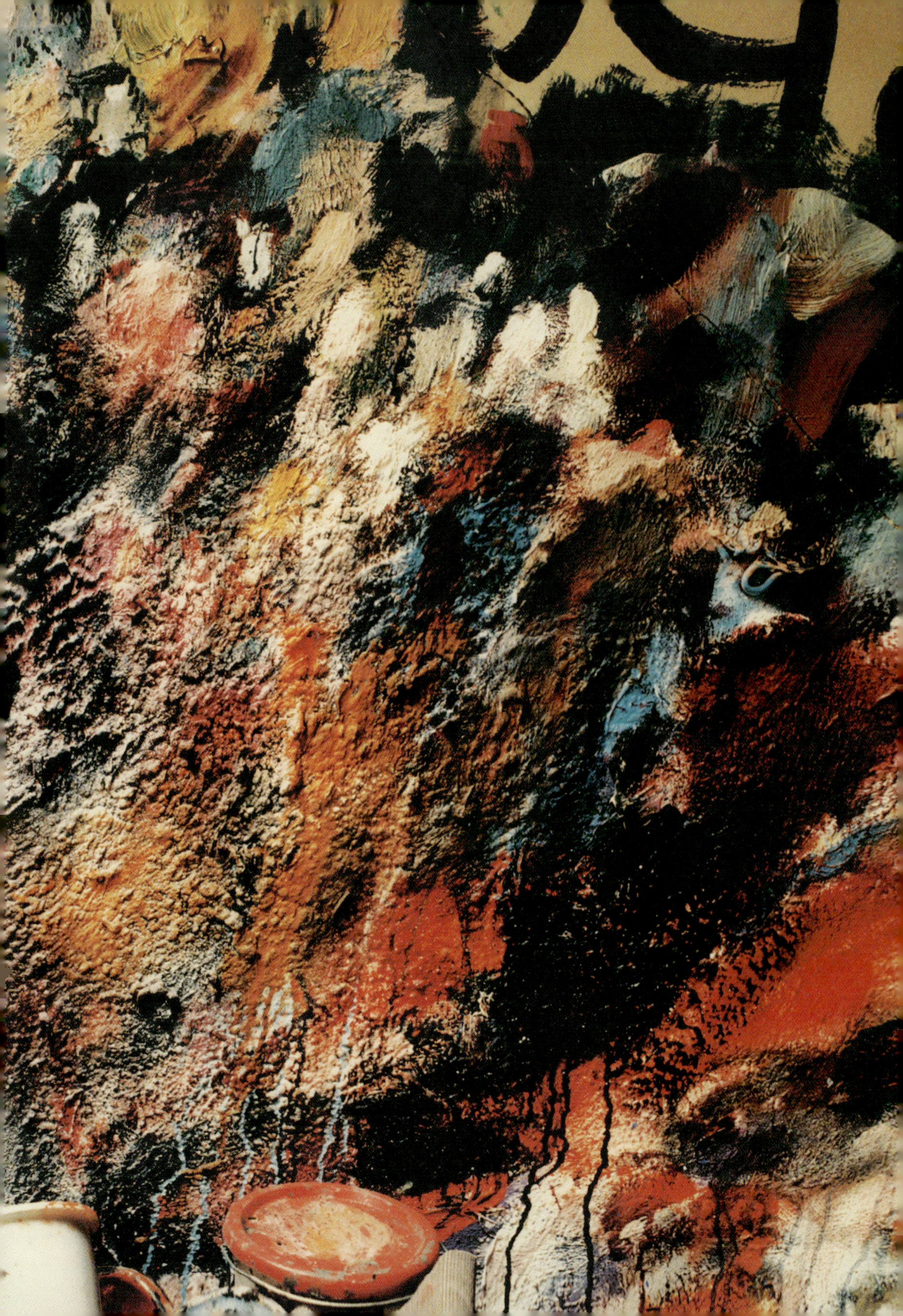

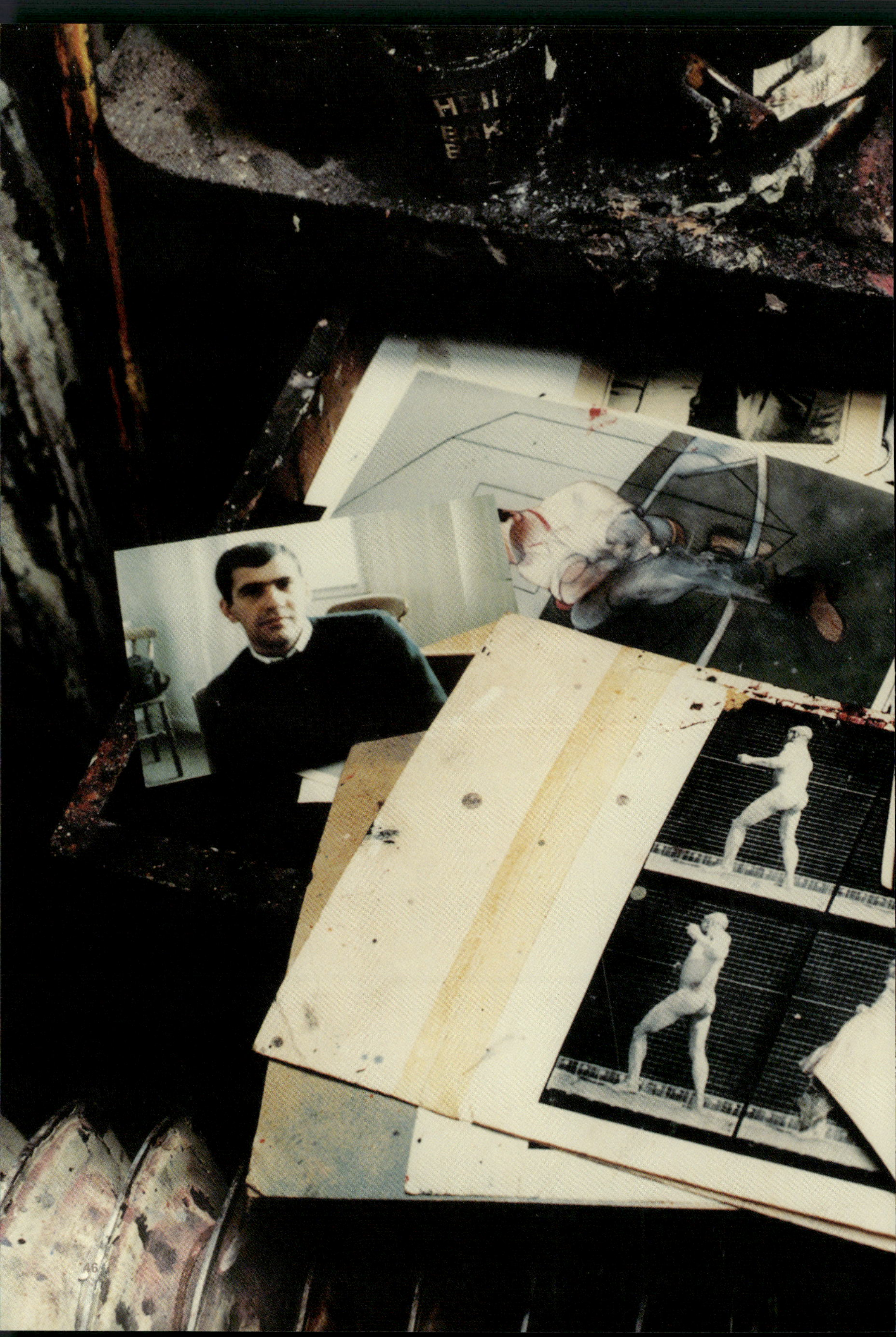

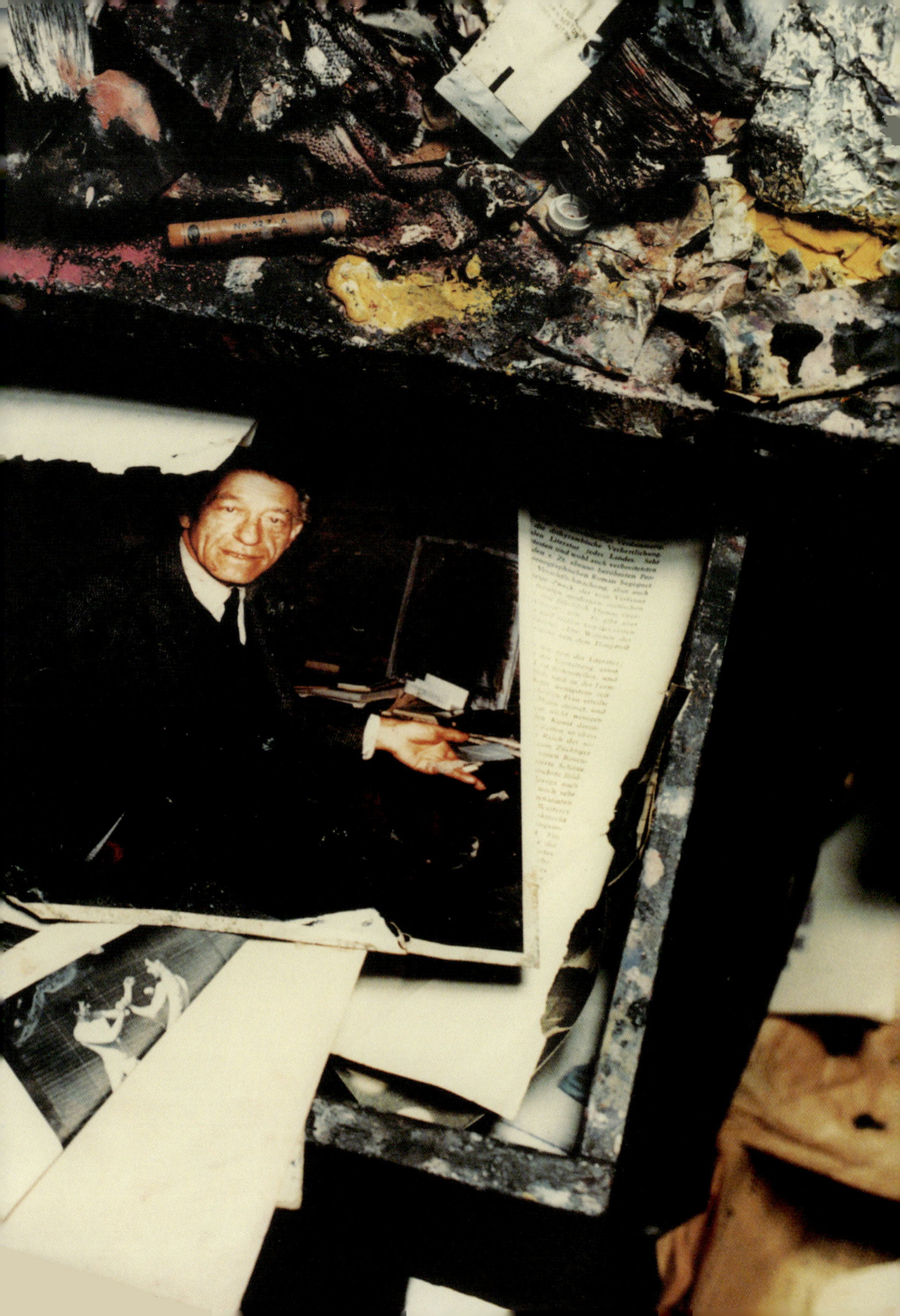

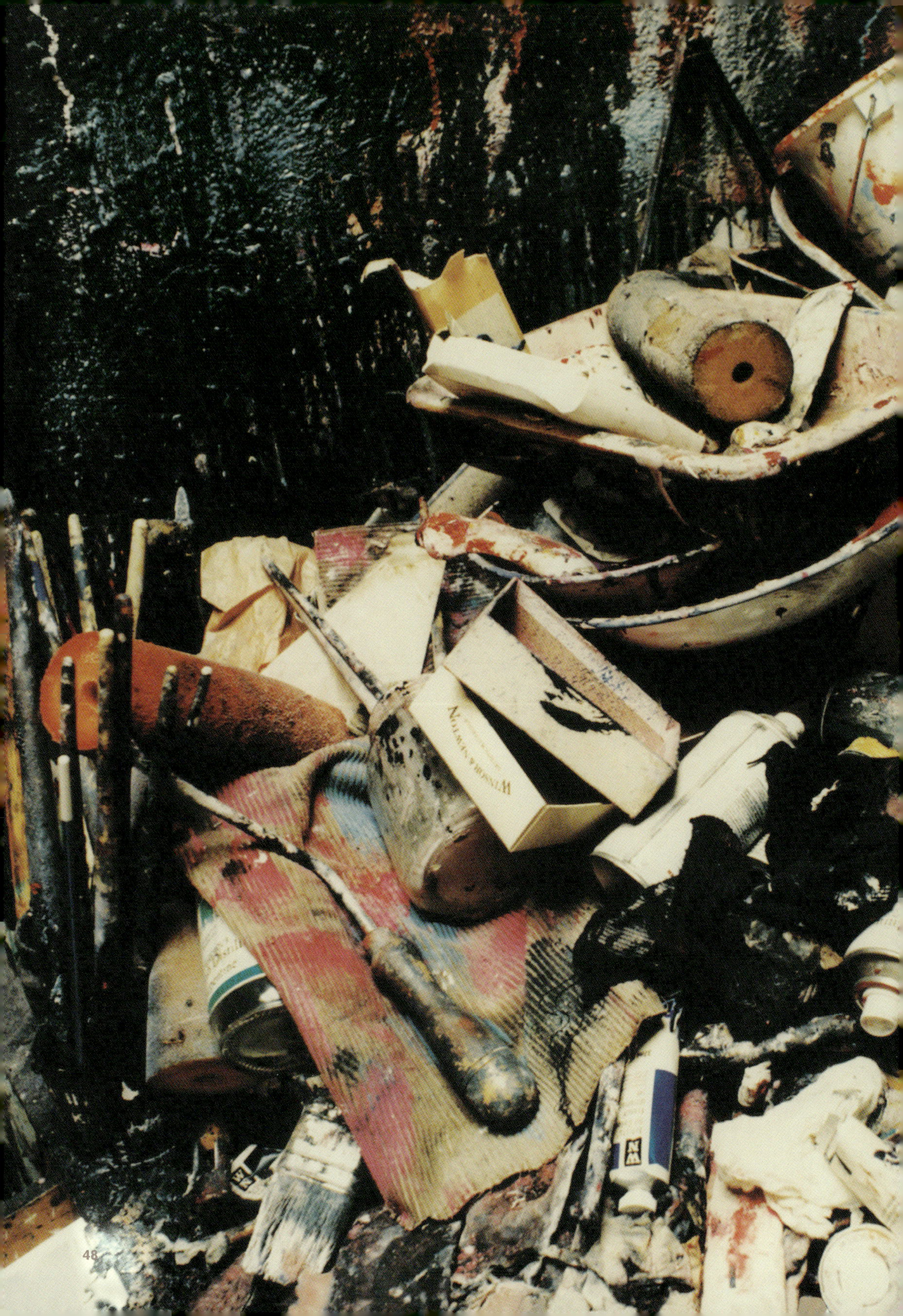

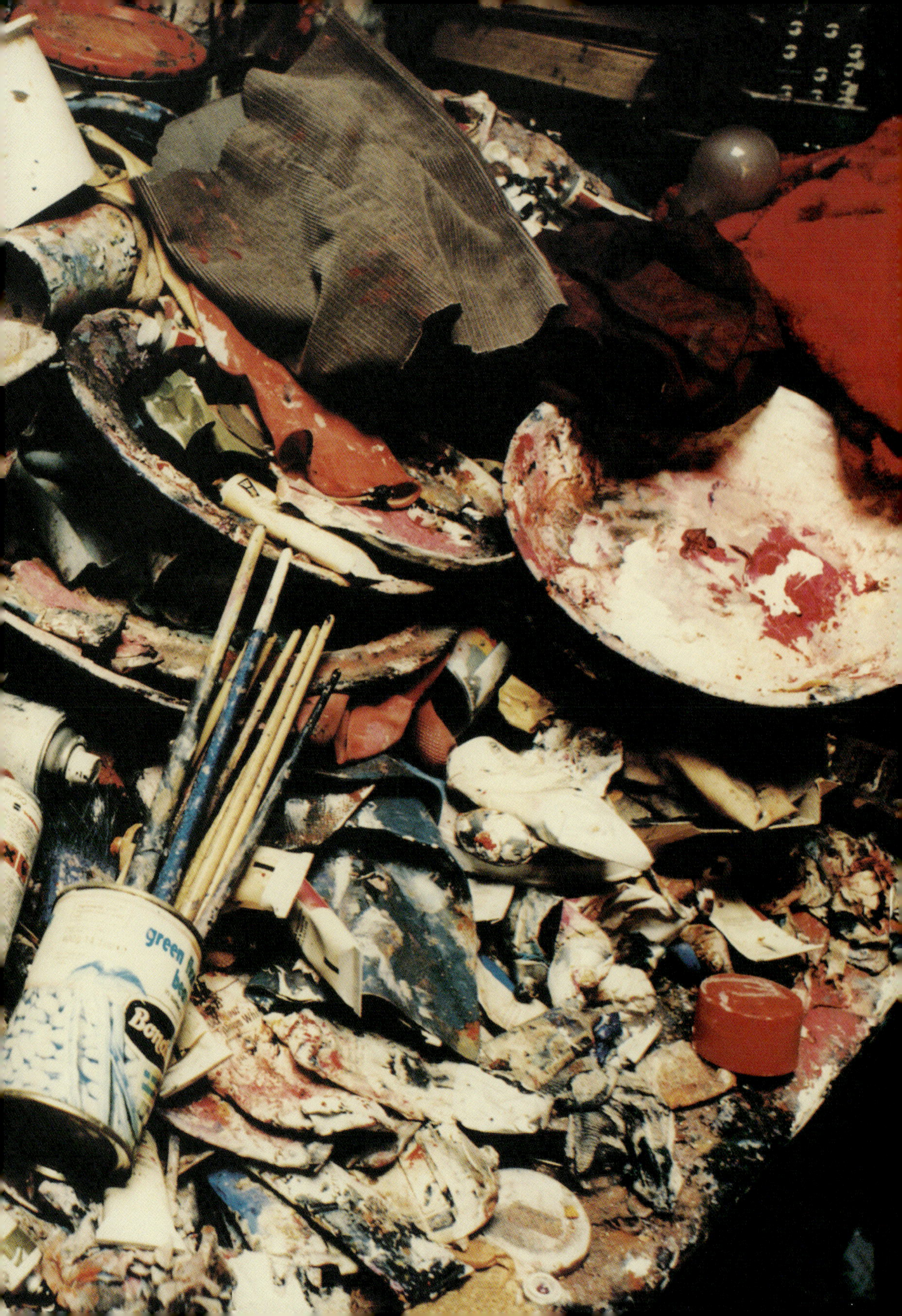

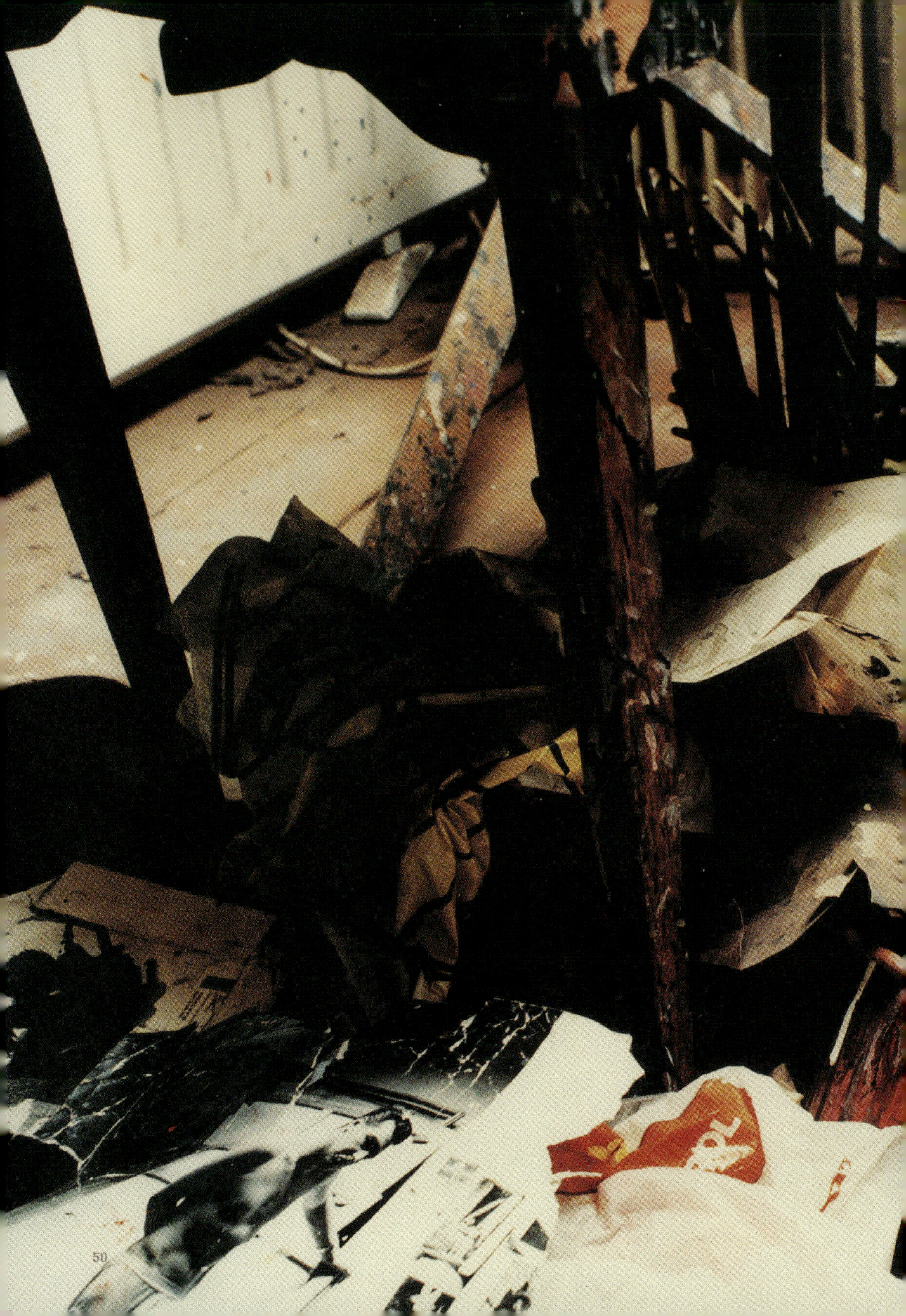

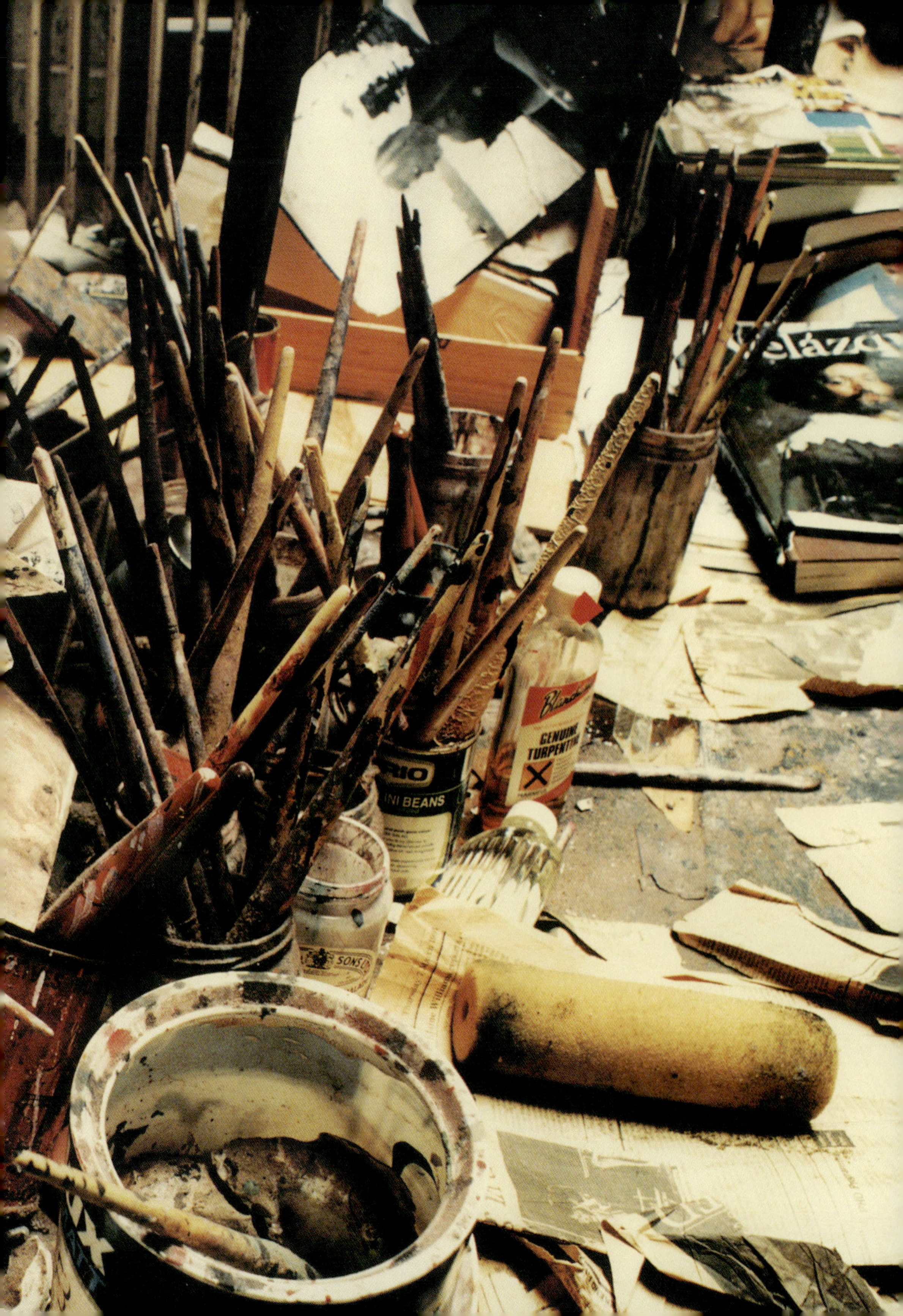
Velázquez
OIL
NI BEANS
Blanche...
GENUINE
TURPENTINE
SONS

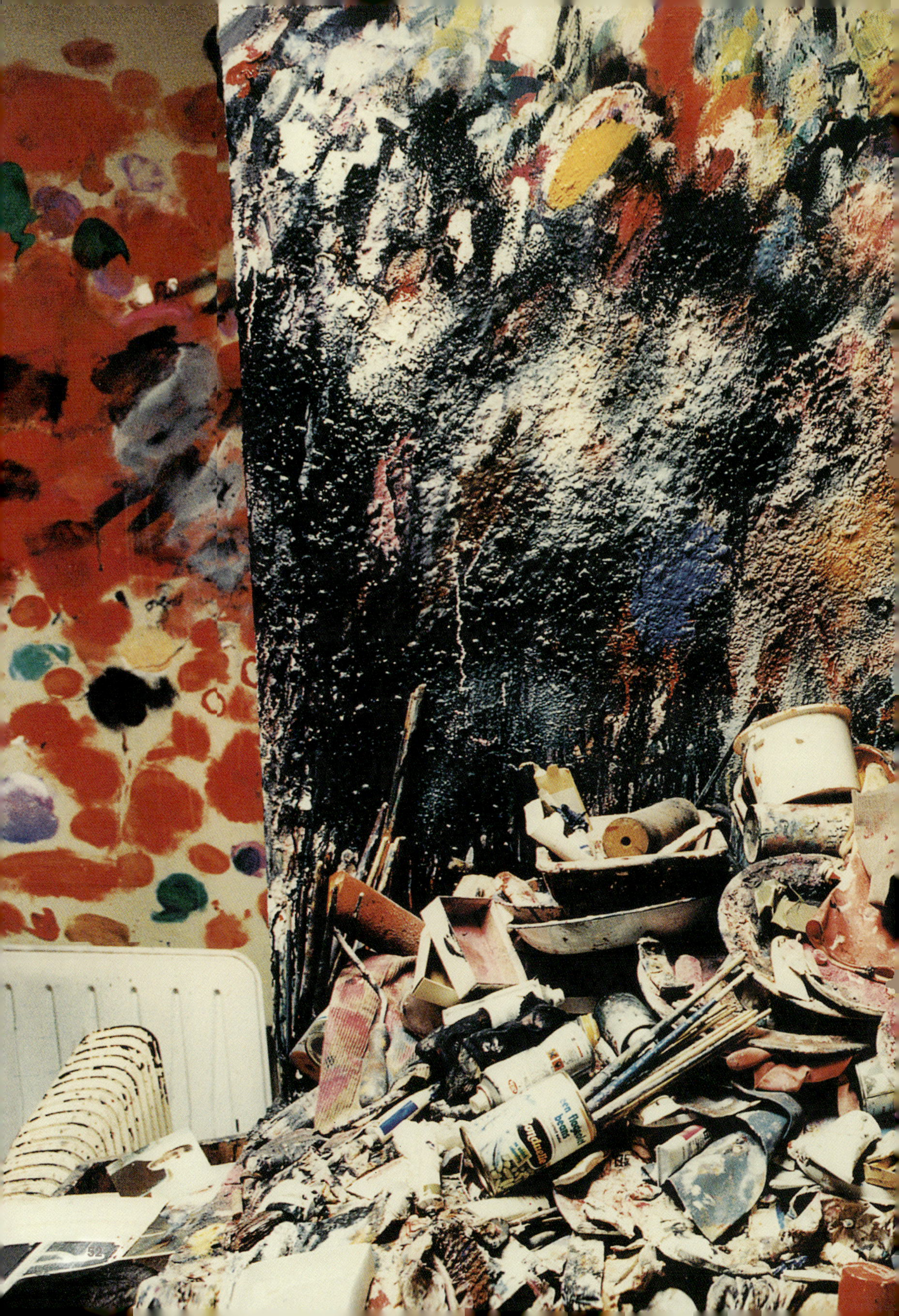

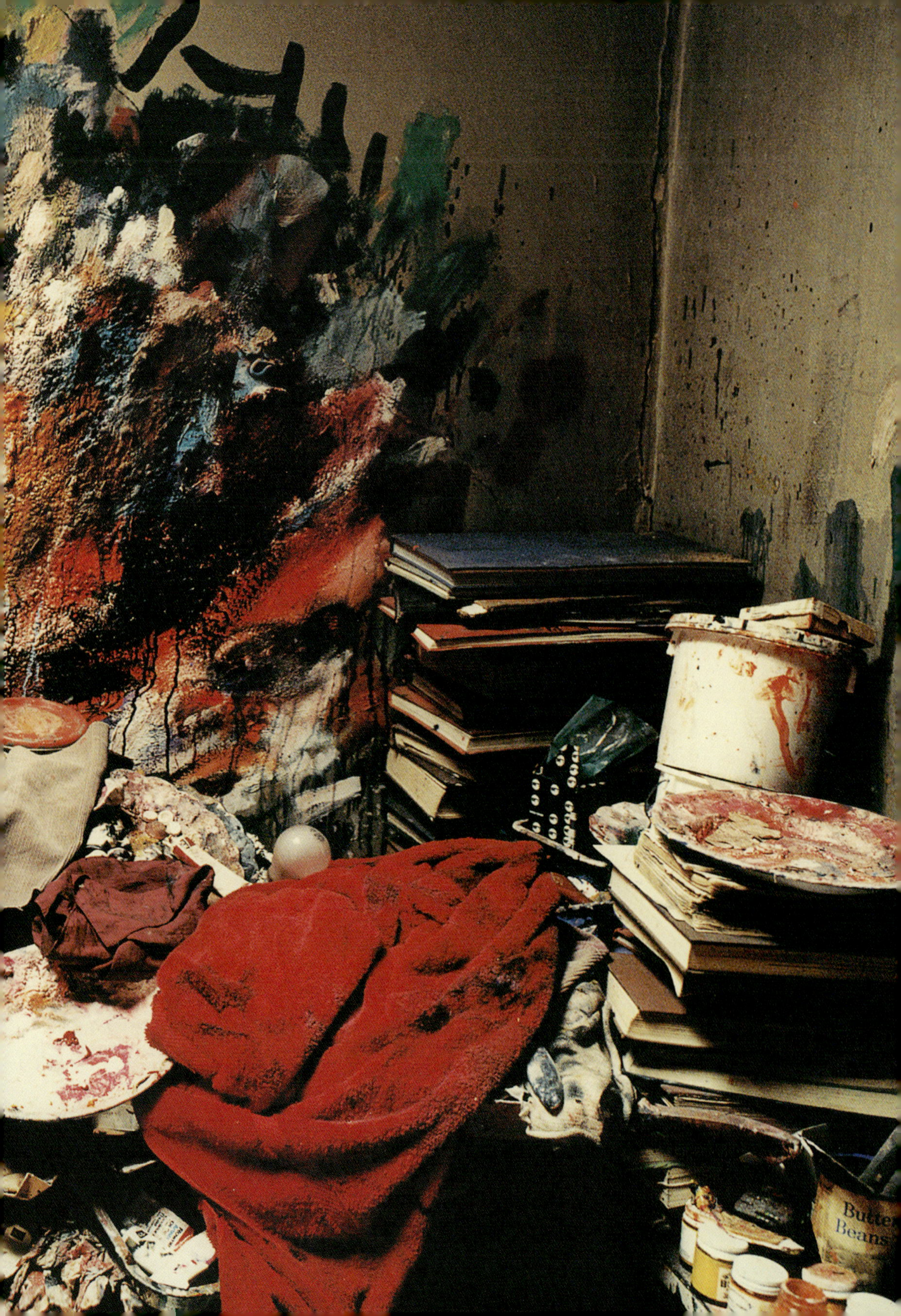

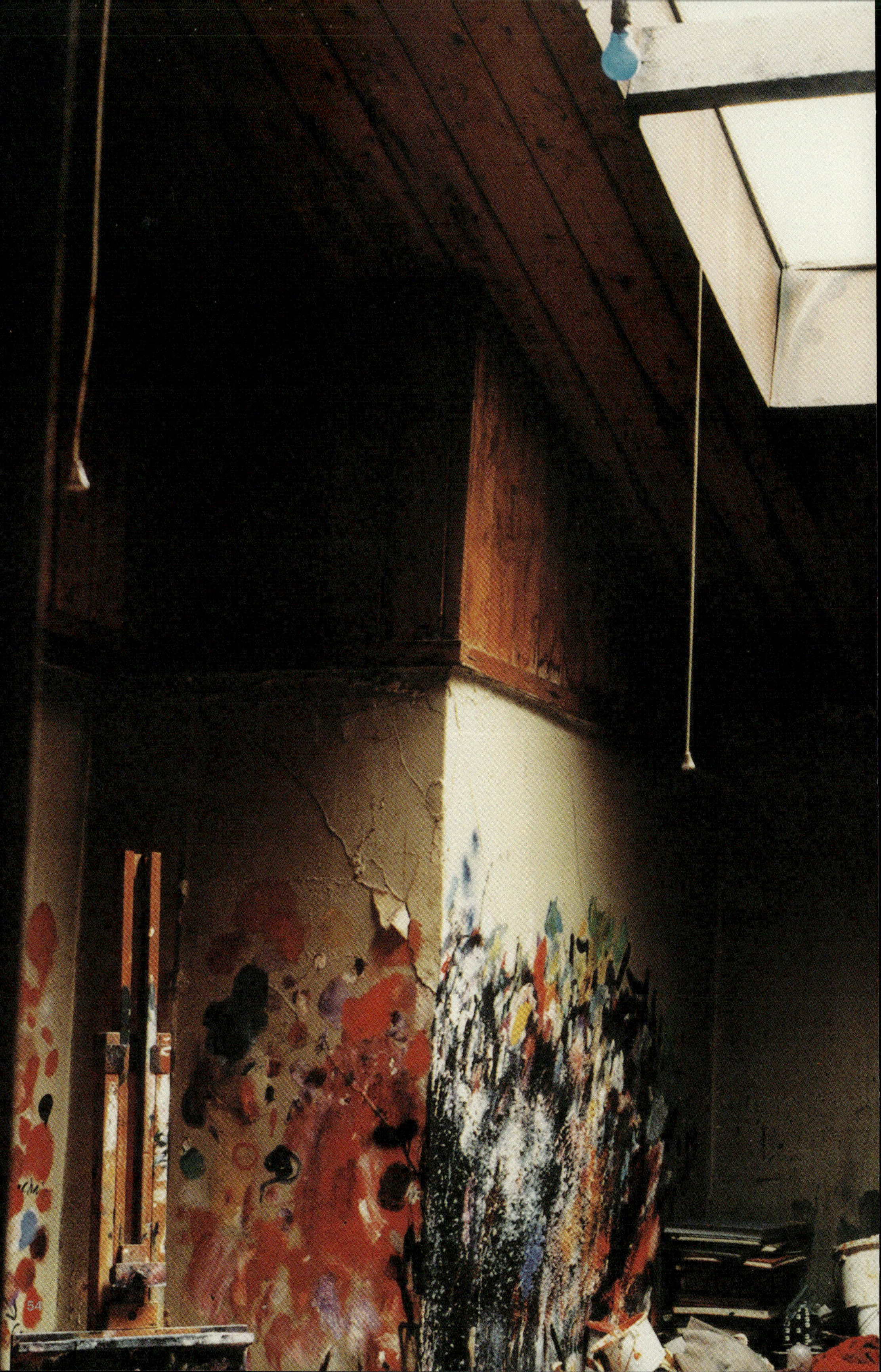

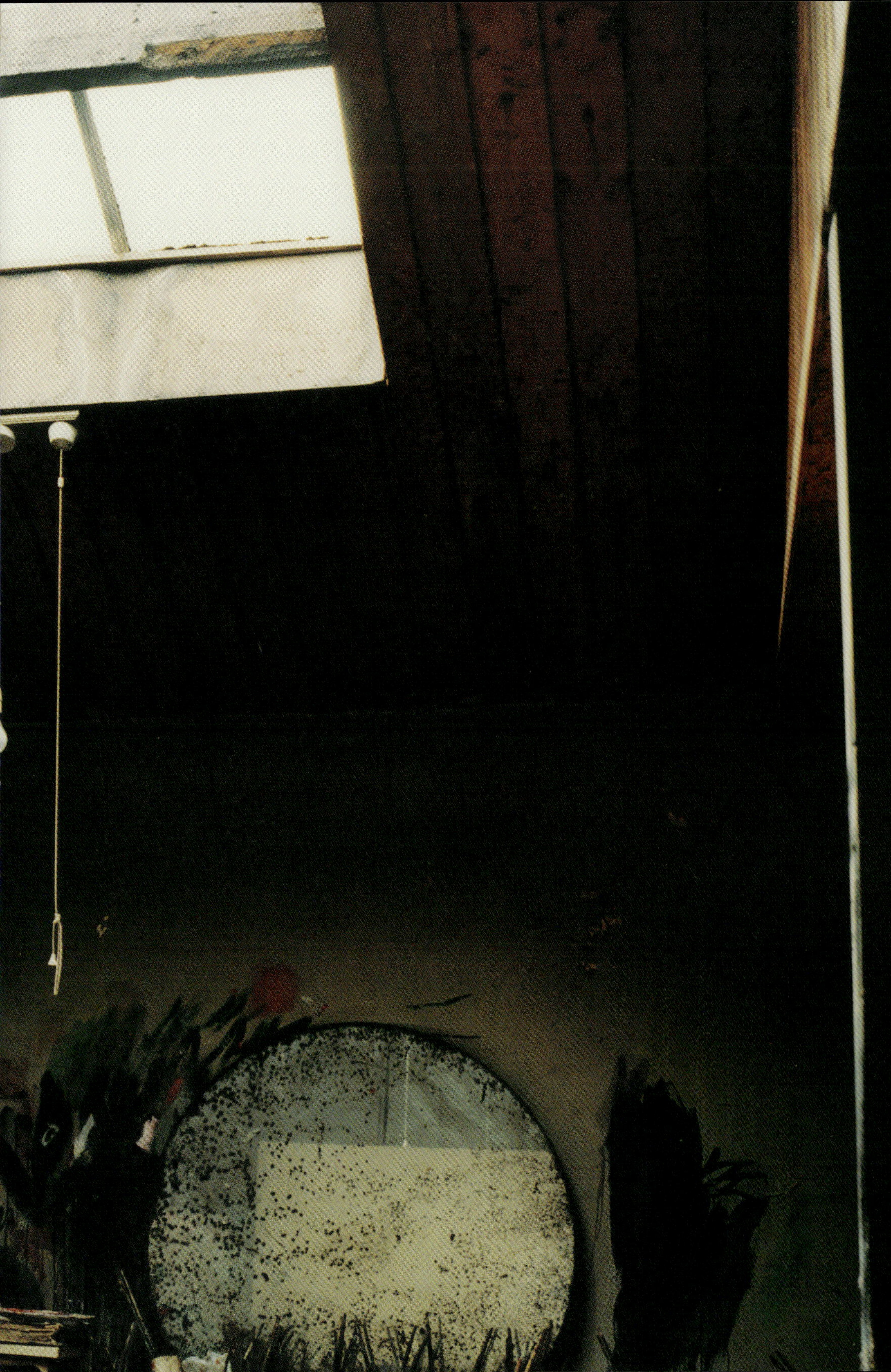

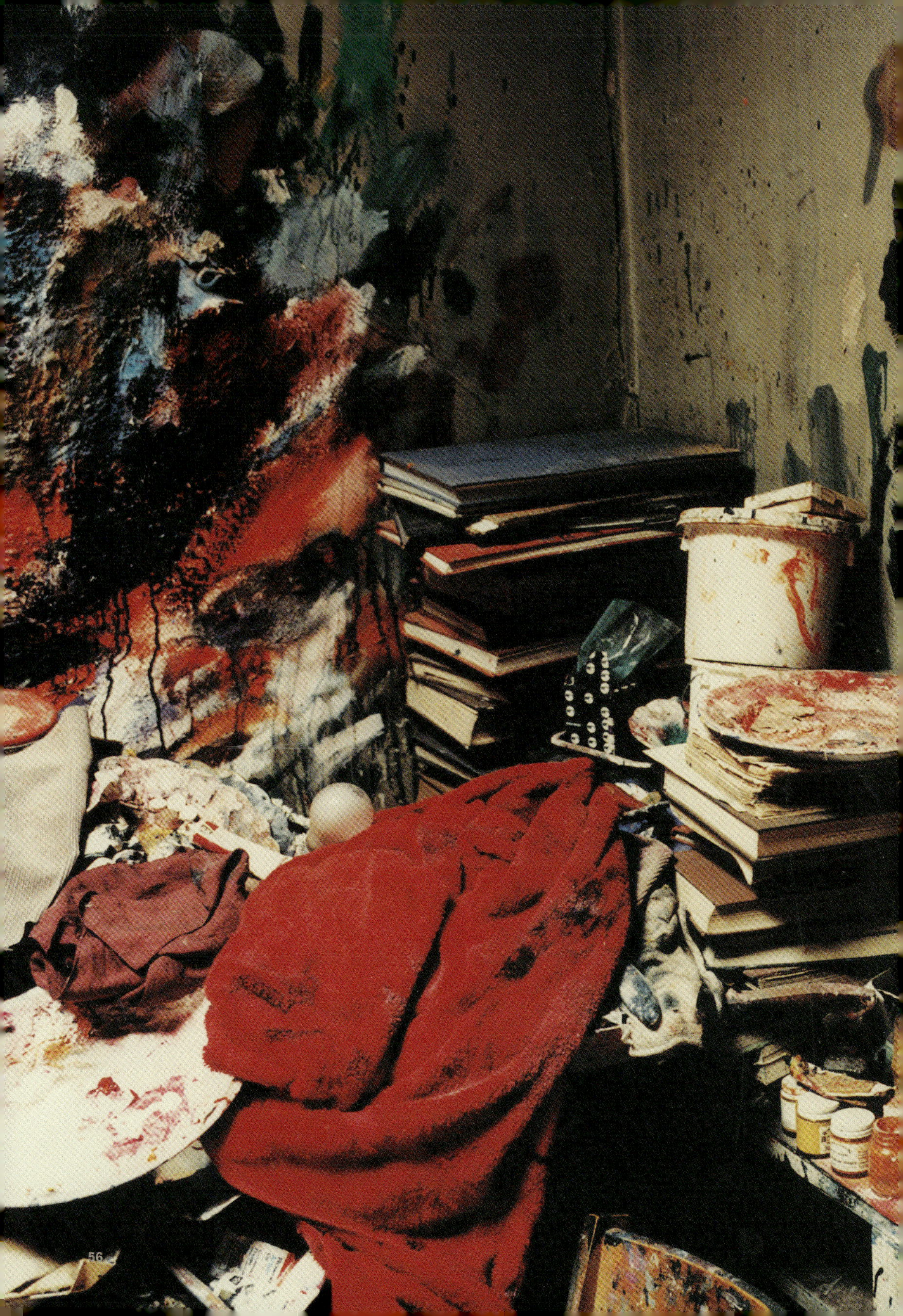

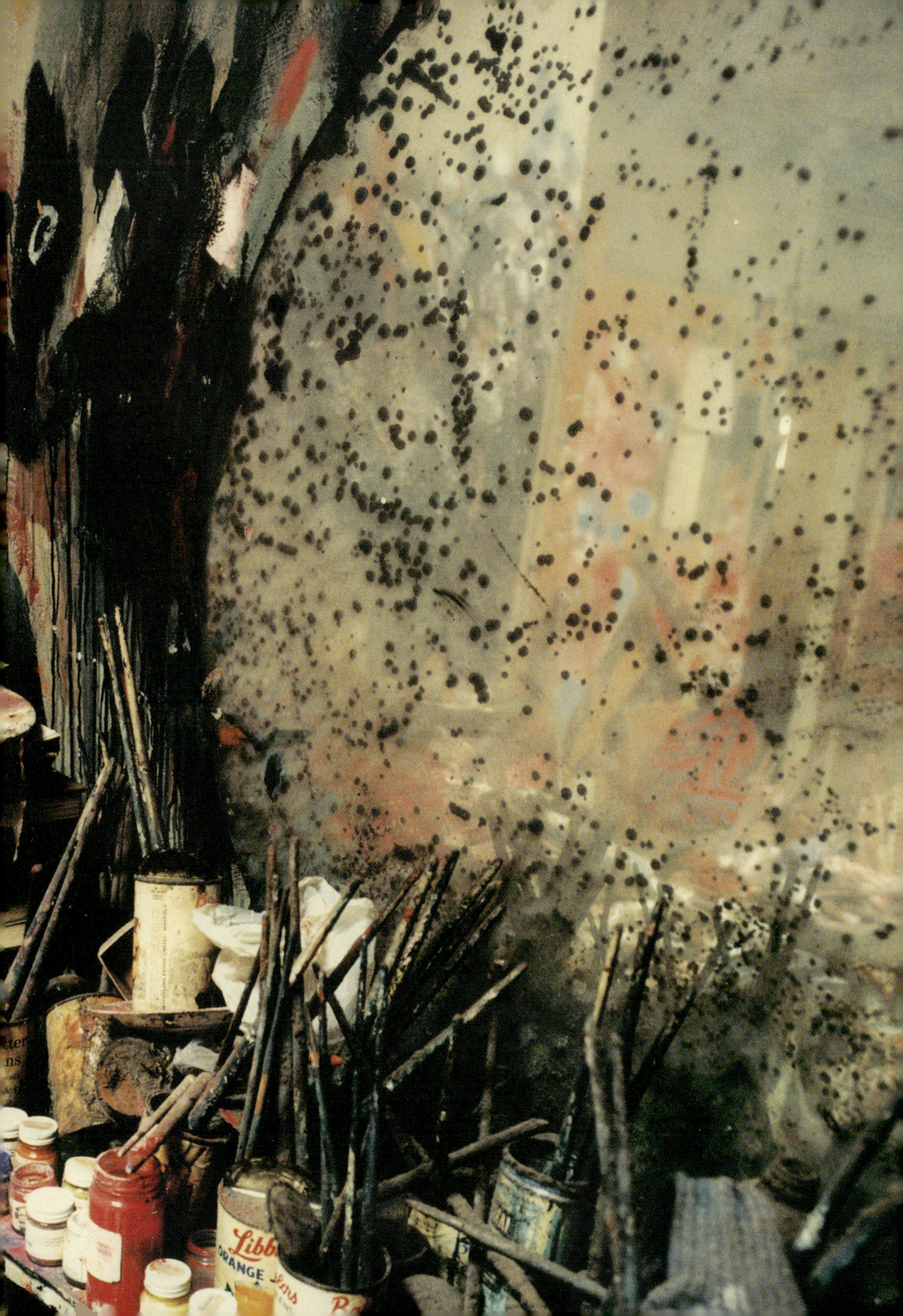

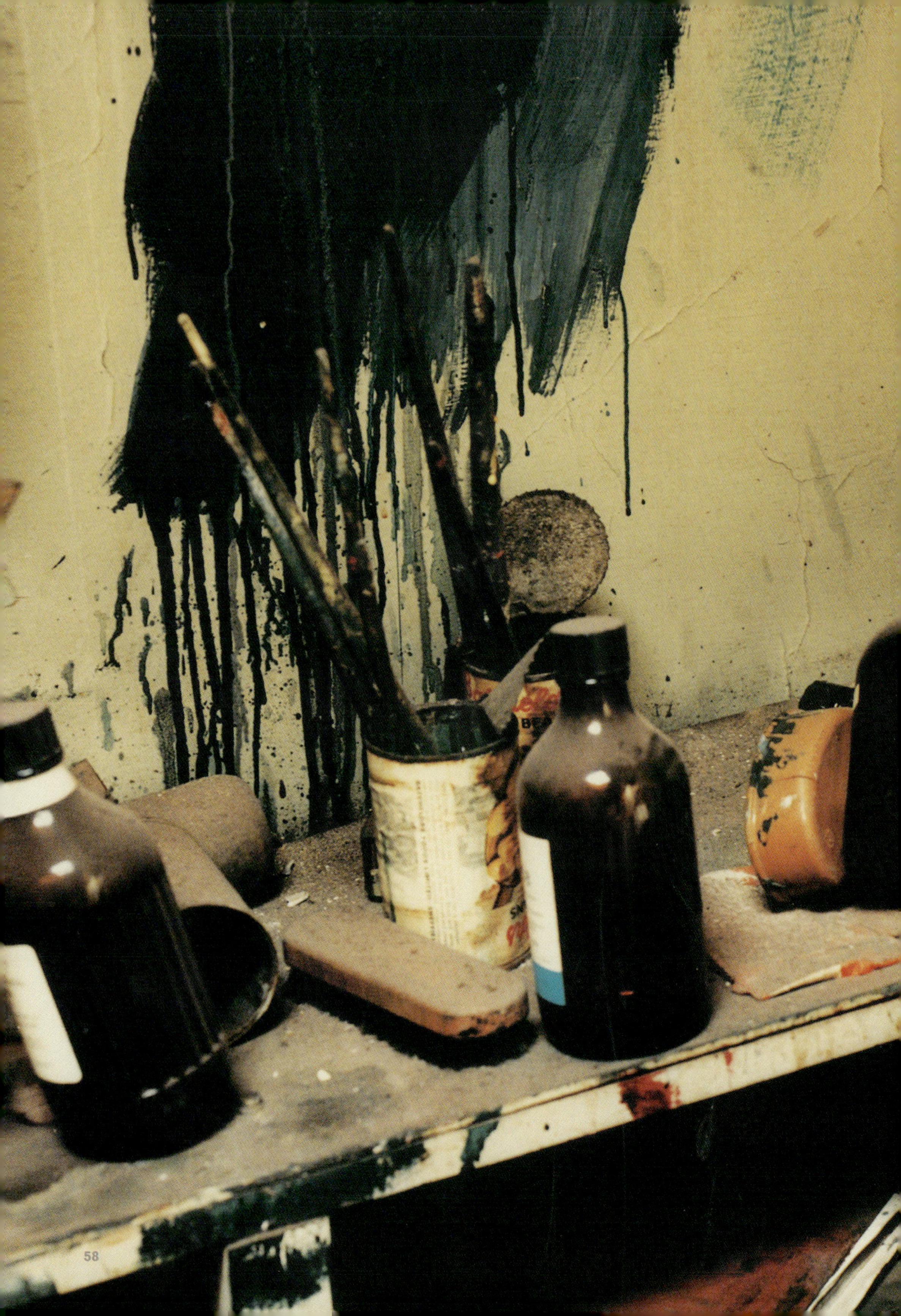

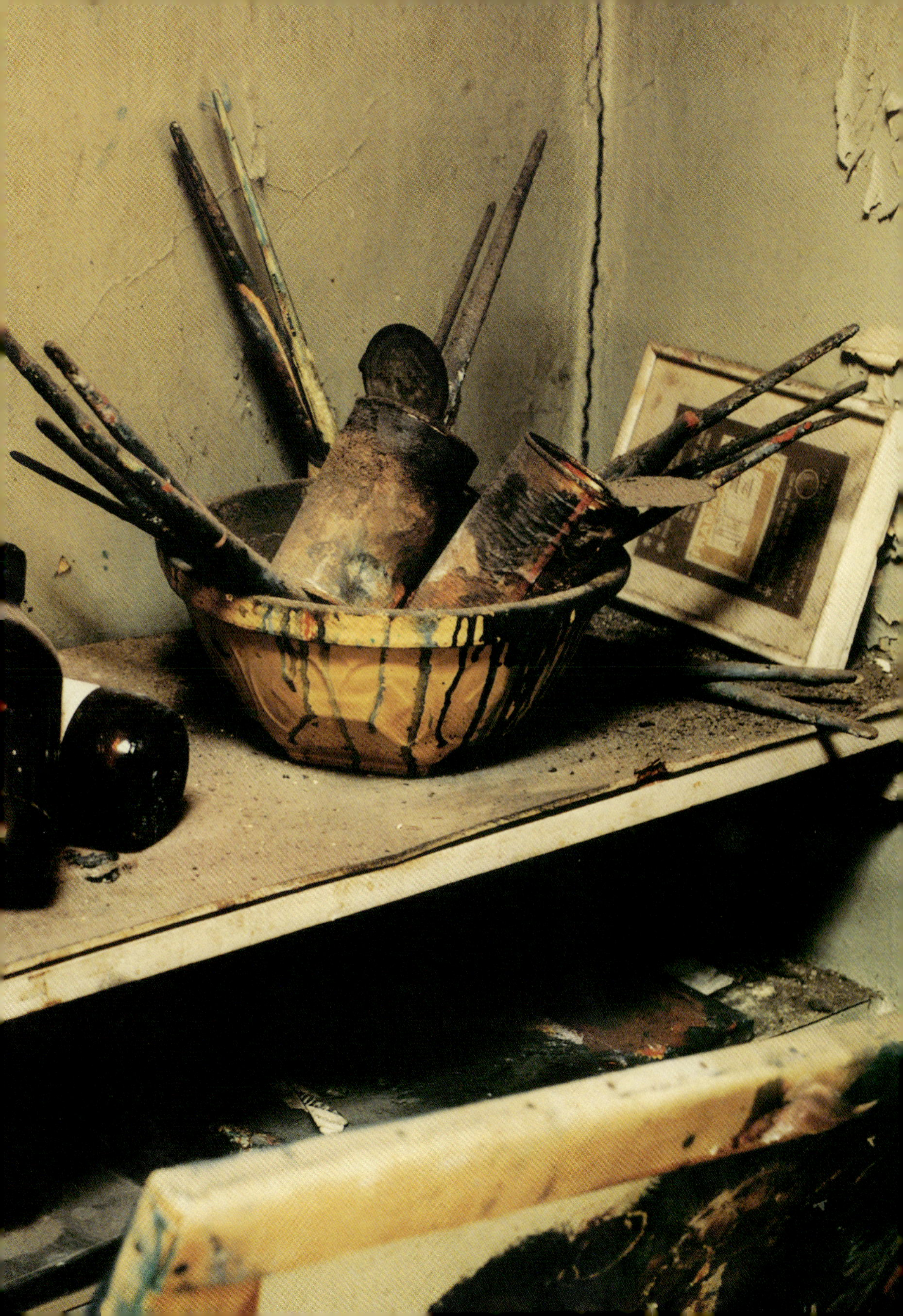

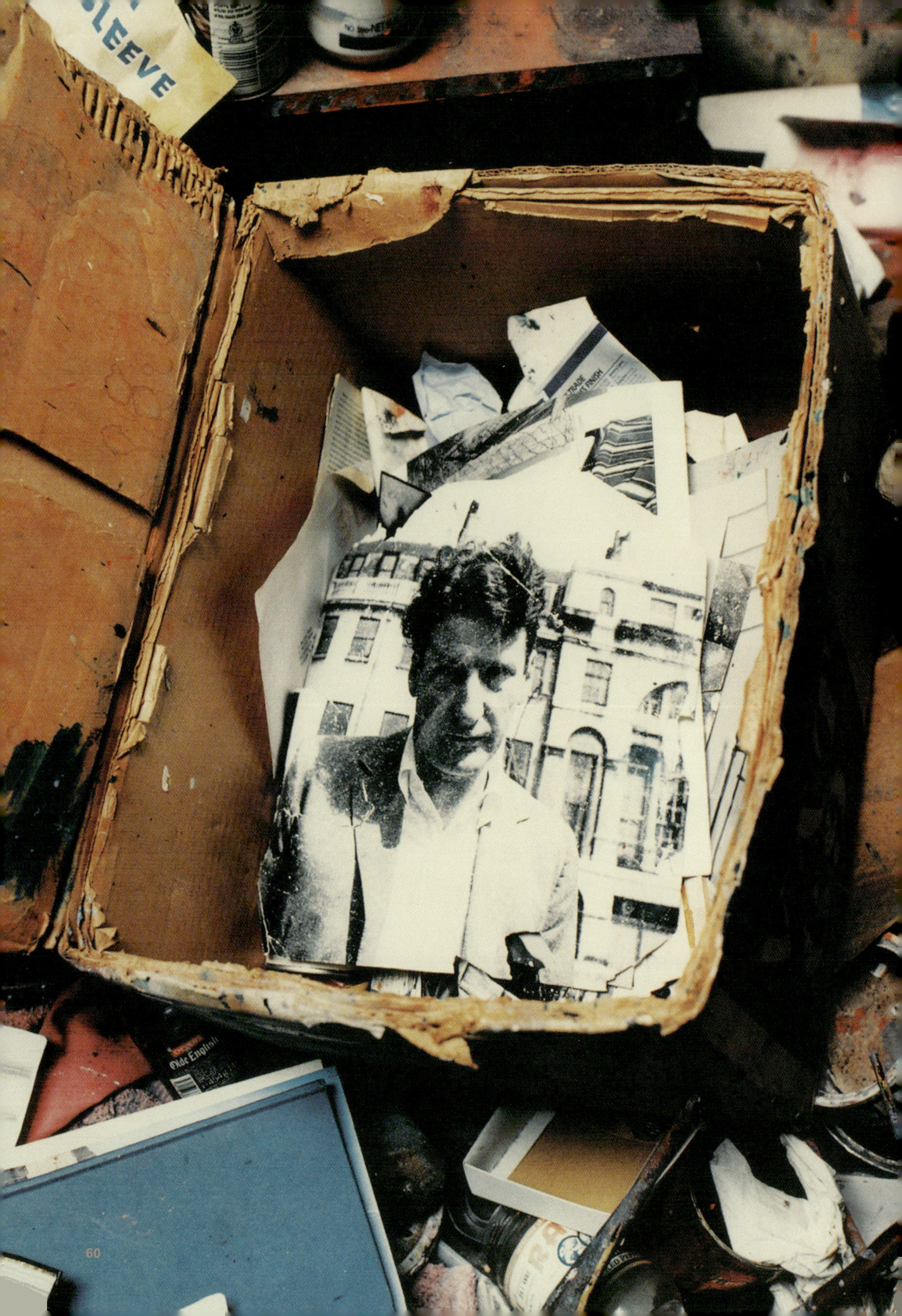
SLEEVE
Olde English

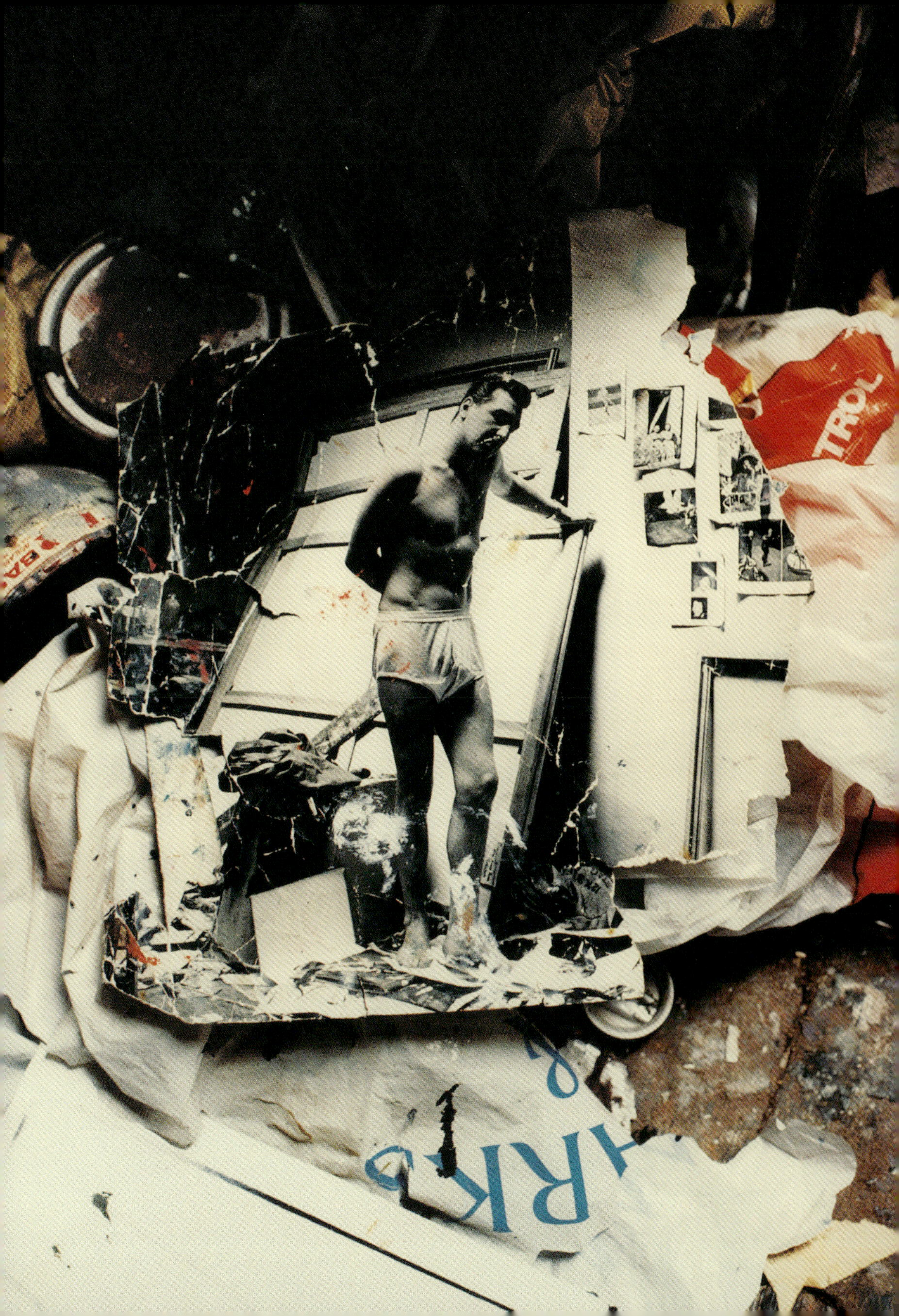
TROL
RKS

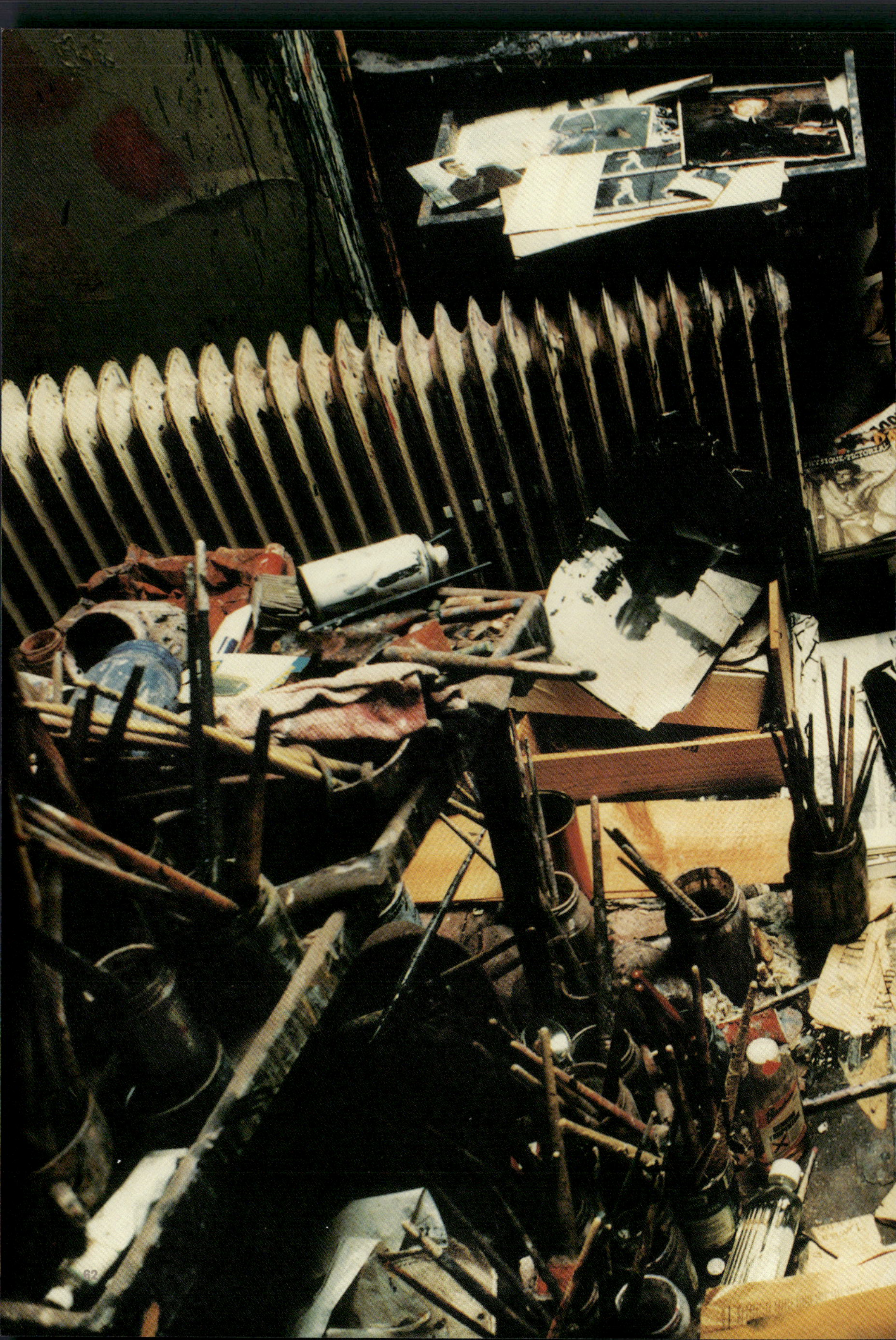
PHYSIQUE PICTORIAL

azquez
l'esquisse
Science
CRT
HISTORY OF PHOTOGRAPHY

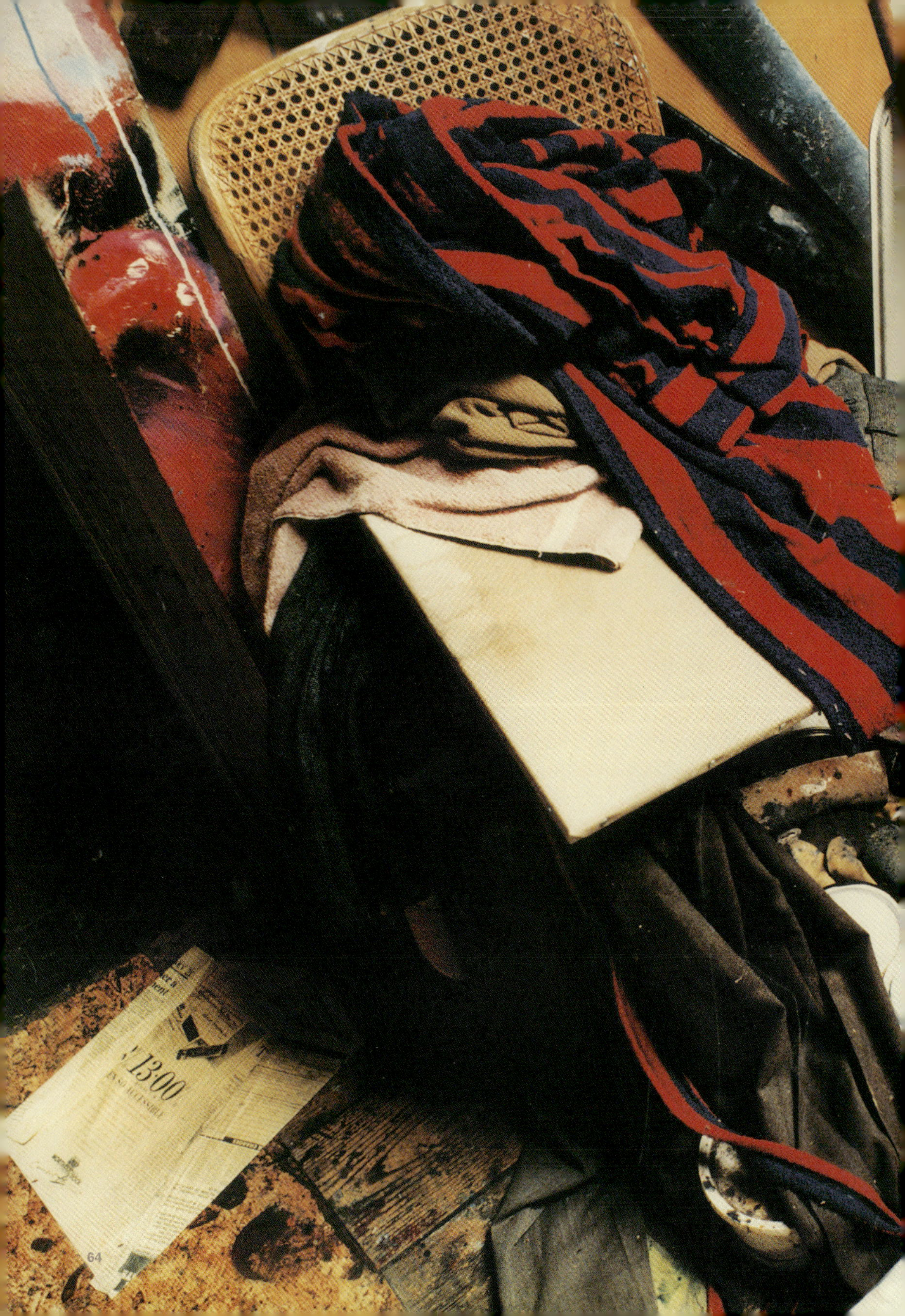

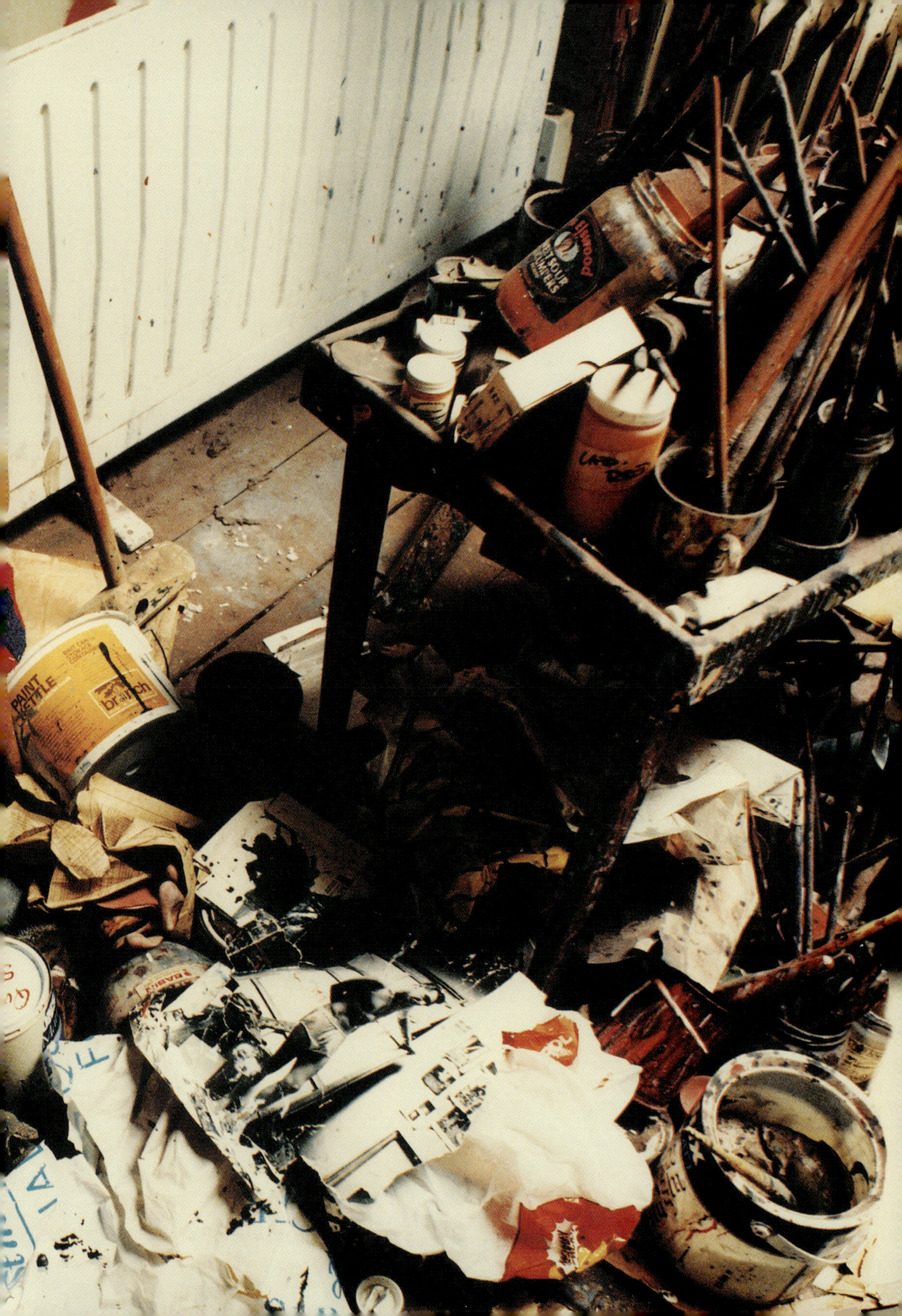

PAINT
KETTLE
branch

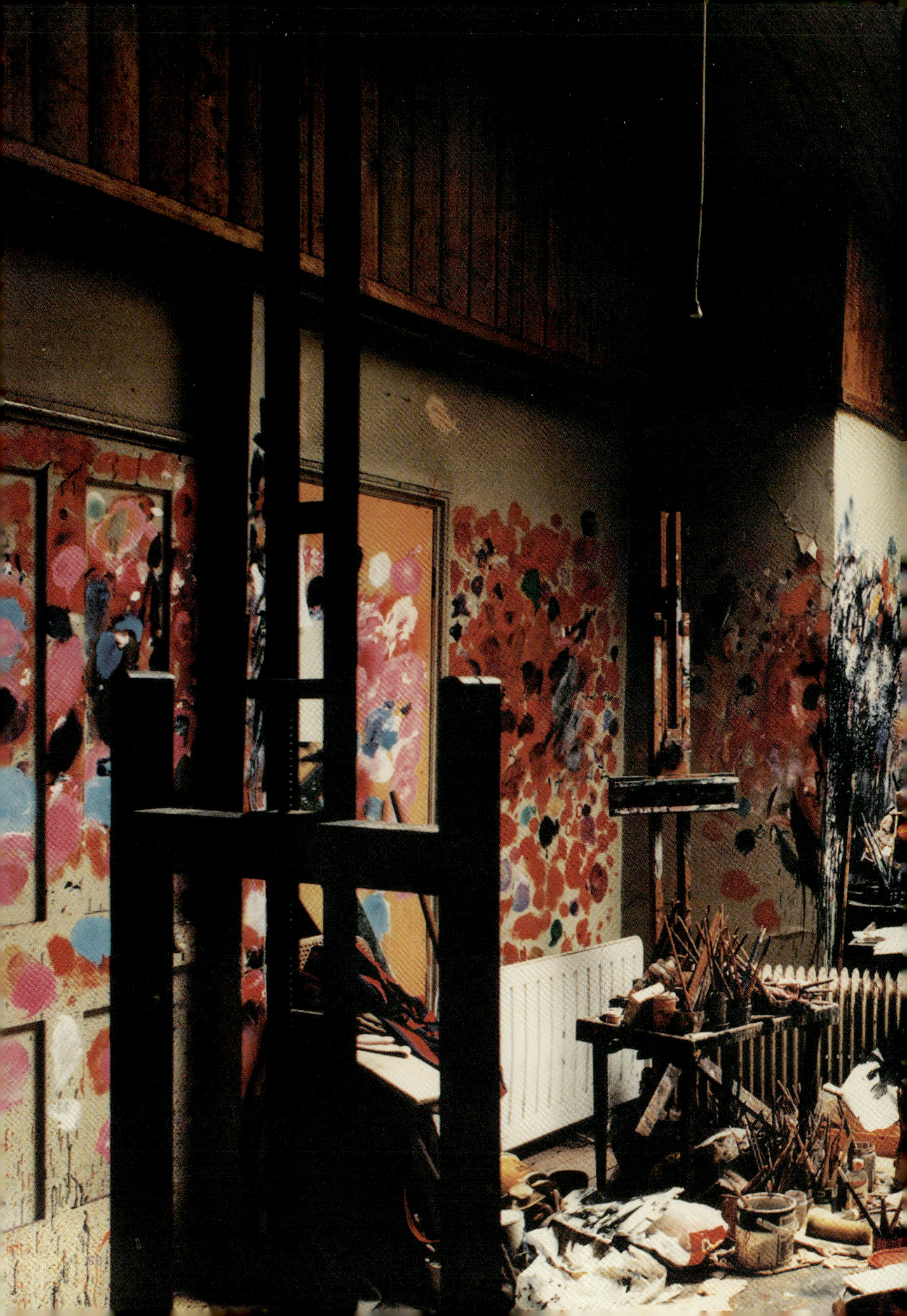

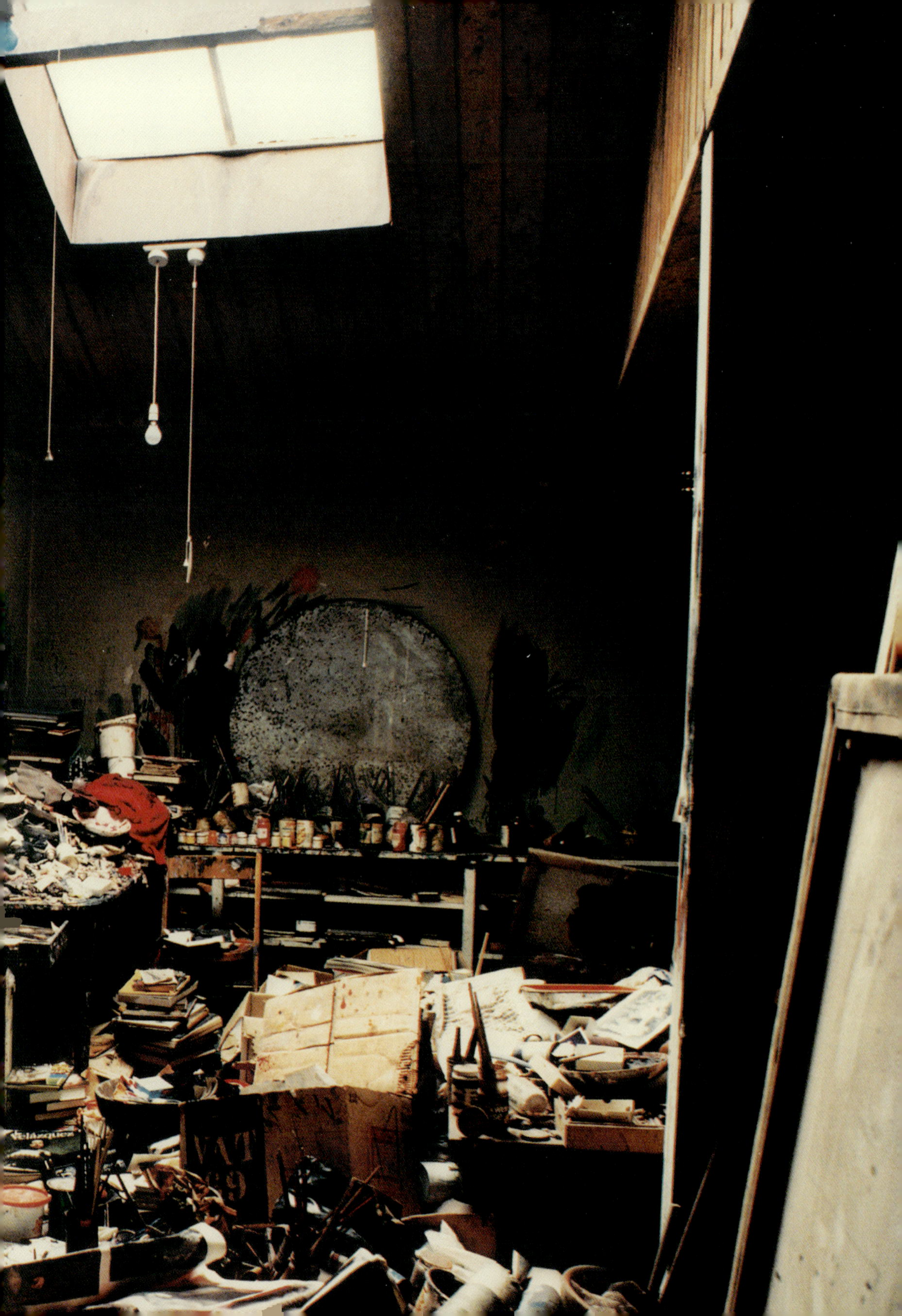

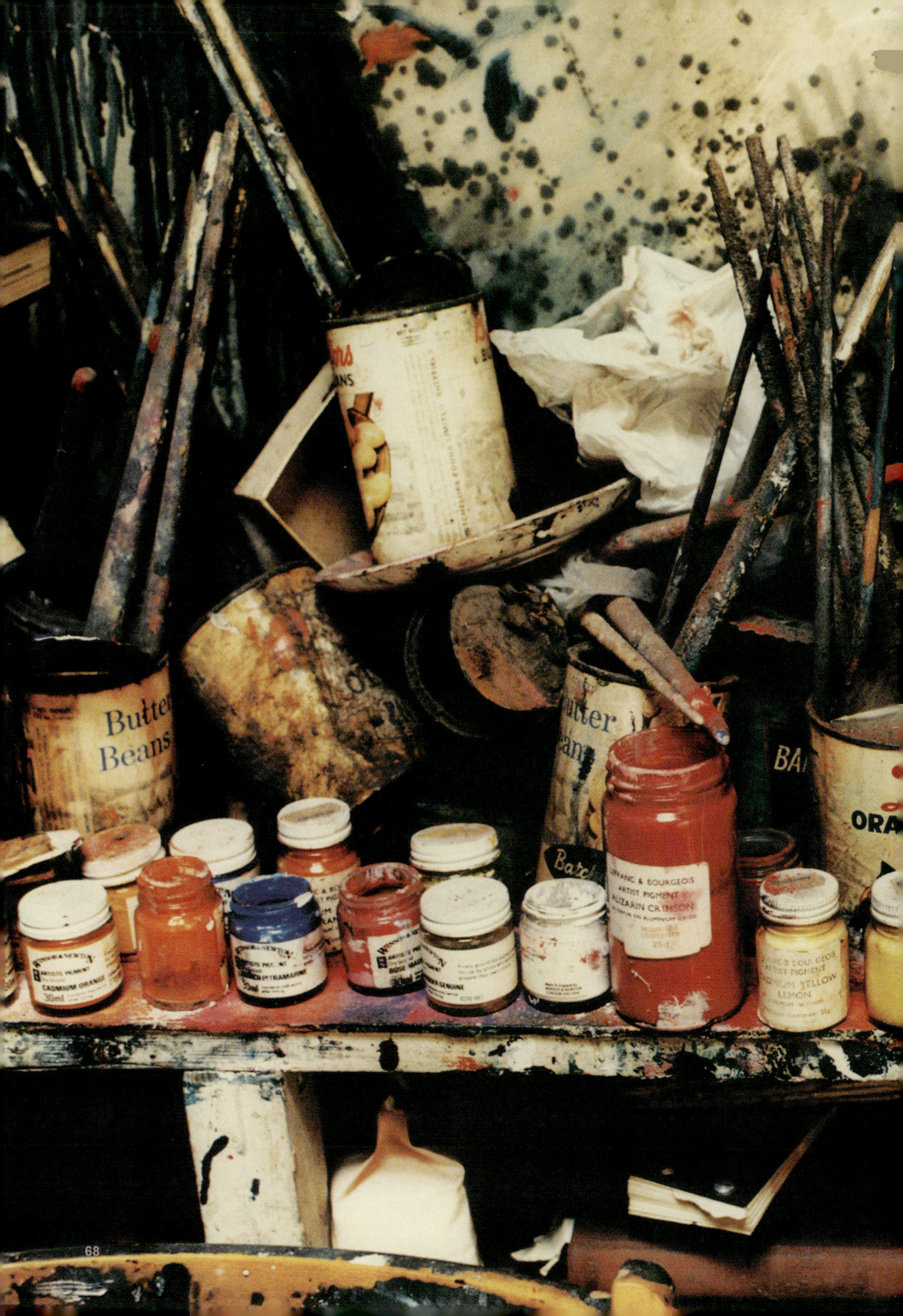

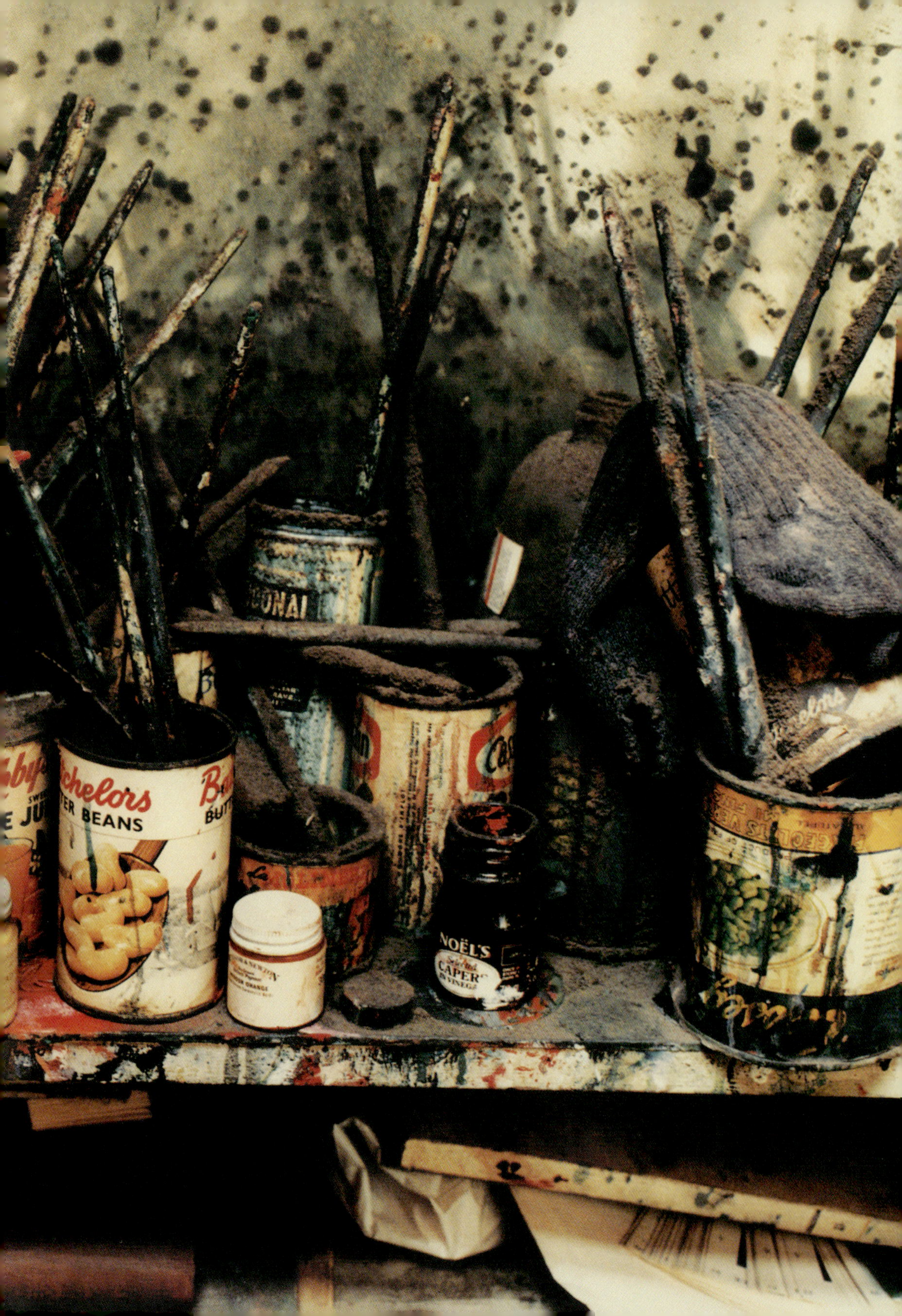

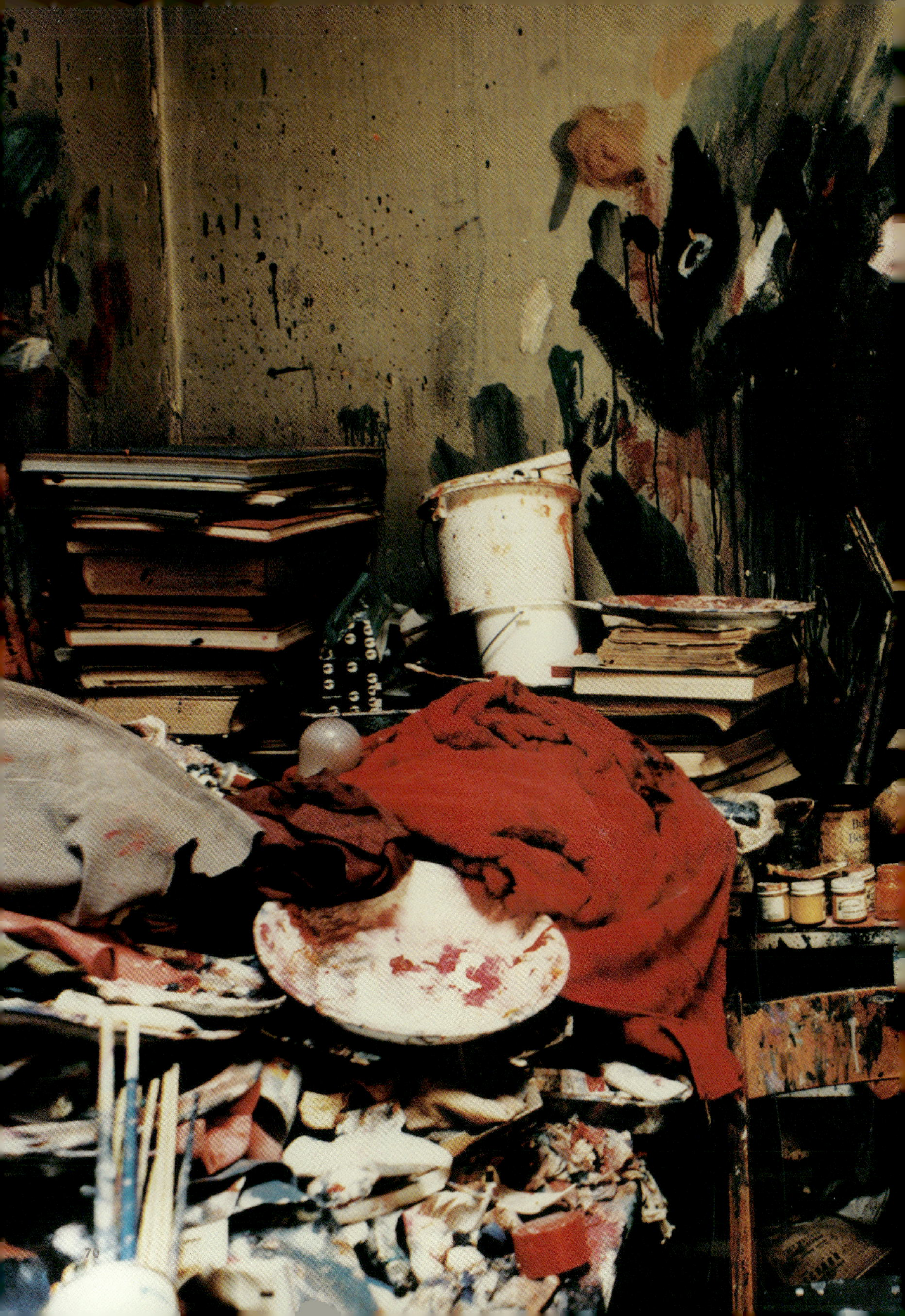

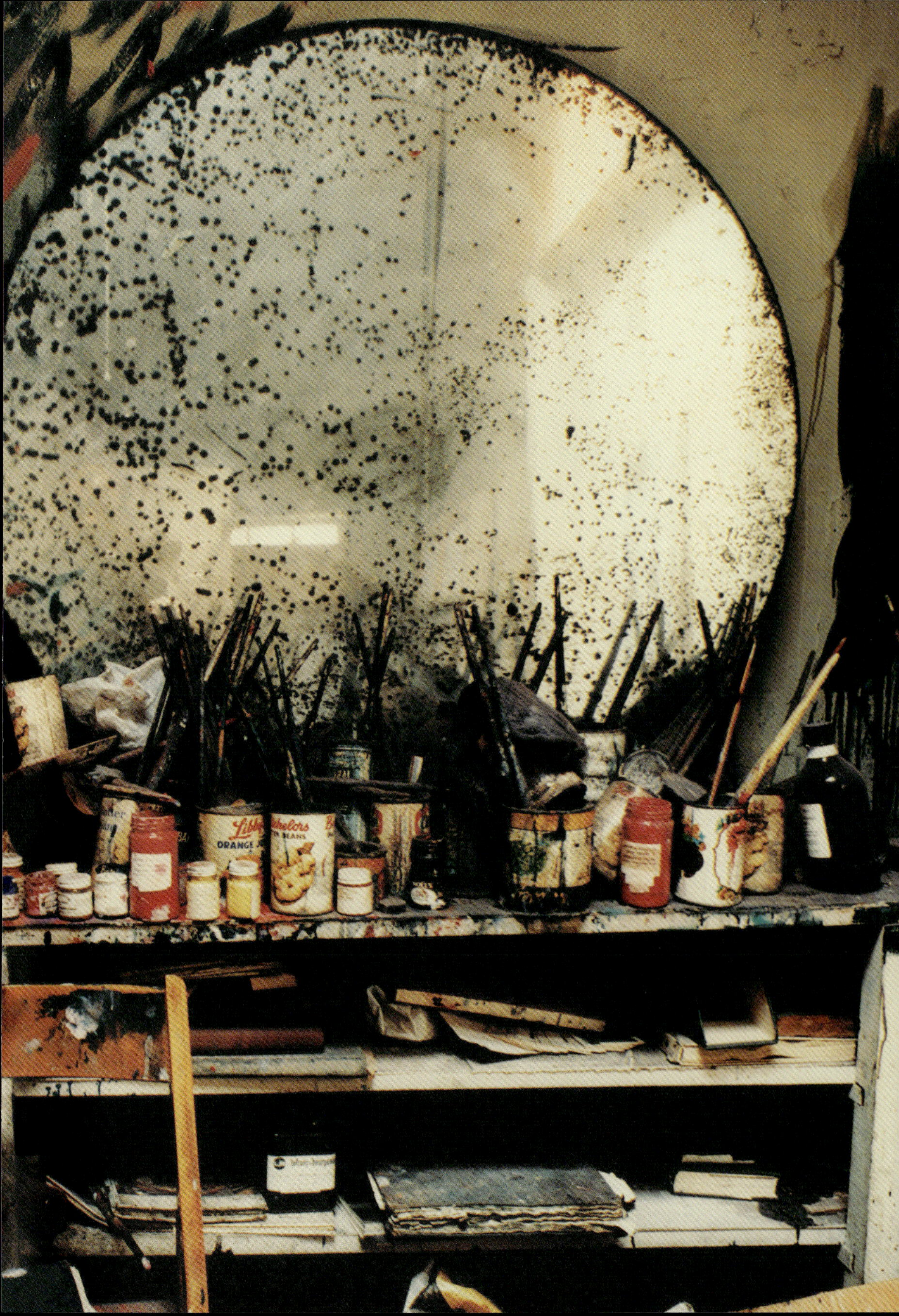

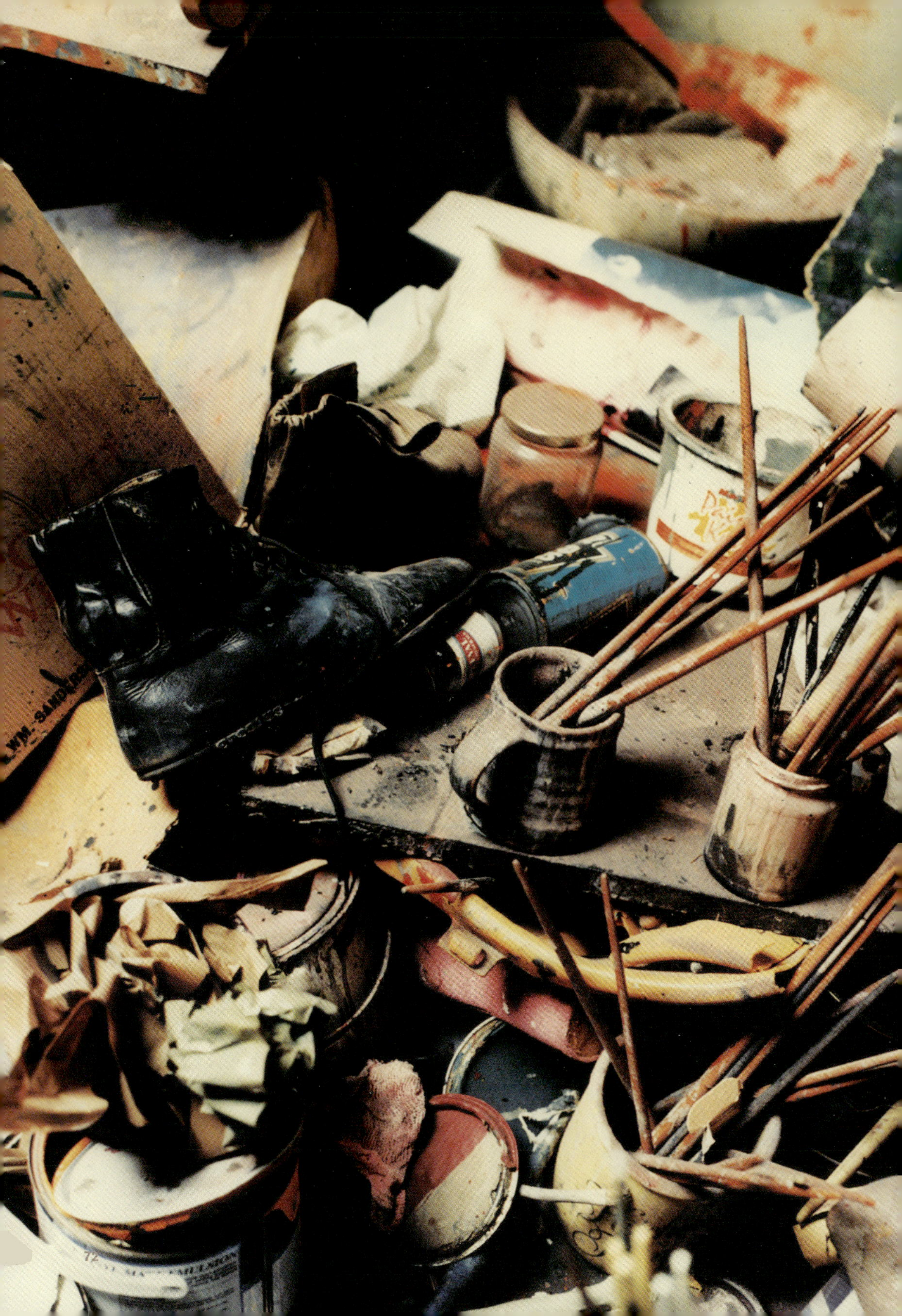

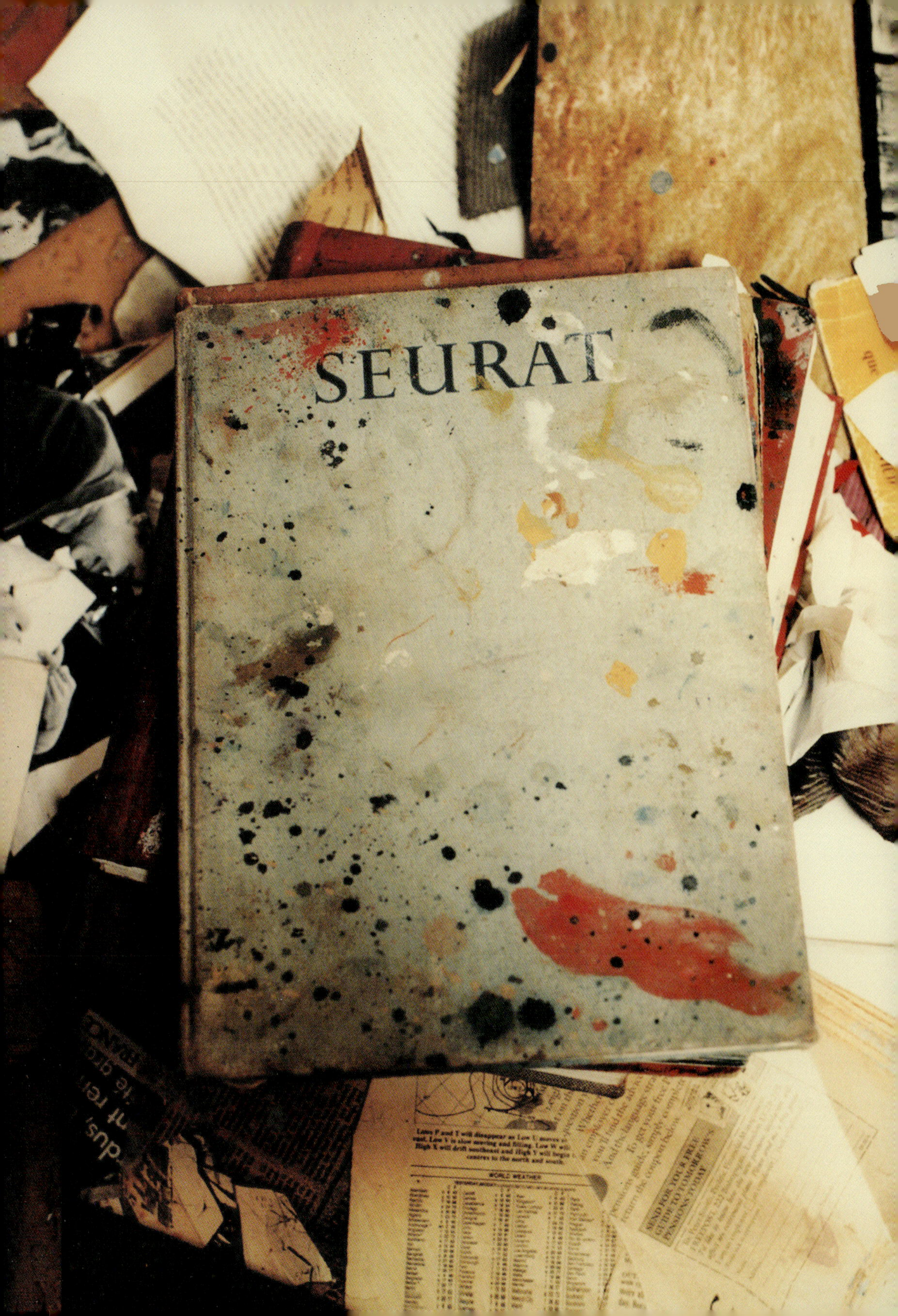
SEURAT

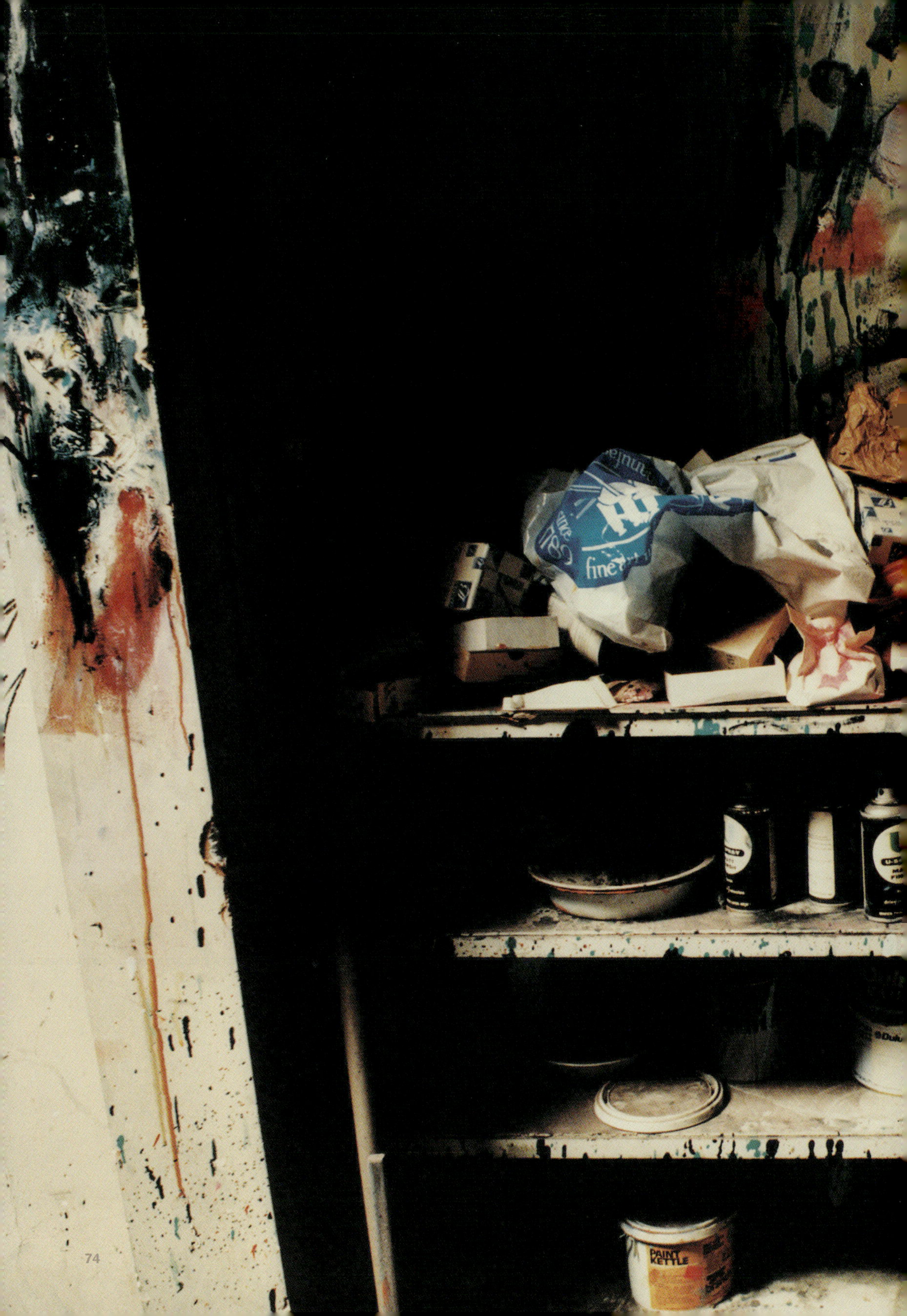

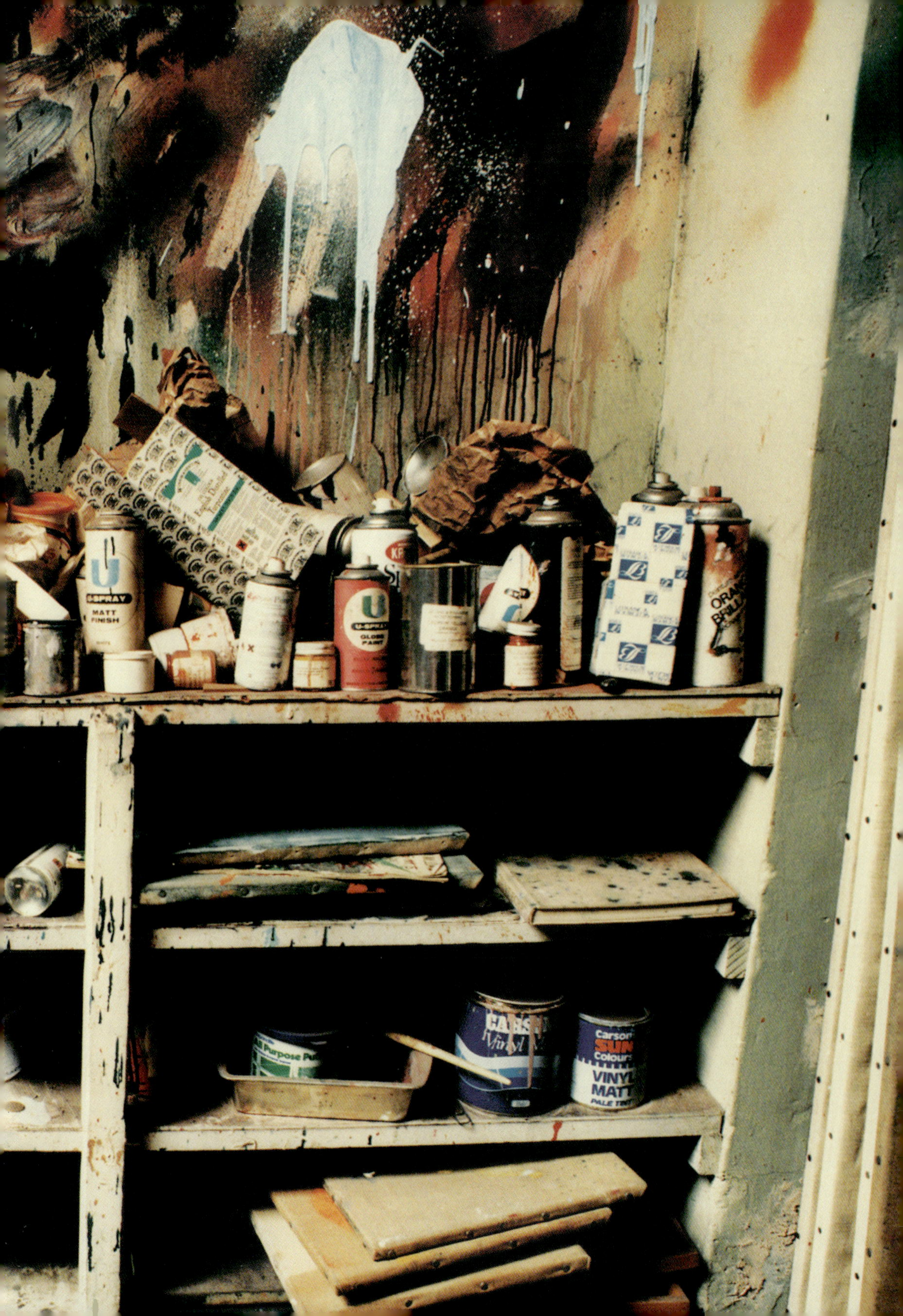

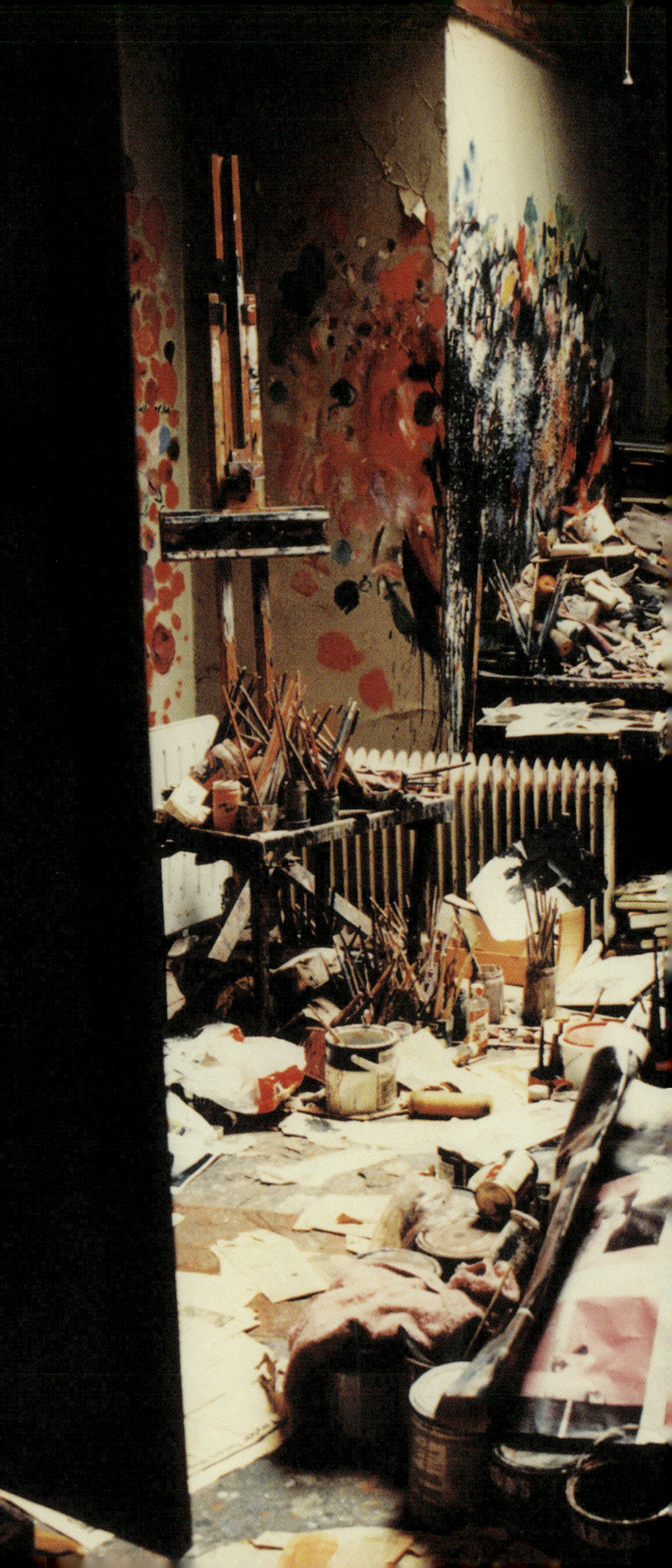

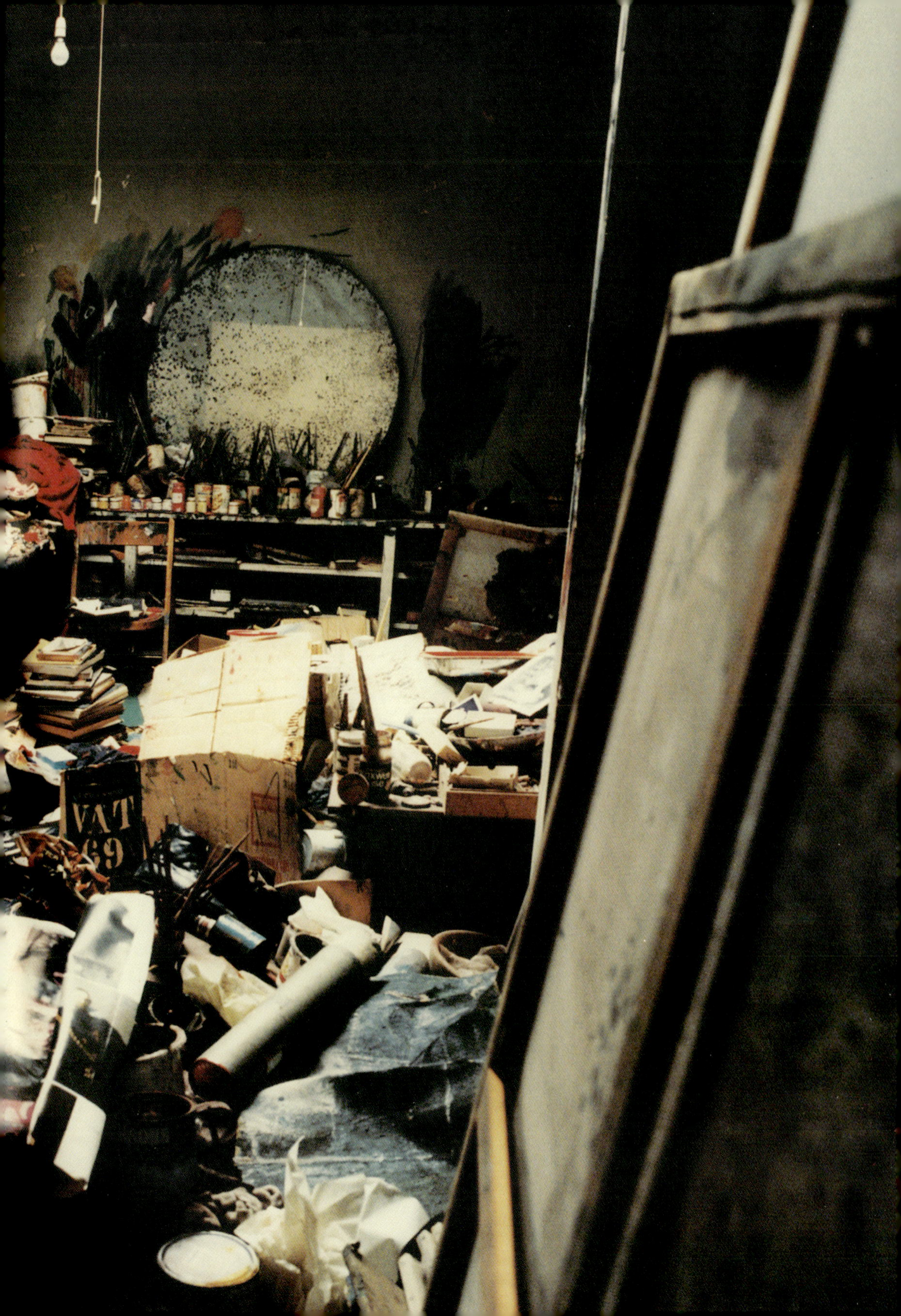

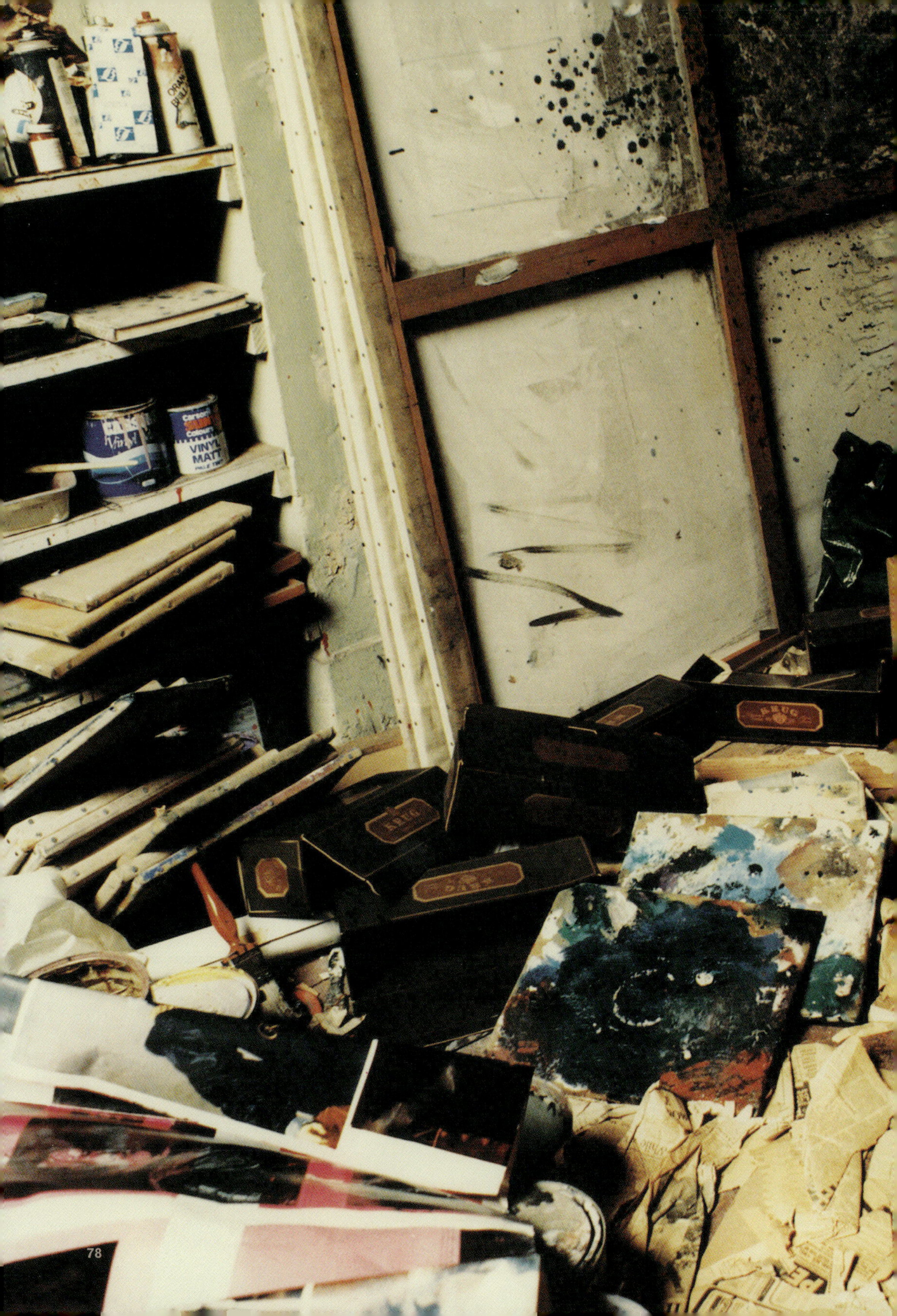

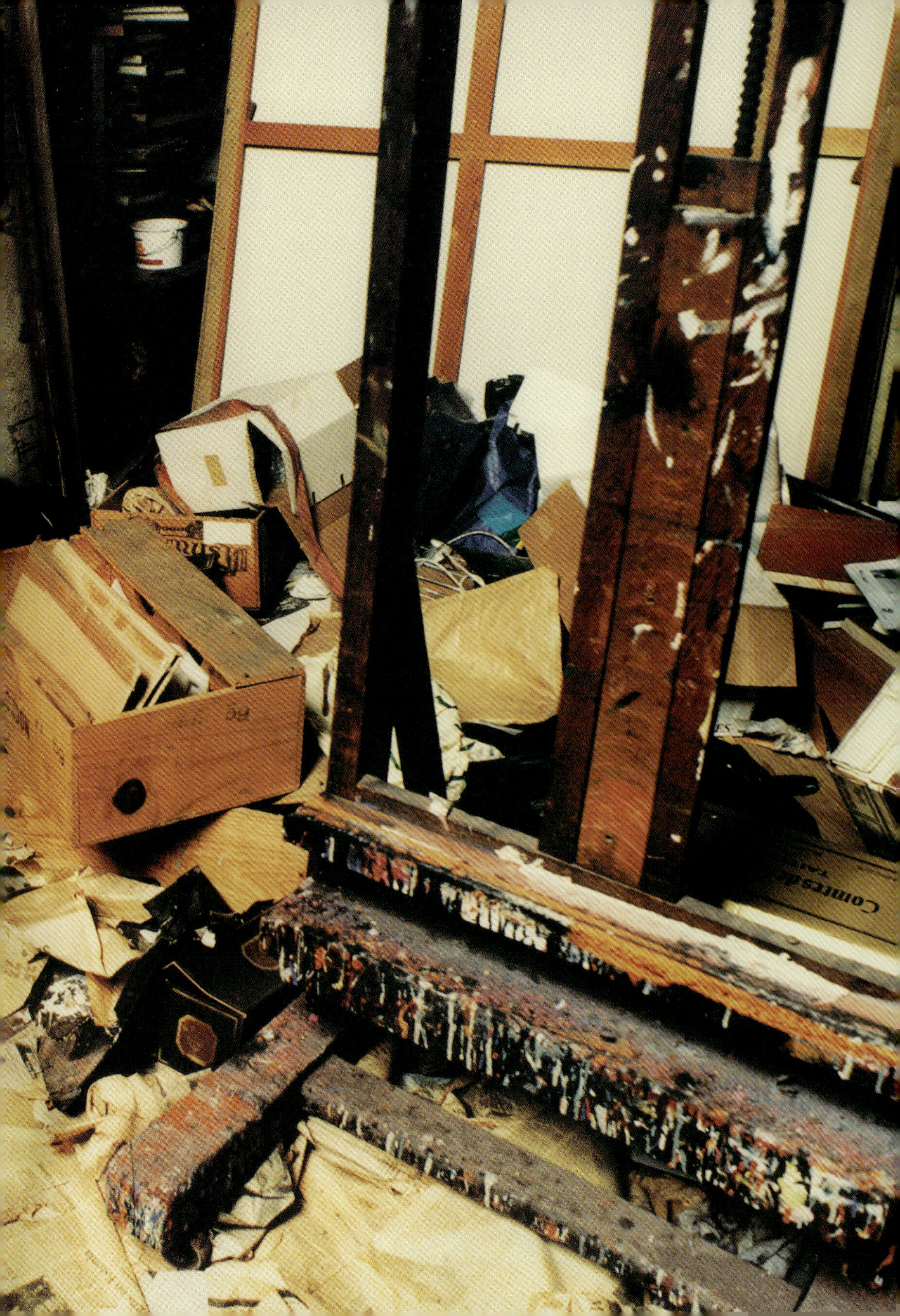

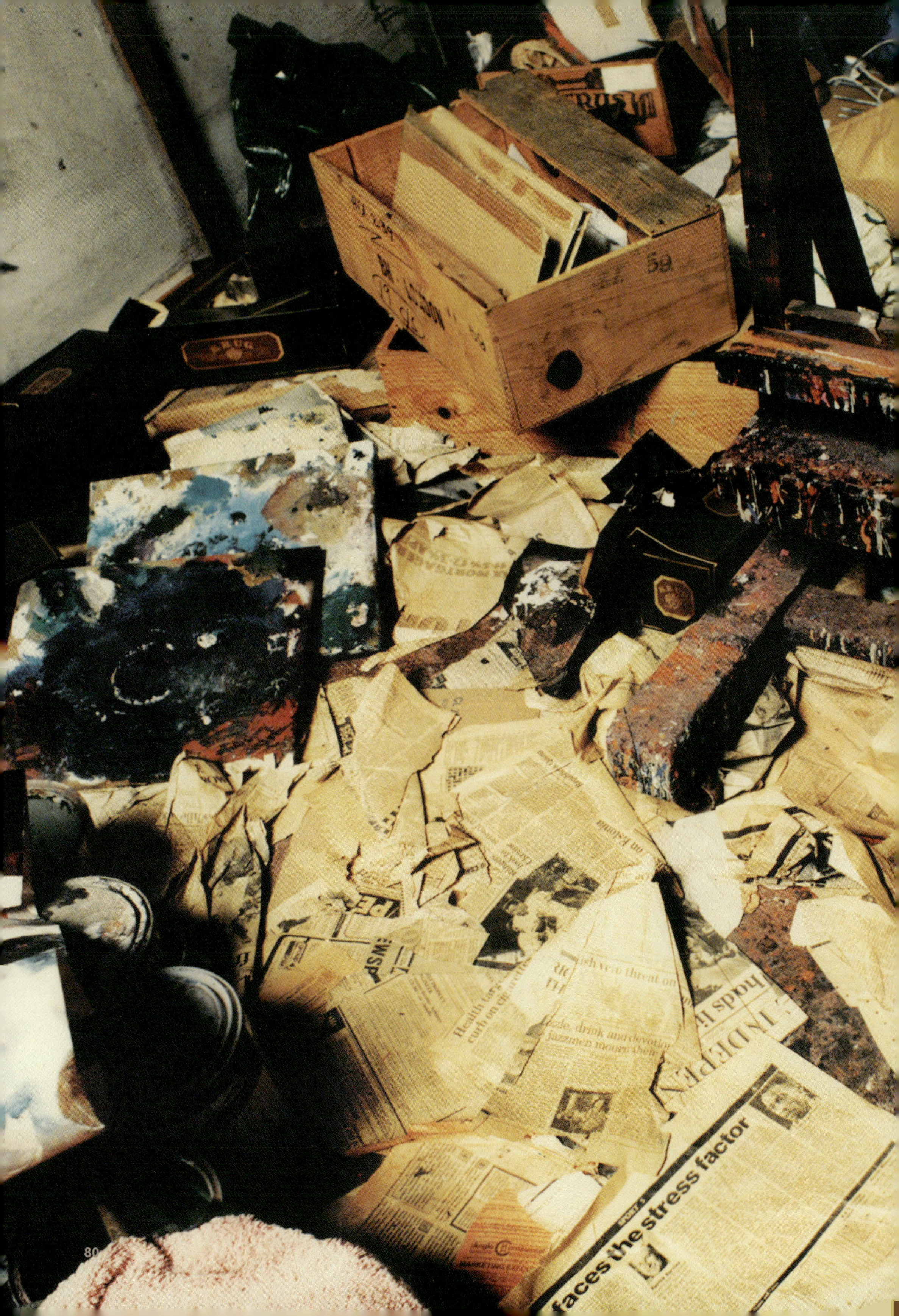
faces the stress factor

FRAGILE
DISCARD
ADNAMS
CHAMPAGNE
LE MESNIL
BLANC de BLANCS
Off the beaten track
Comtesse de

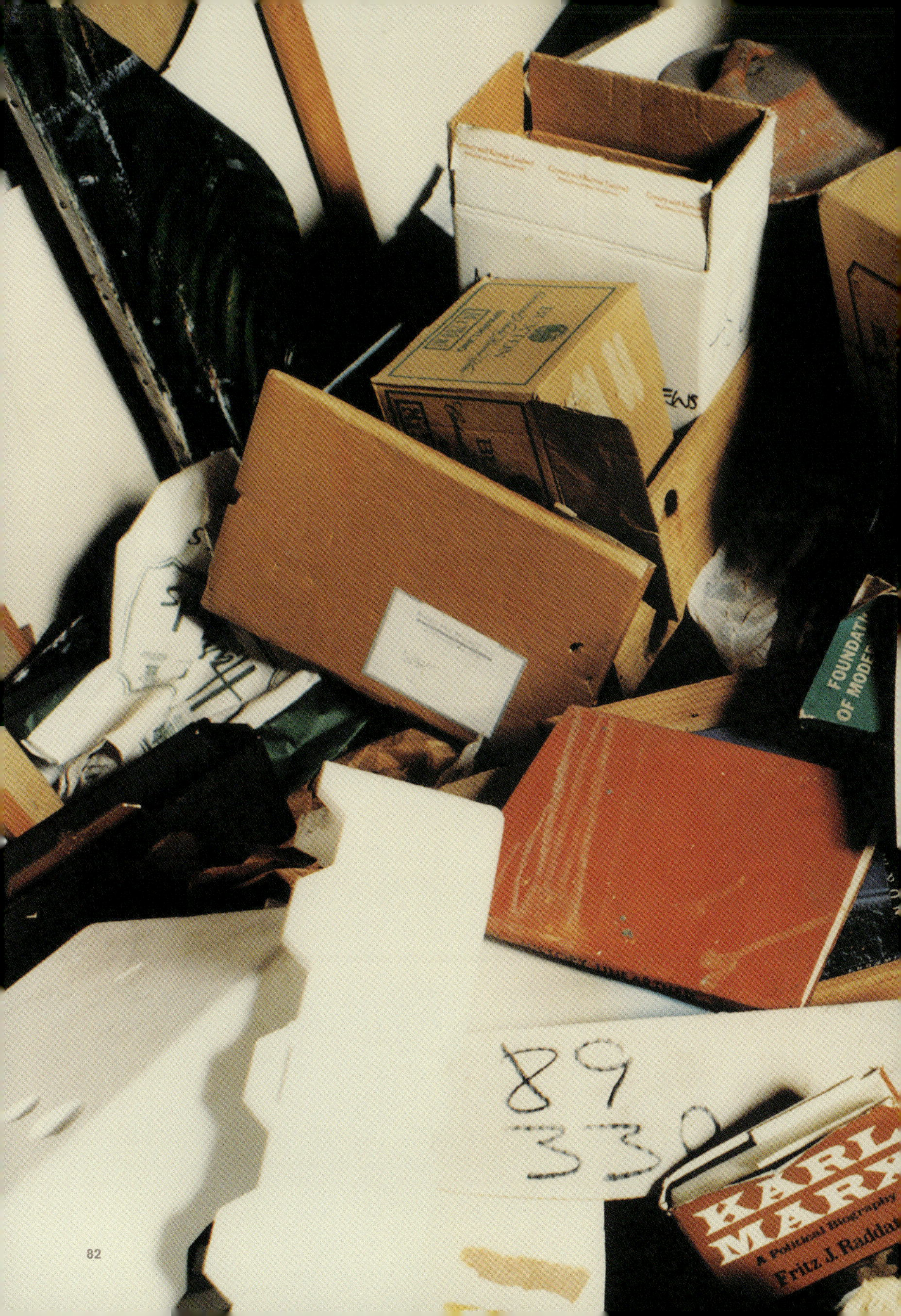

89
33
KARL
MARX
A Political Biography
Fritz J. Raddatz
FOUNDATIONS
OF MODERN

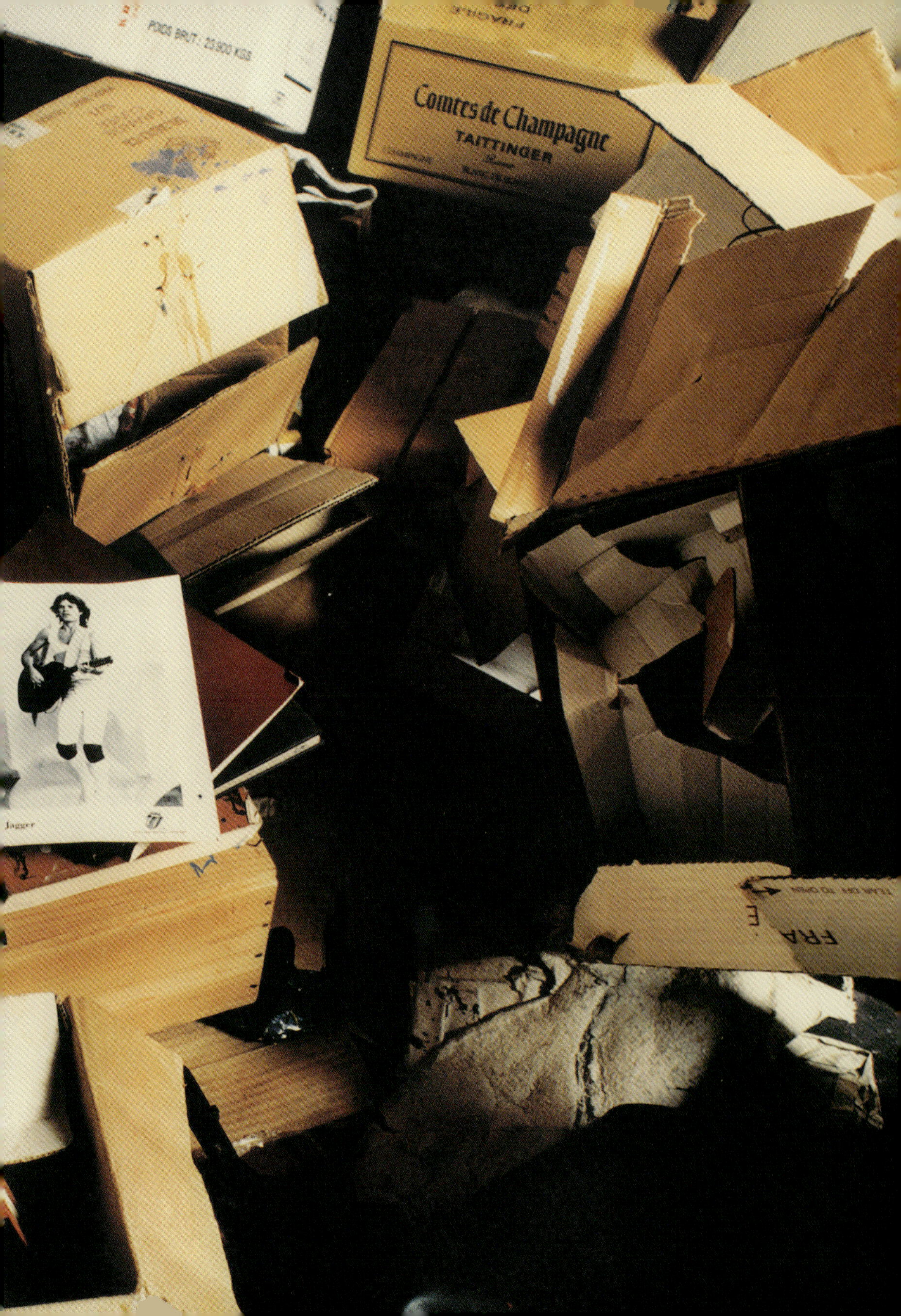
POIDS BRUT : 23,900 KGS
FRAGILE
Comtes de Champagne
TAITTINGER
Jagger
FRA
E

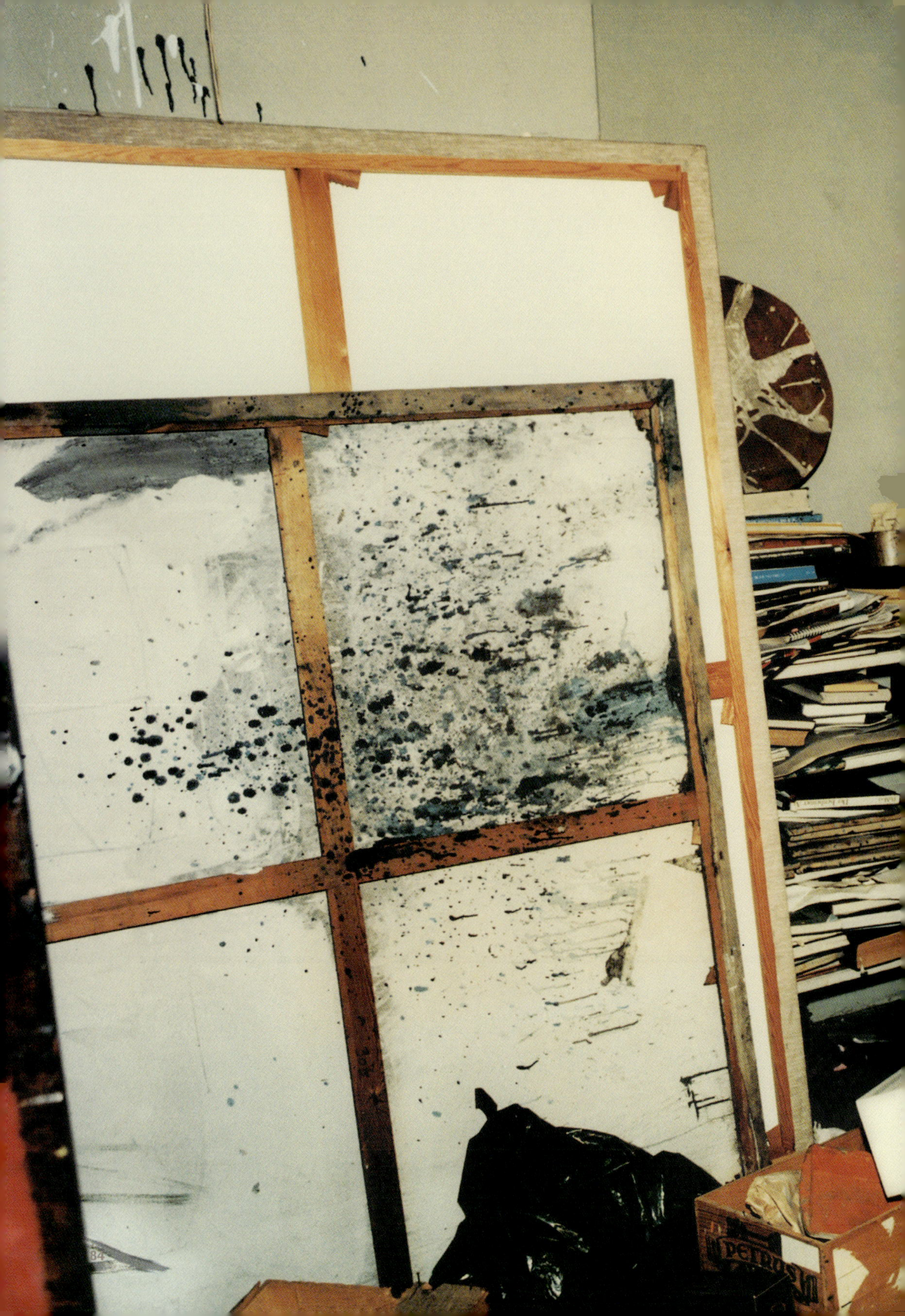

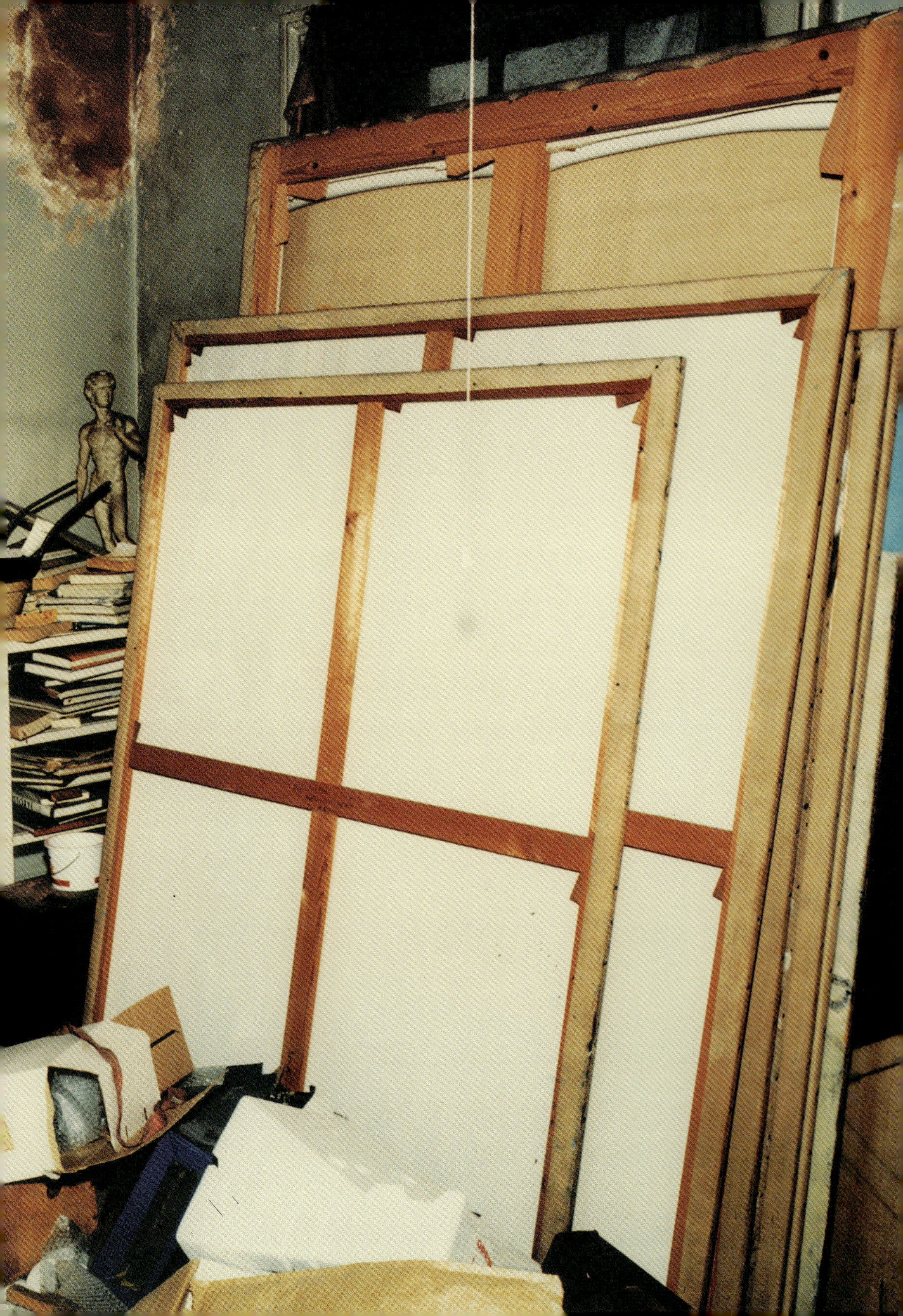

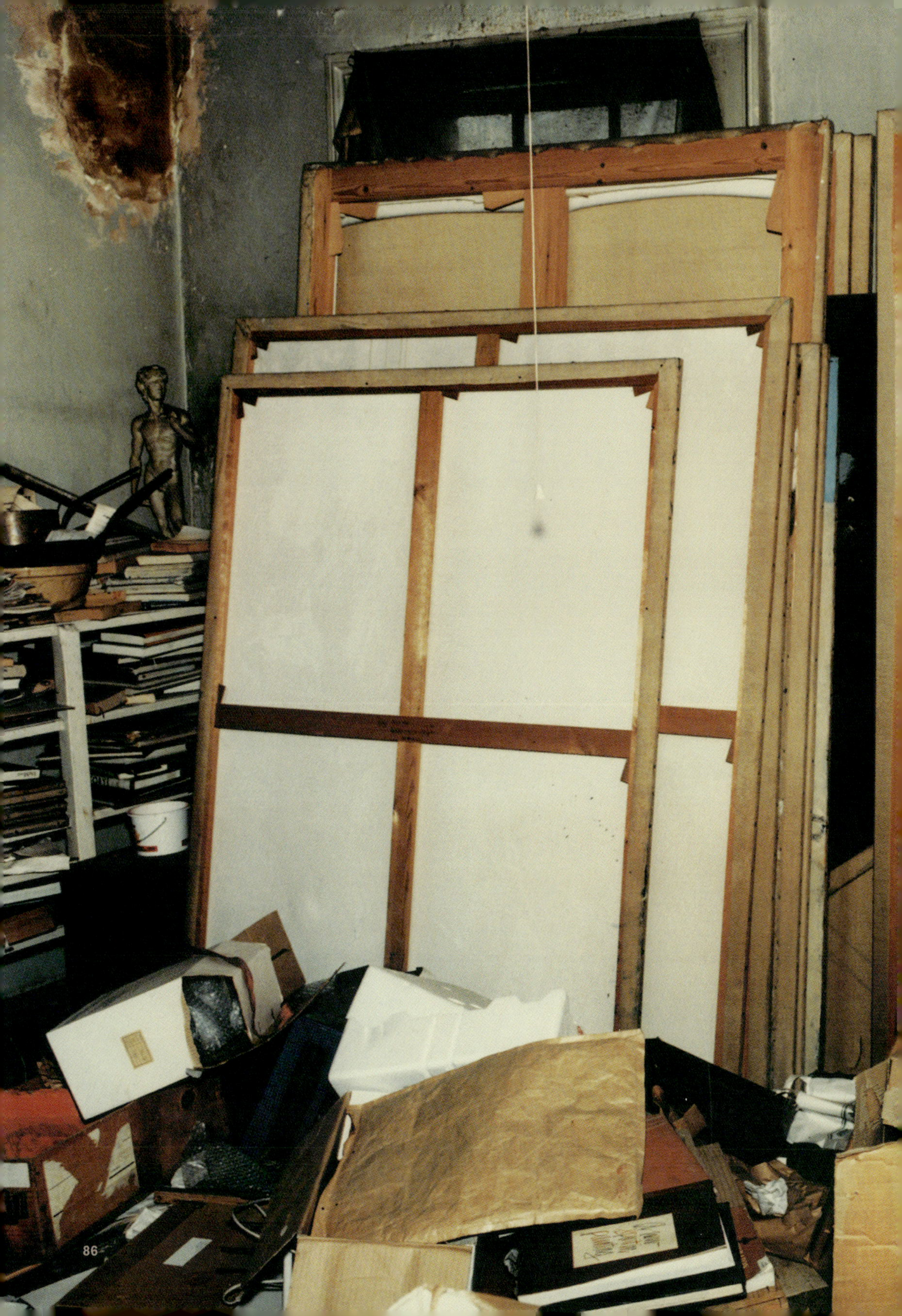

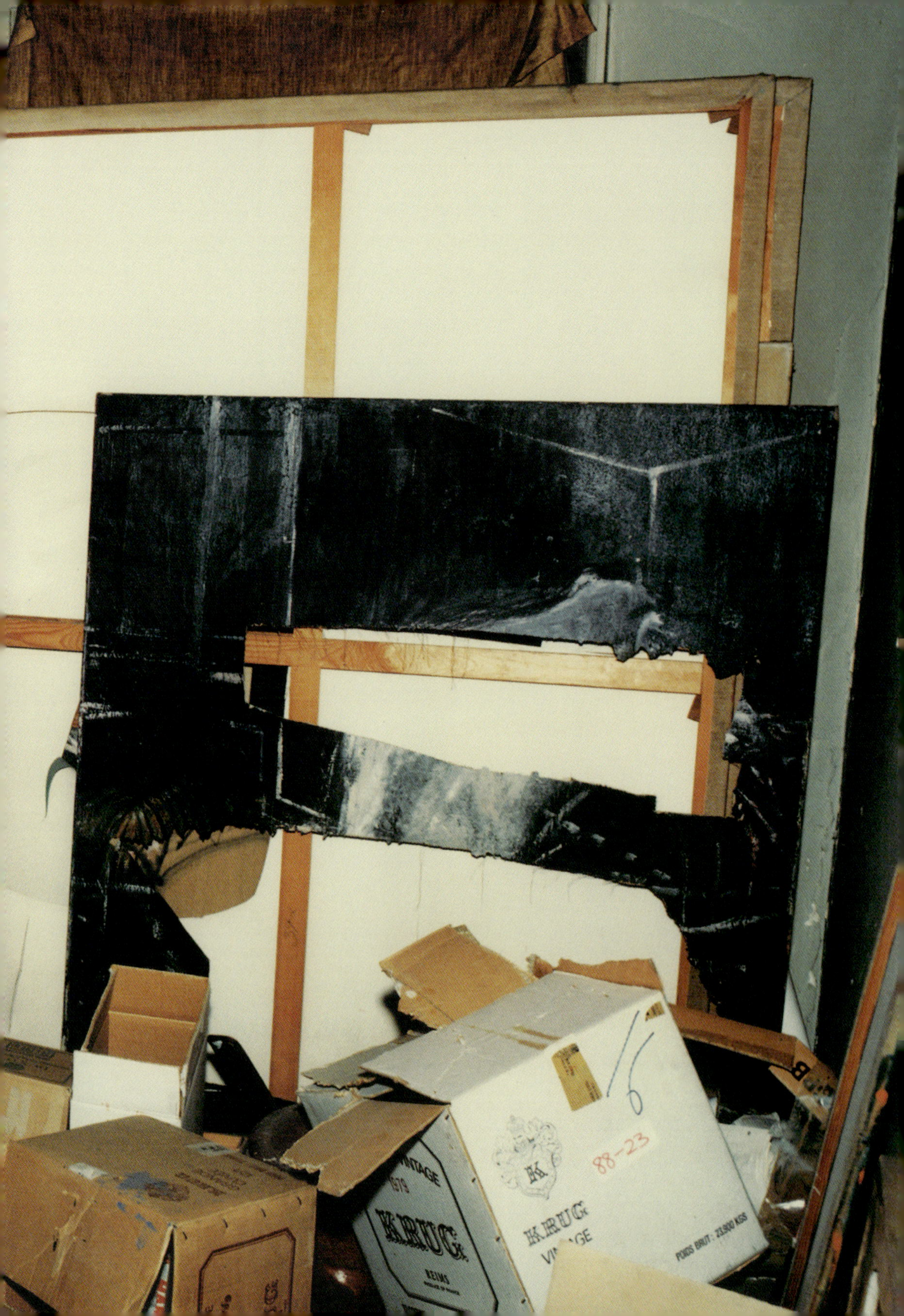

VINTAGE
1979
KRUG
REIMS
K.
KRUG
VINTAGE
88-23
POIDS BRUT: 22,900 KGS

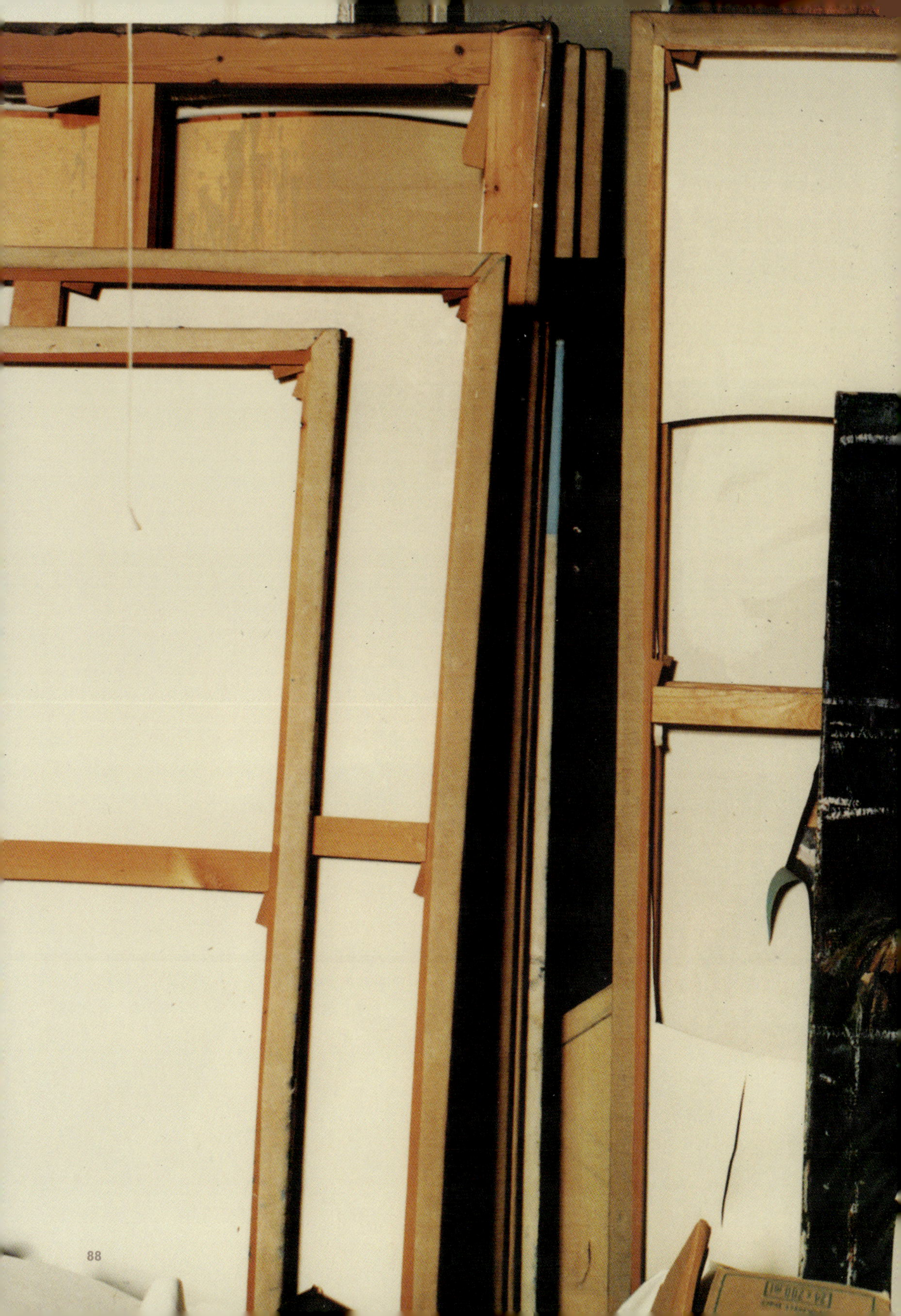

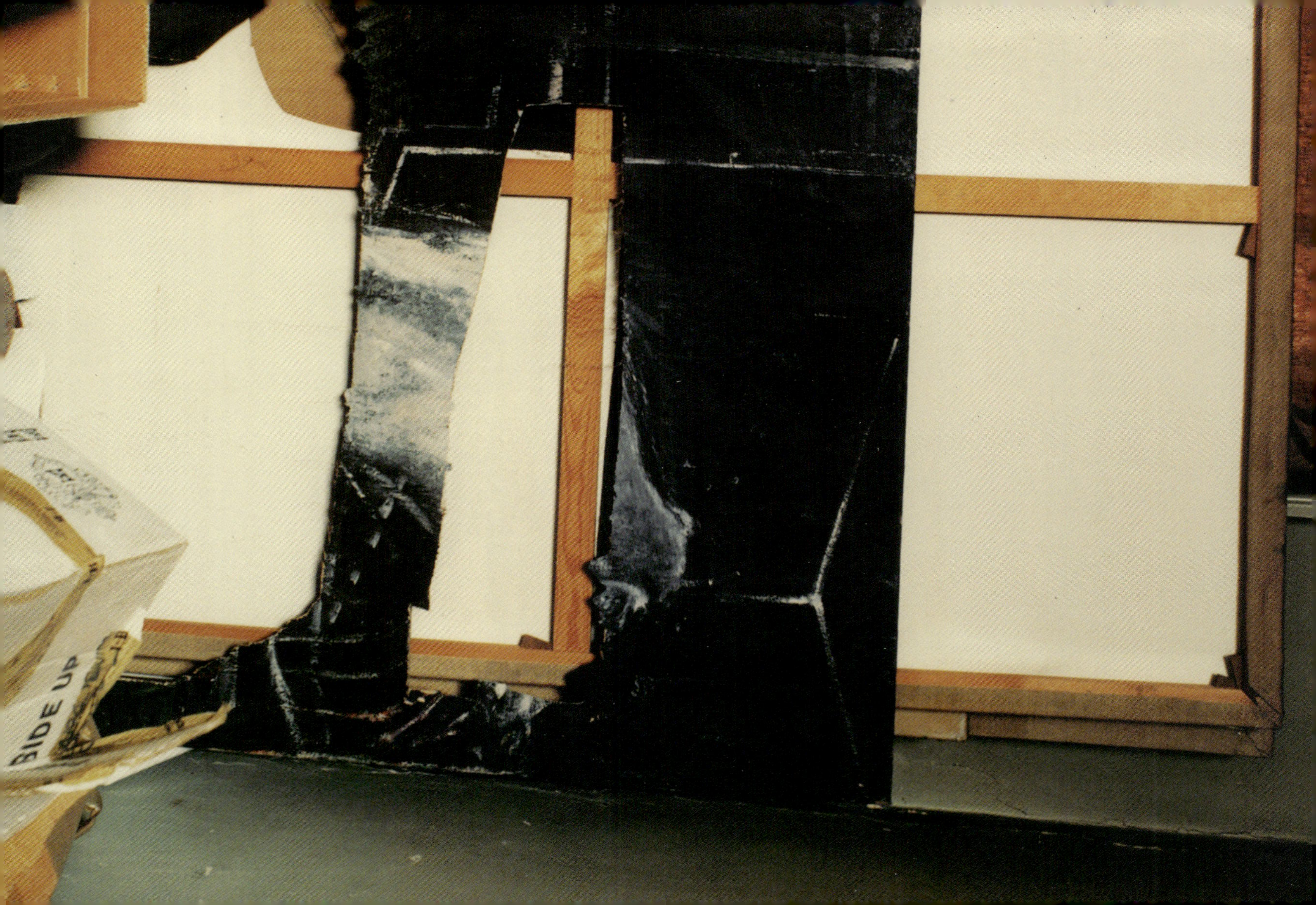
SIDE UP

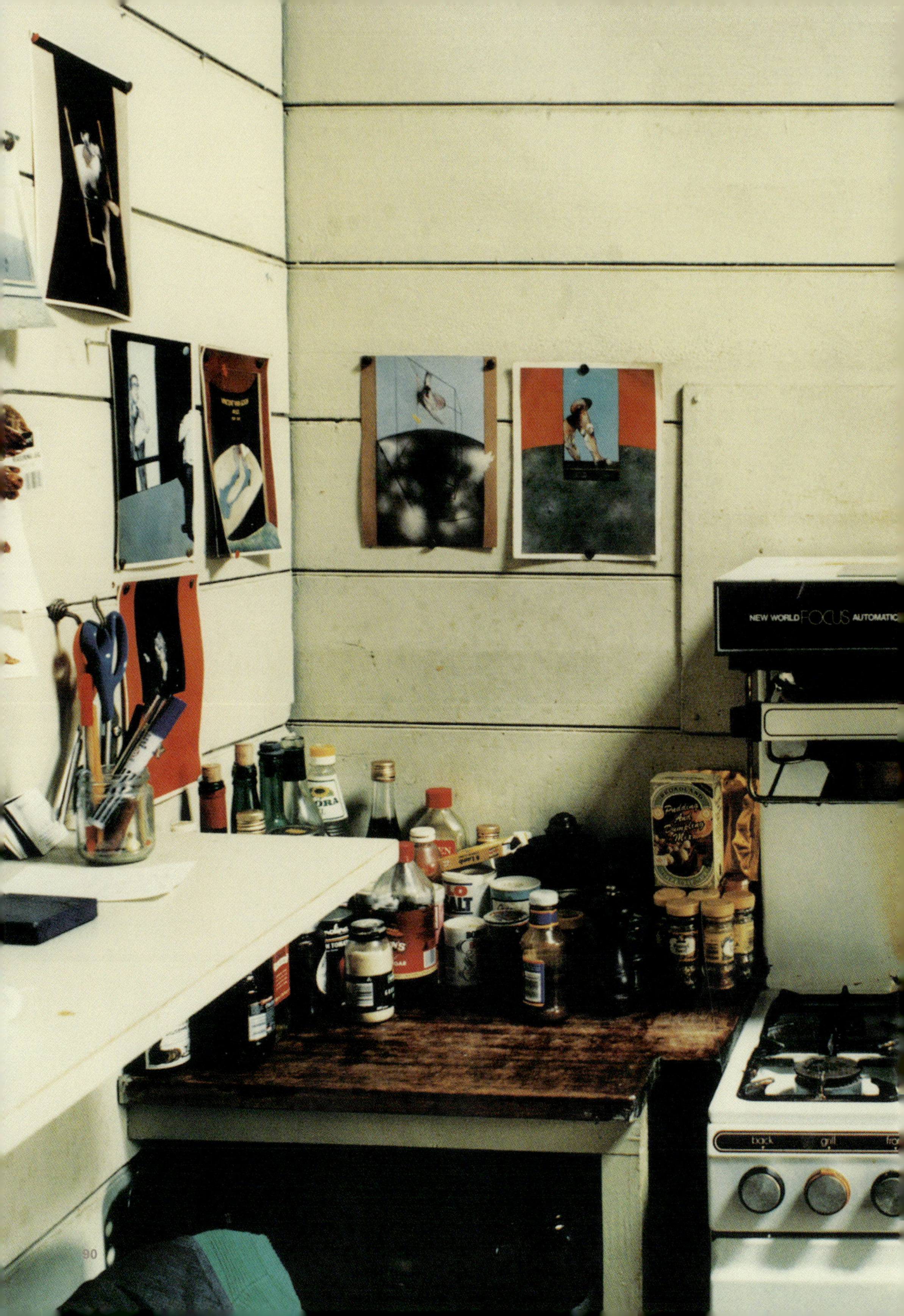

NEW WORLD FOCUS AUTOMATIC
back   grill   fro
90

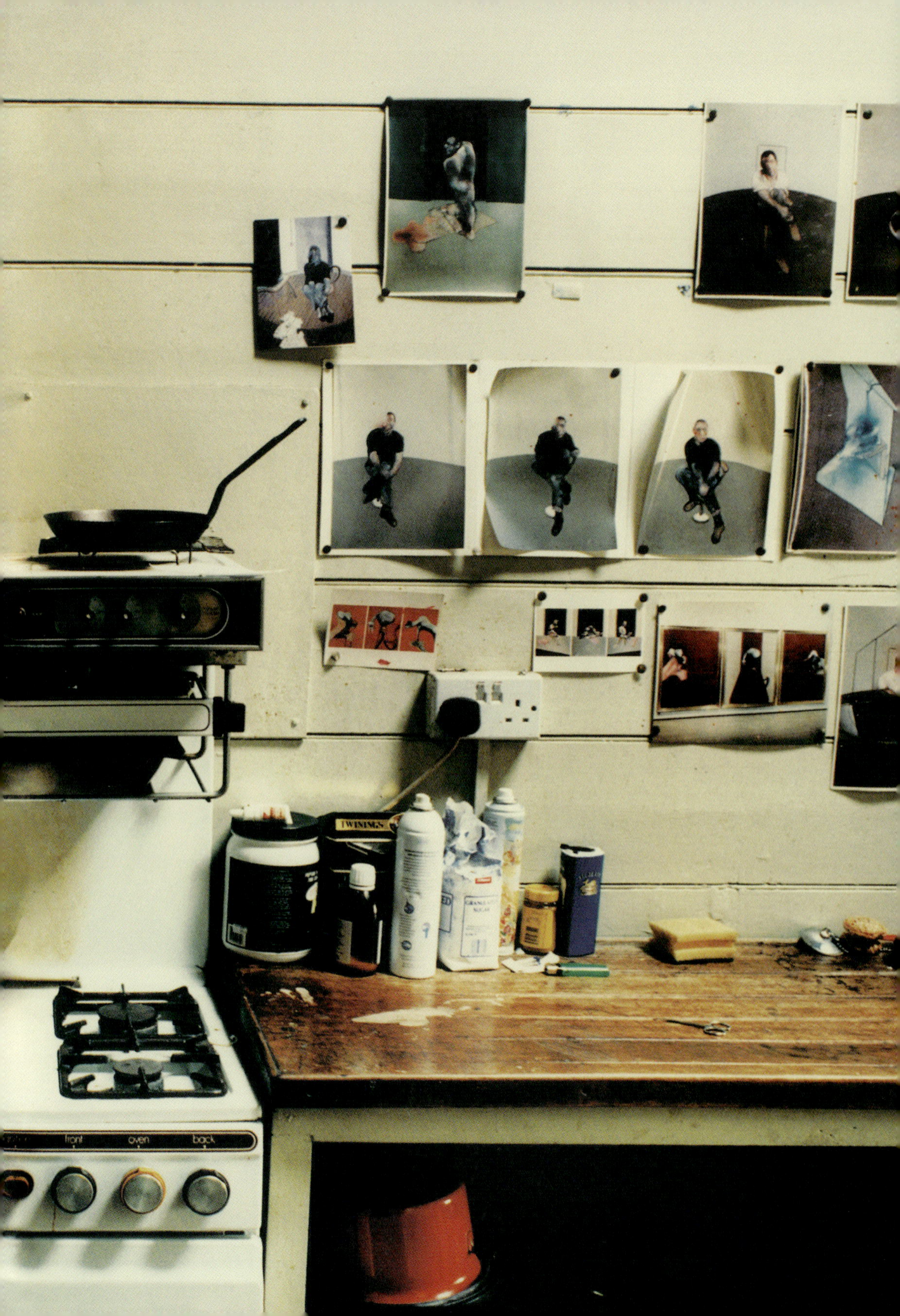

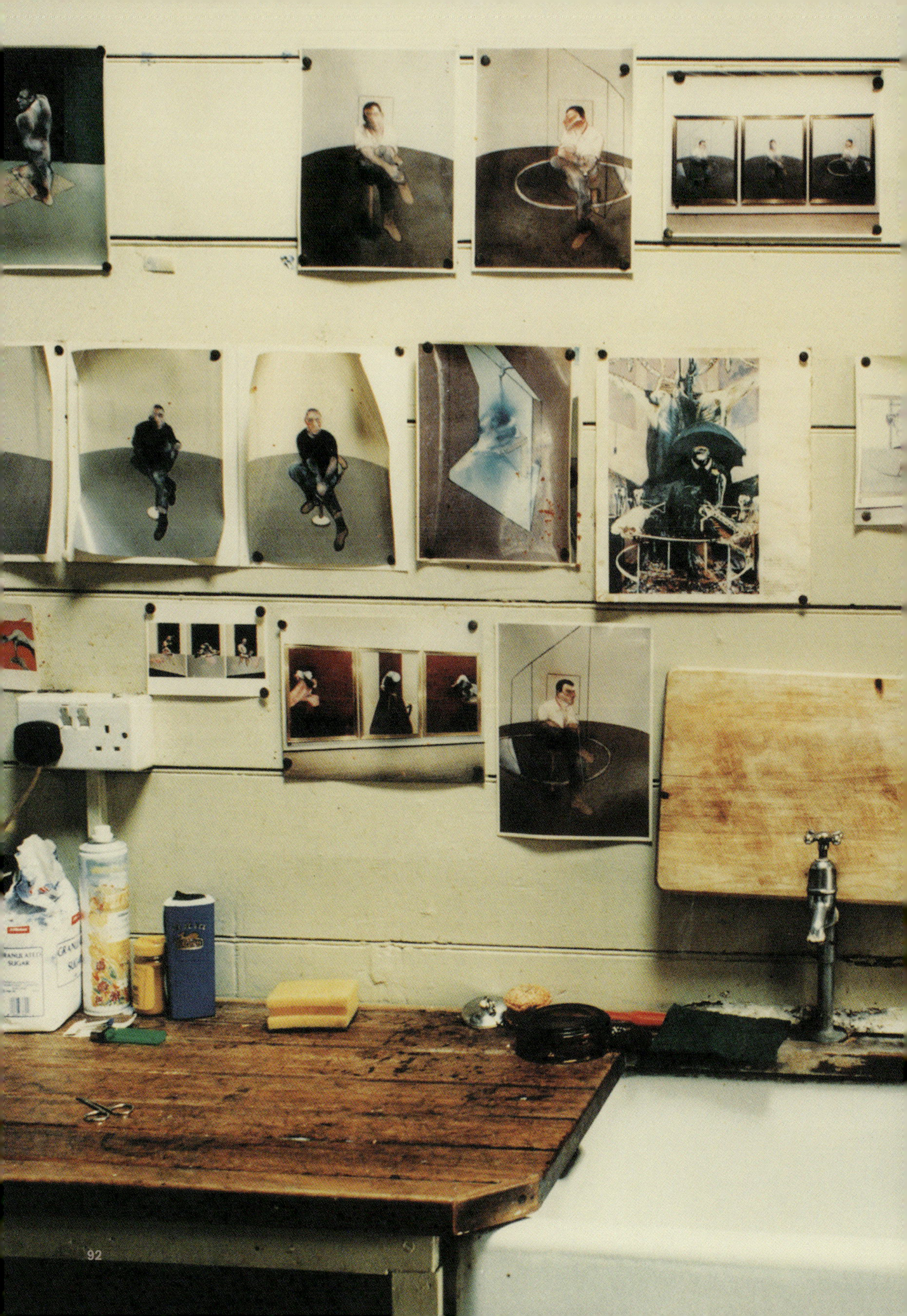

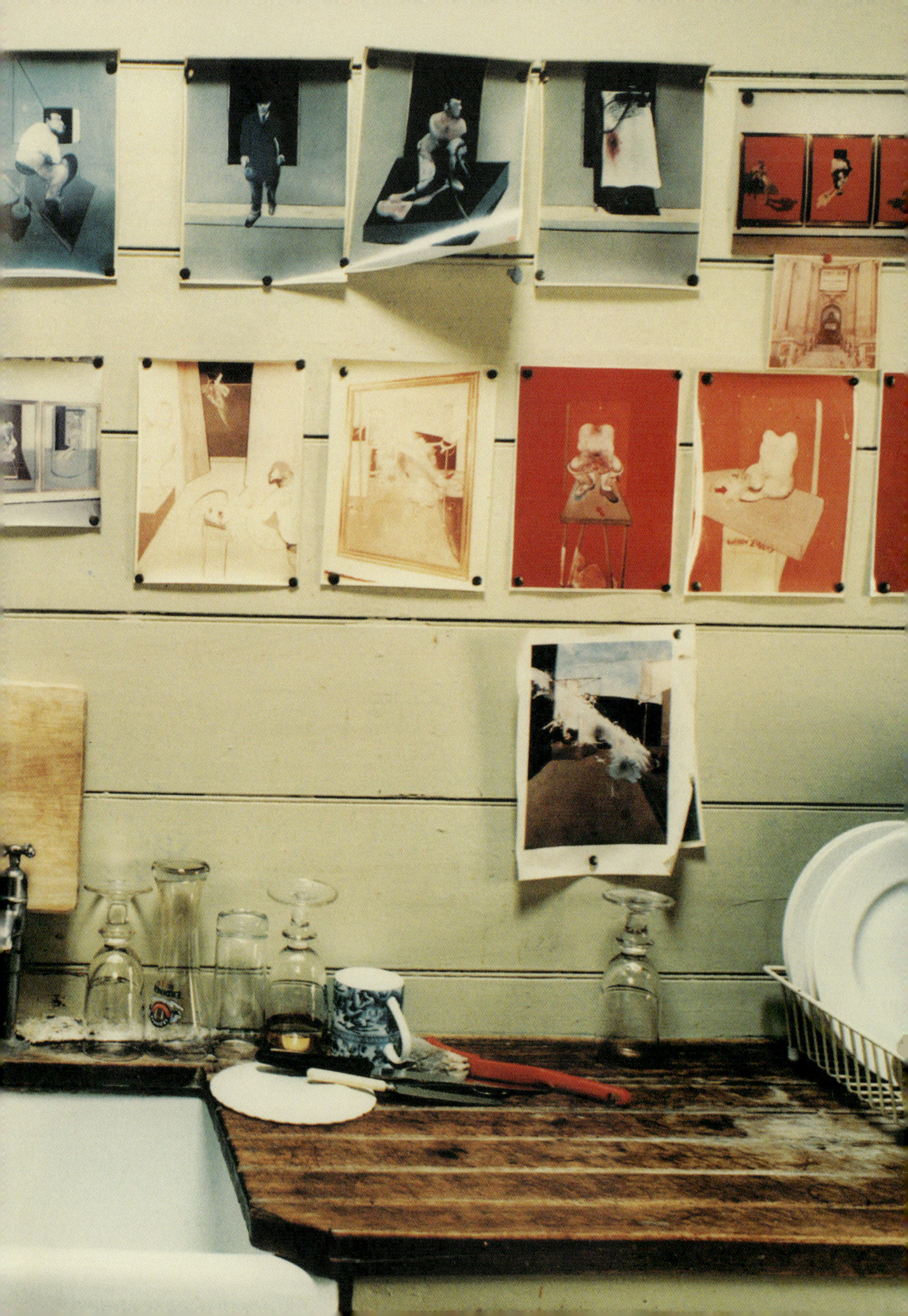

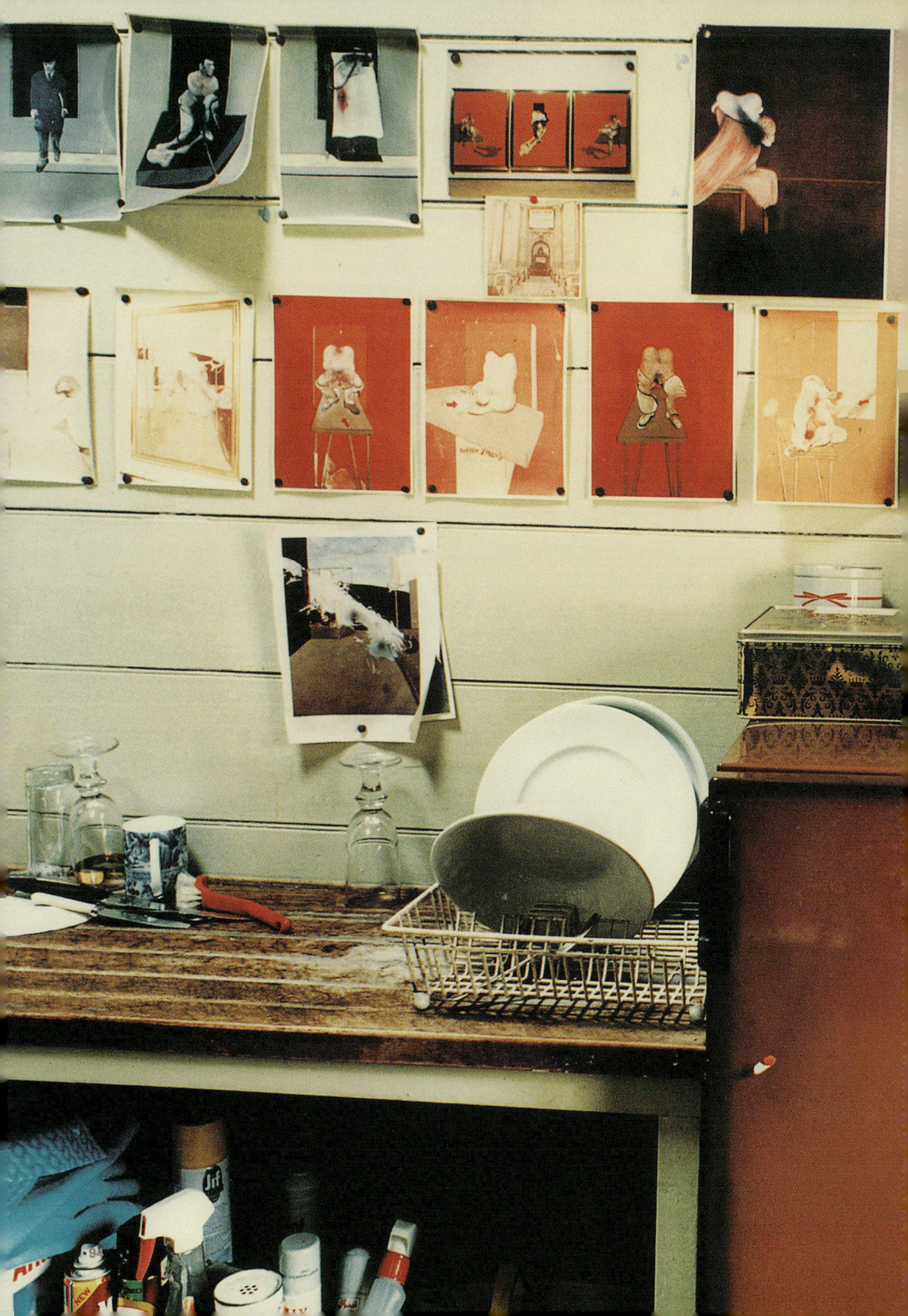

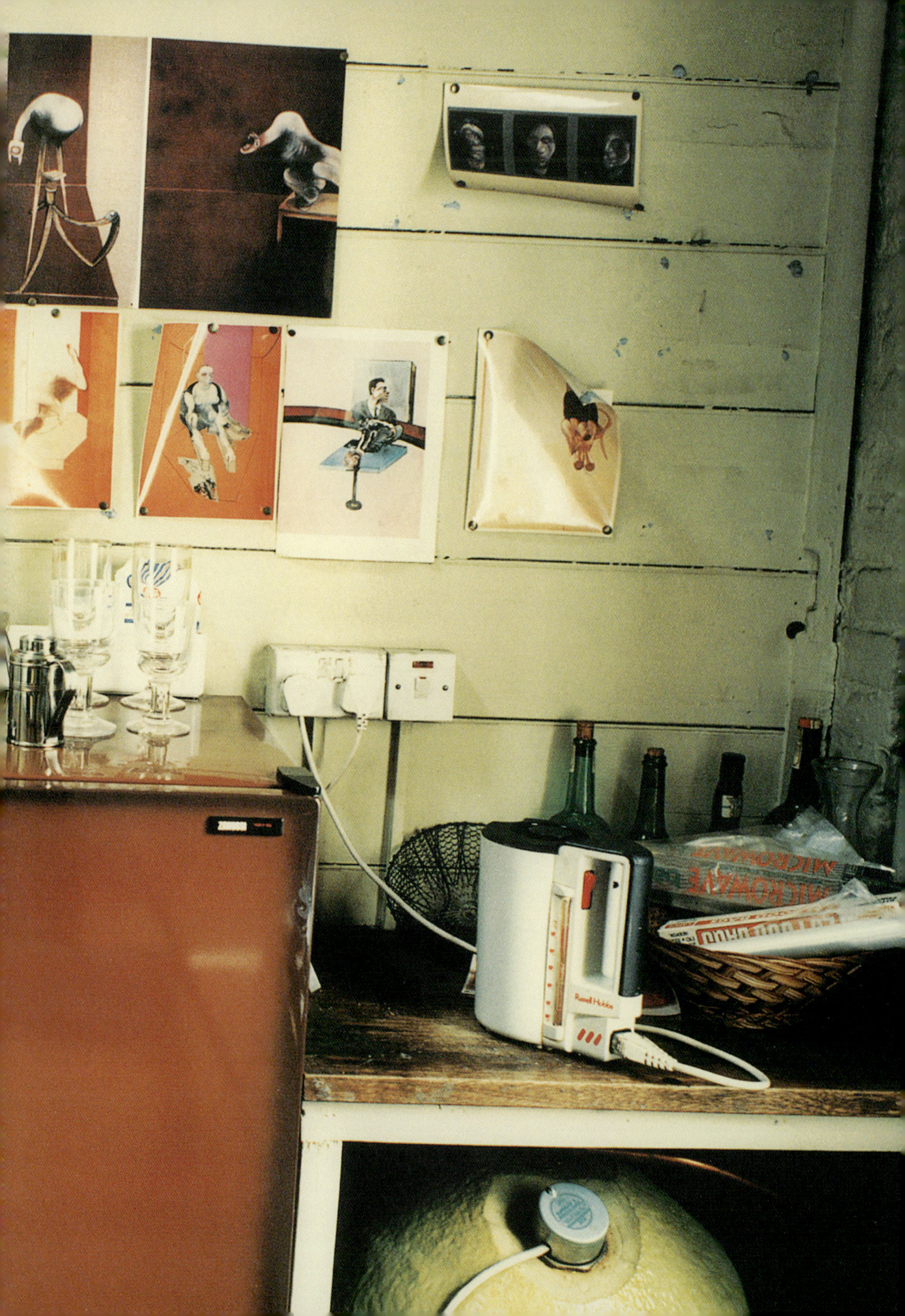

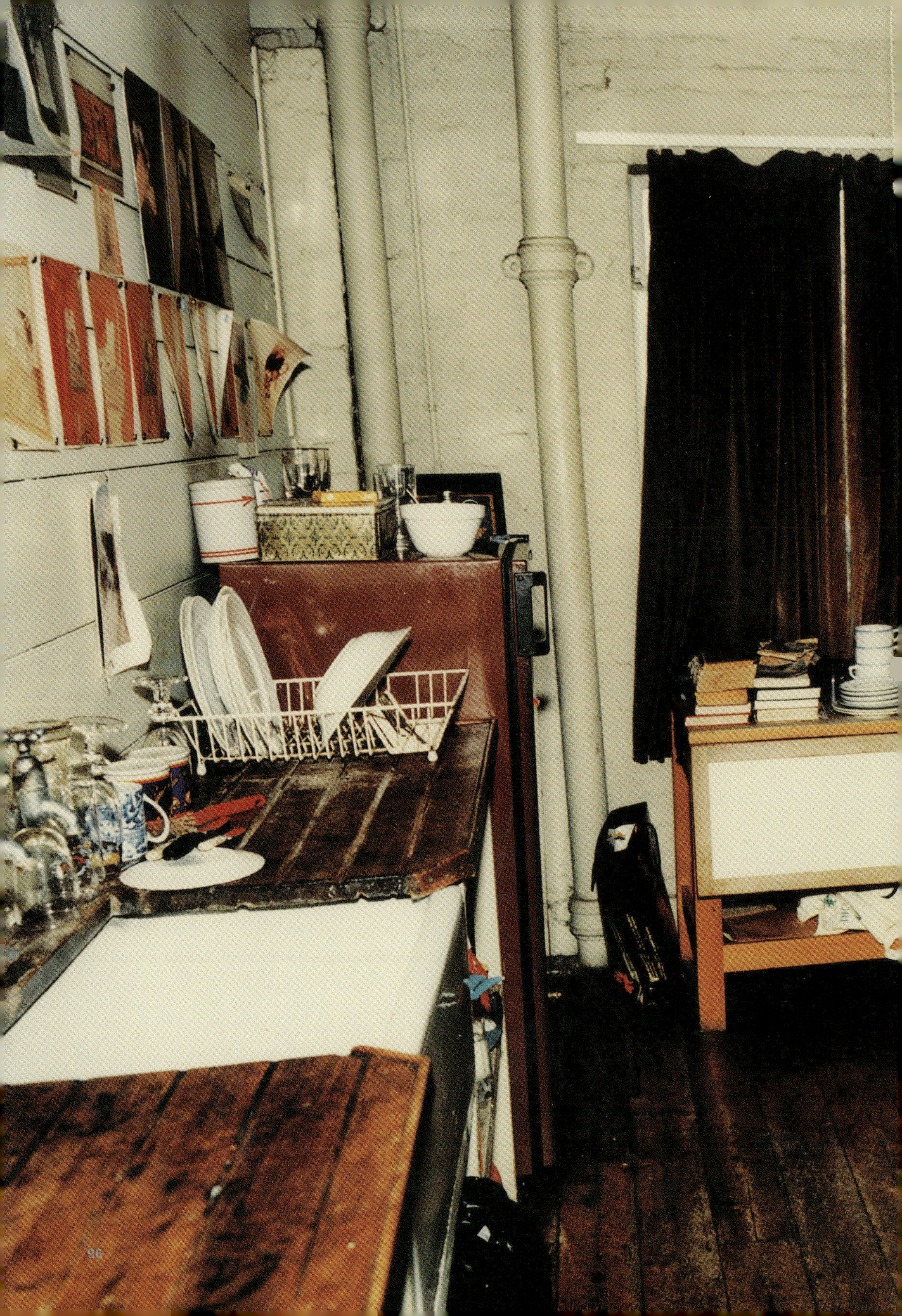

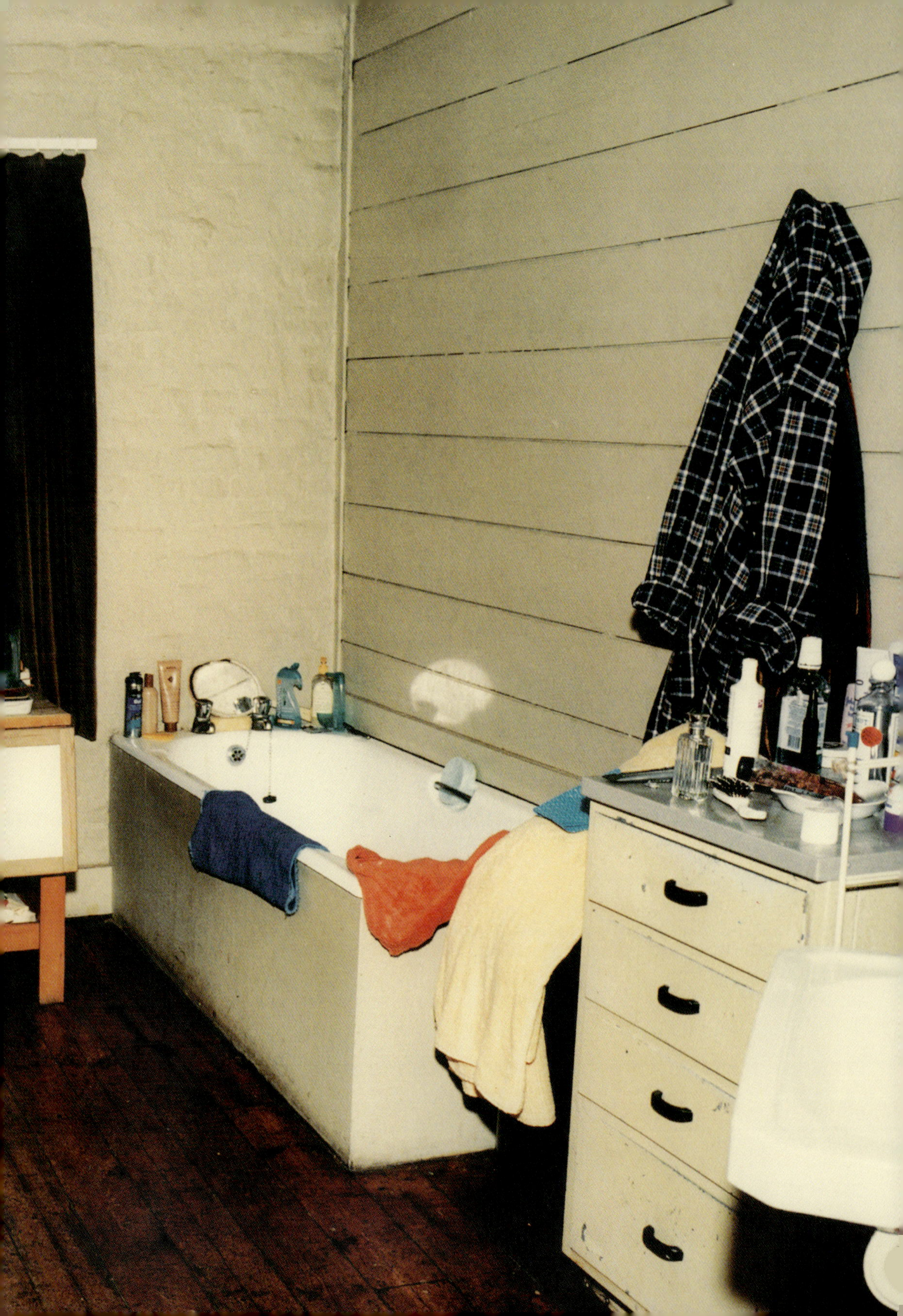

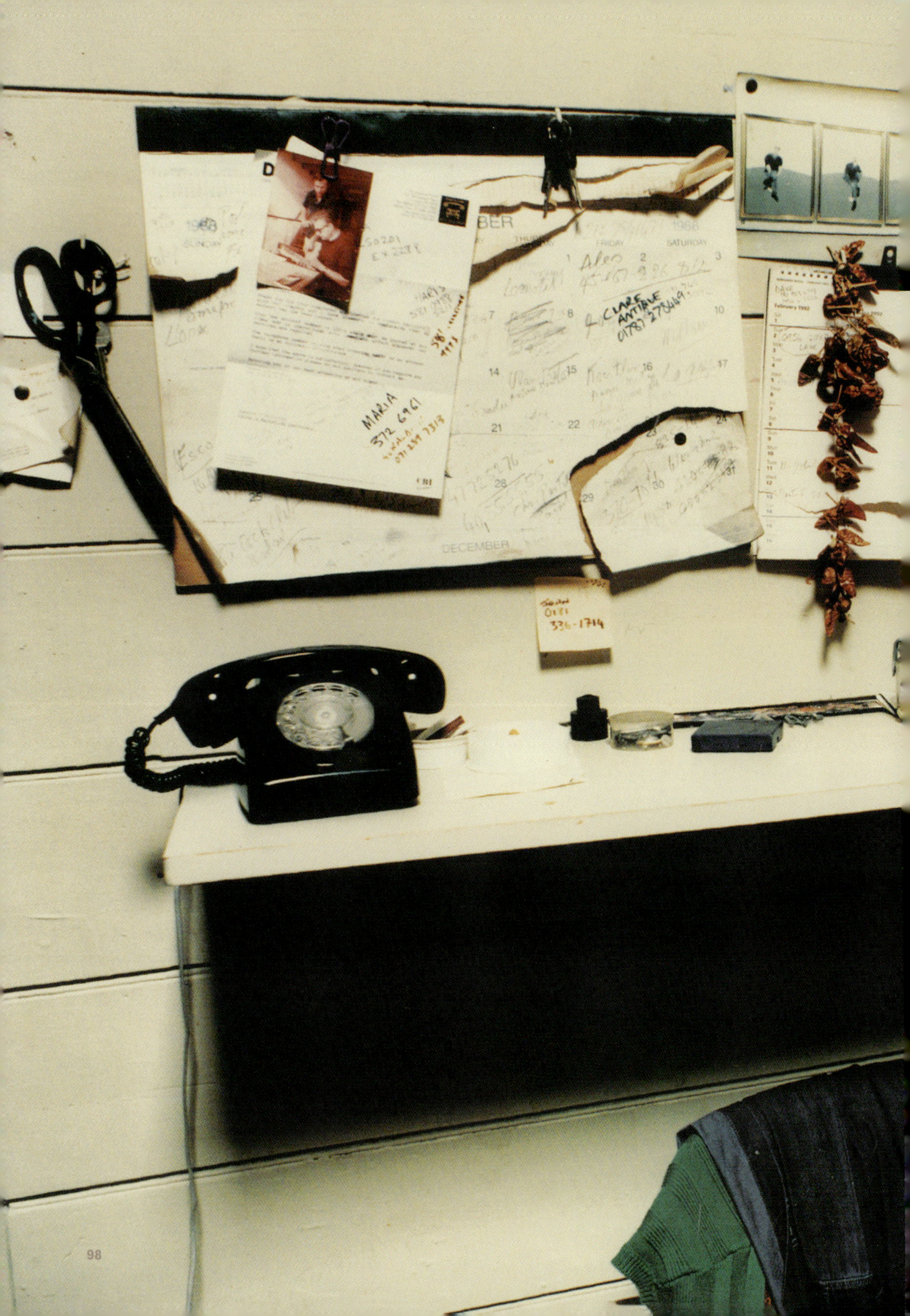

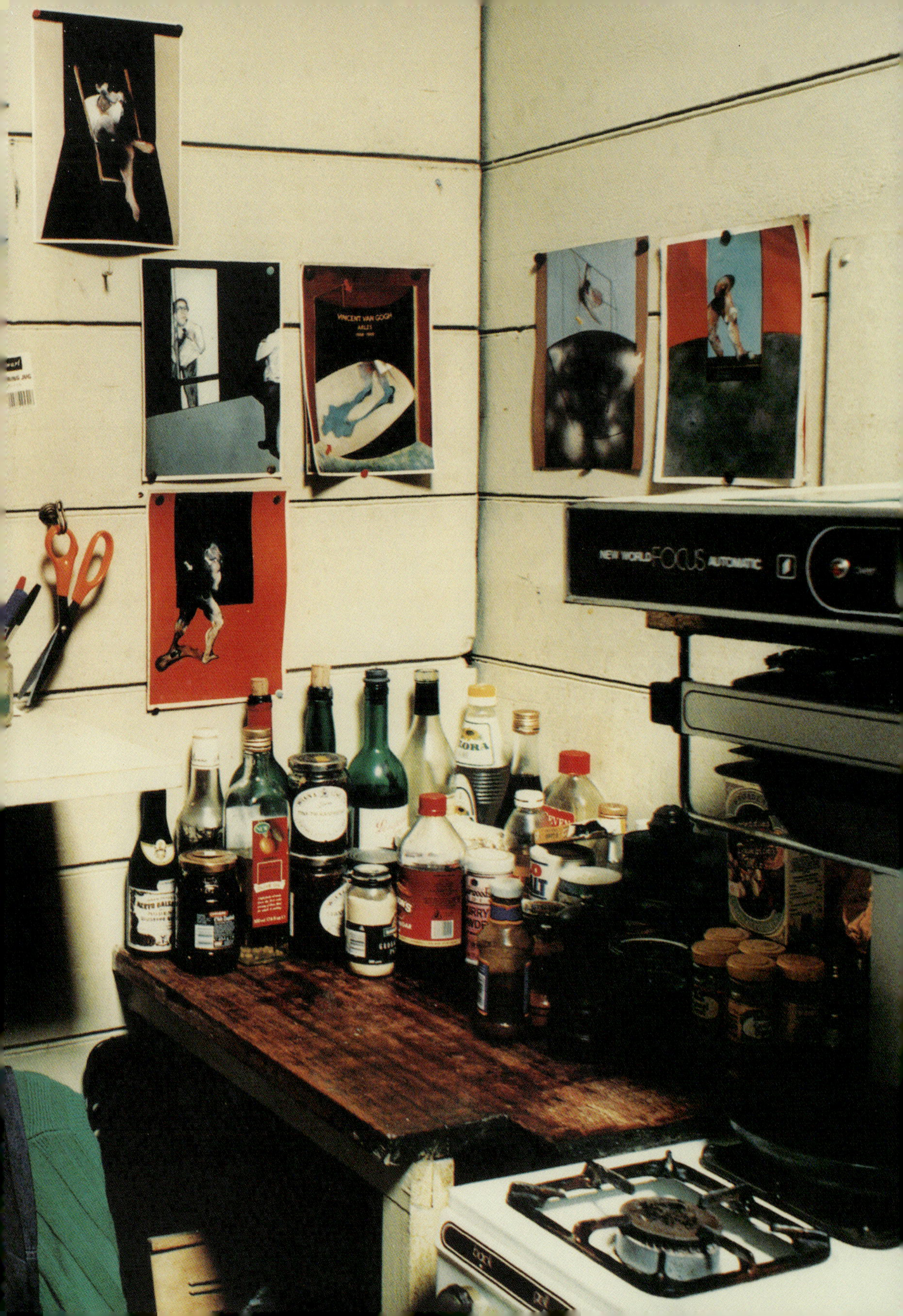

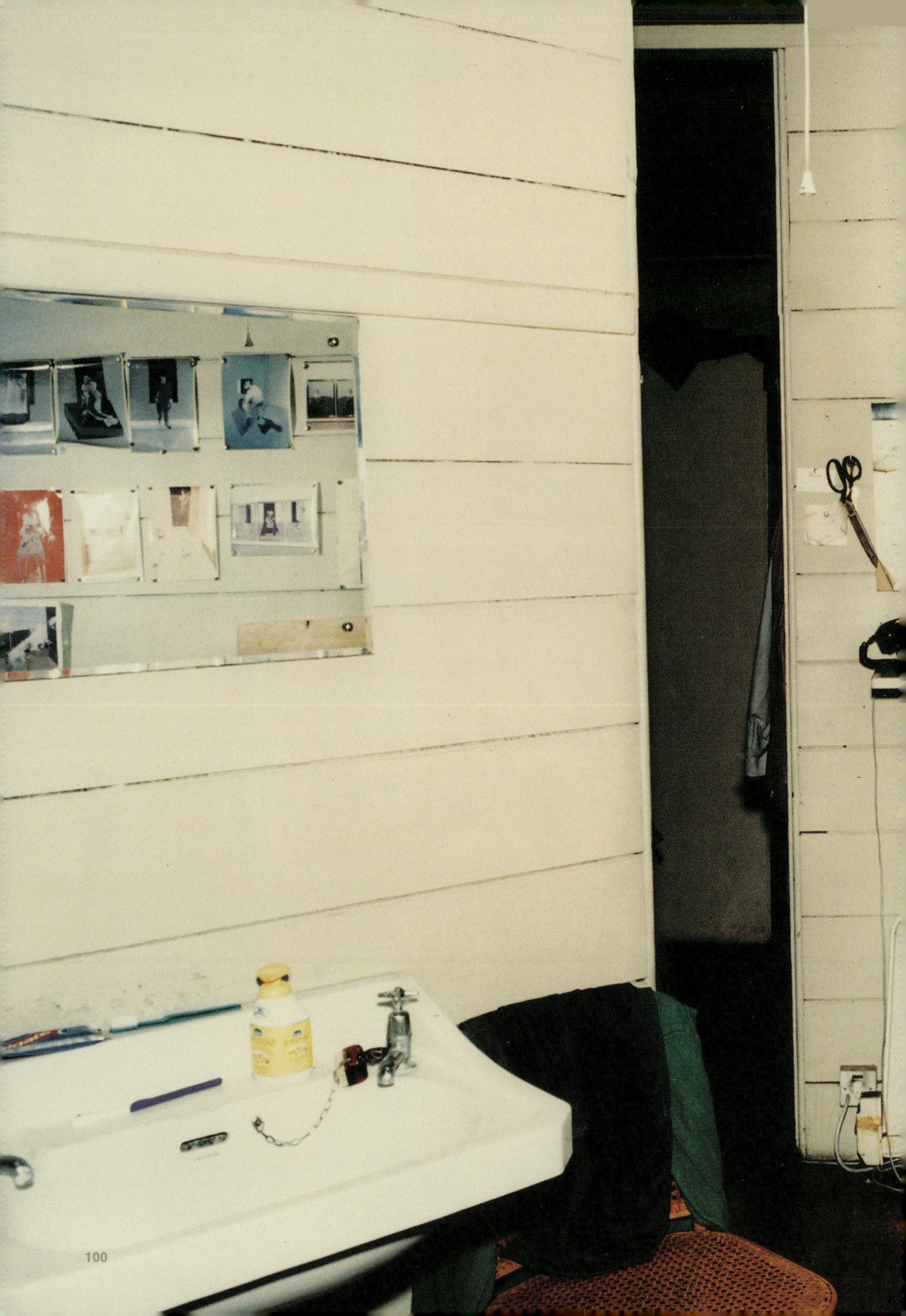

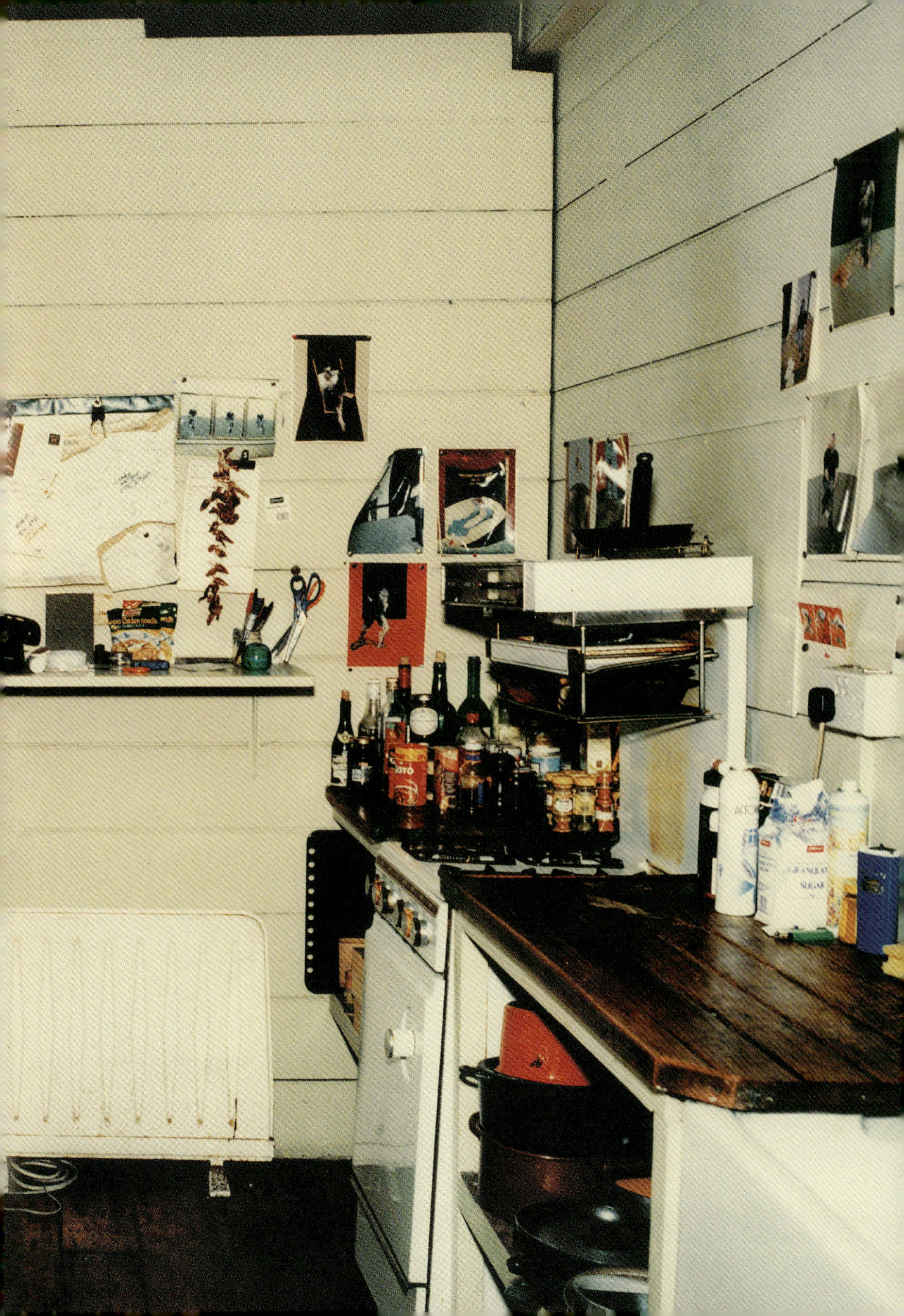

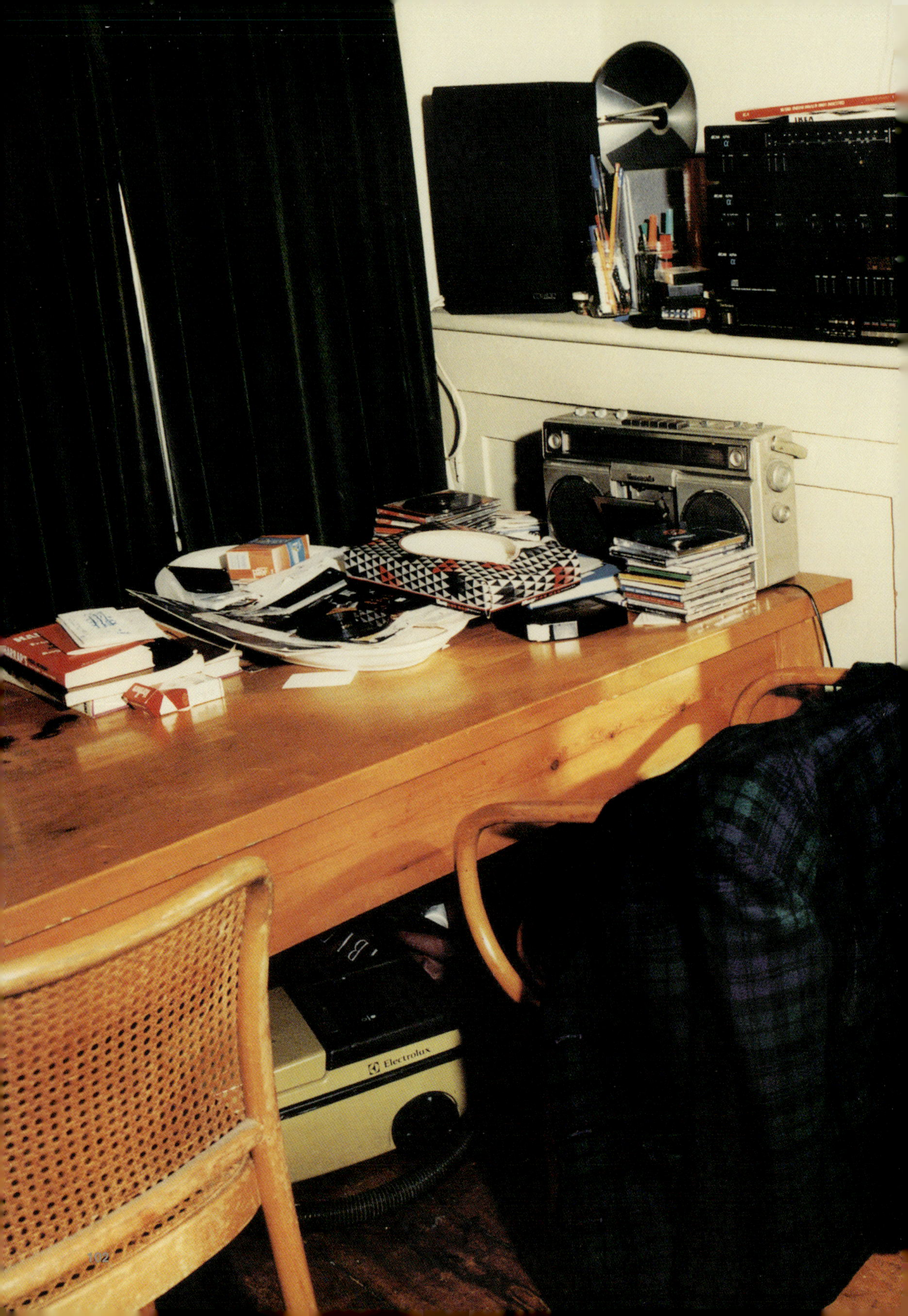

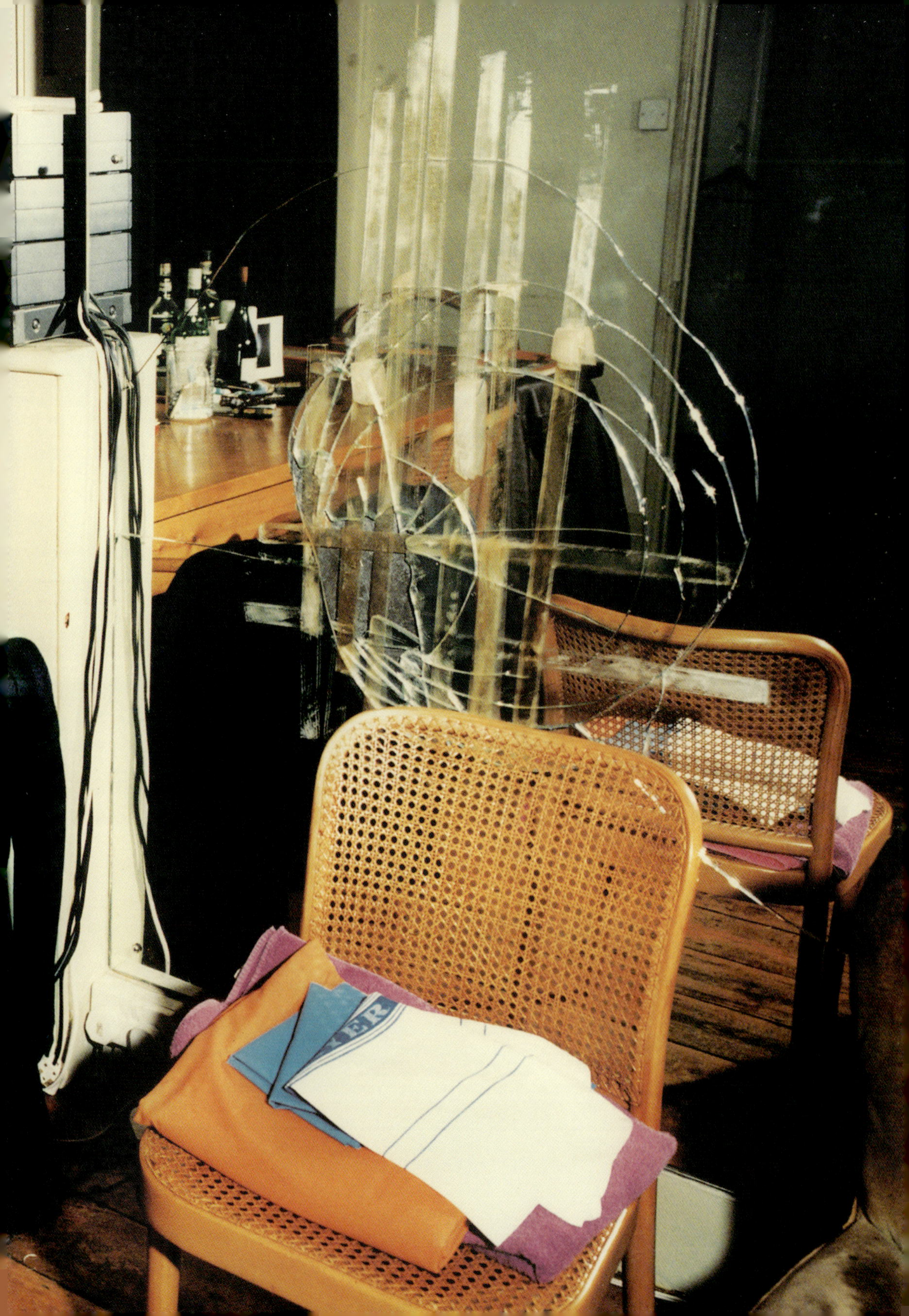

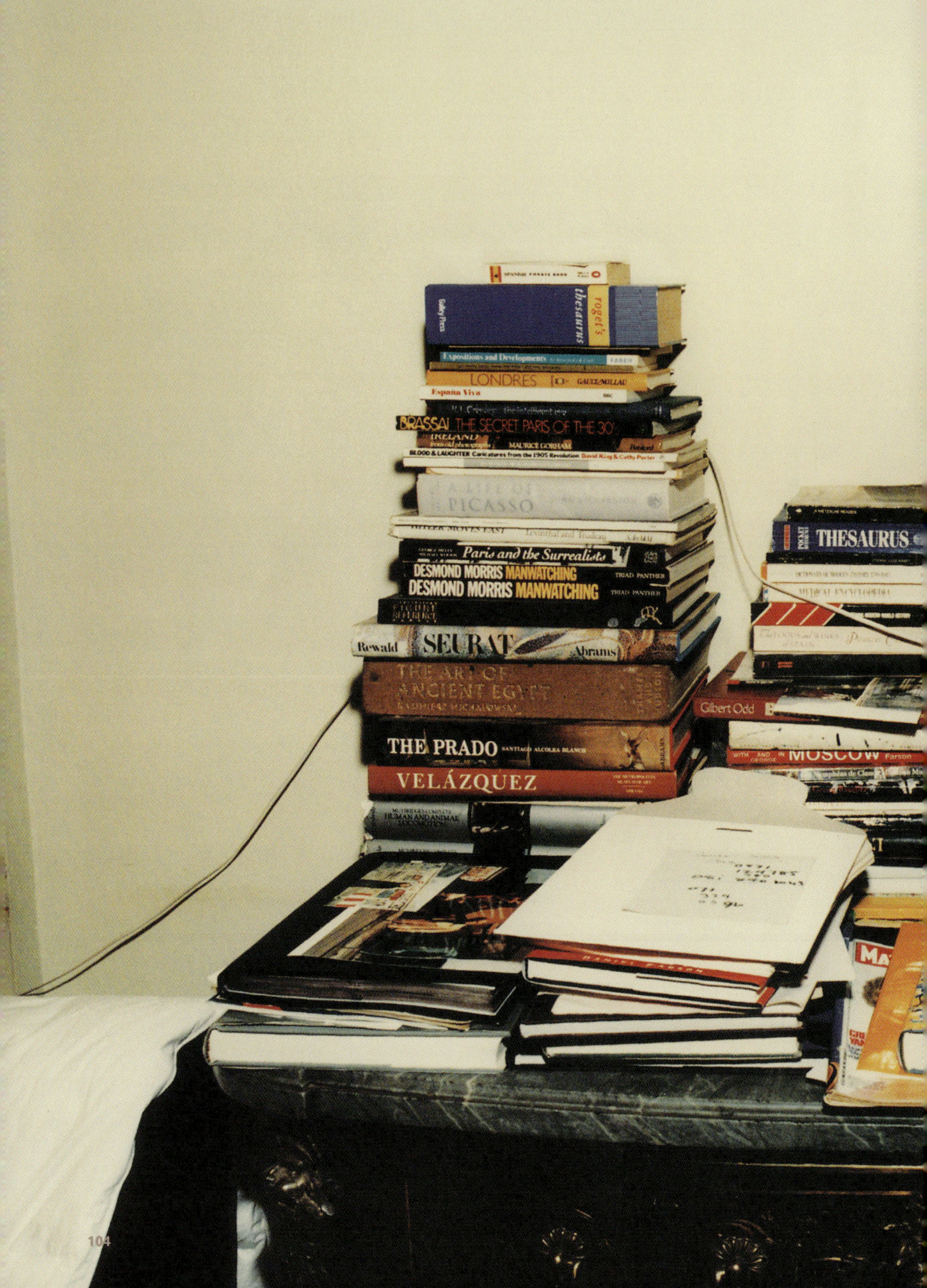

roget's thesaurus
Galley Press
SPANISH PHRASE BOOK
Expositions and Developments   FABER
LONDRES   ICI   GALLIMARD
España Viva   BBC
BRASSAI   THE SECRET PARIS OF THE 30's
IRELAND   MAURICE GORHAM
BLOOD & LAUGHTER Caricatures from the 1905 Revolution   David King & Cathy Porter
A LIFE OF
PICASSO
Paris and the Surrealists
DESMOND MORRIS MANWATCHING   TRIAD PANTHER
DESMOND MORRIS MANWATCHING   TRIAD PANTHER
Rewald   SEURAT   Abrams
THE ART OF
ANCIENT EGYPT
THE PRADO   SANTIAGO ALCOLEA BLANCH
VELÁZQUEZ
THESAURUS
Gilbert Odd
MOSCOW   Farson
MAN

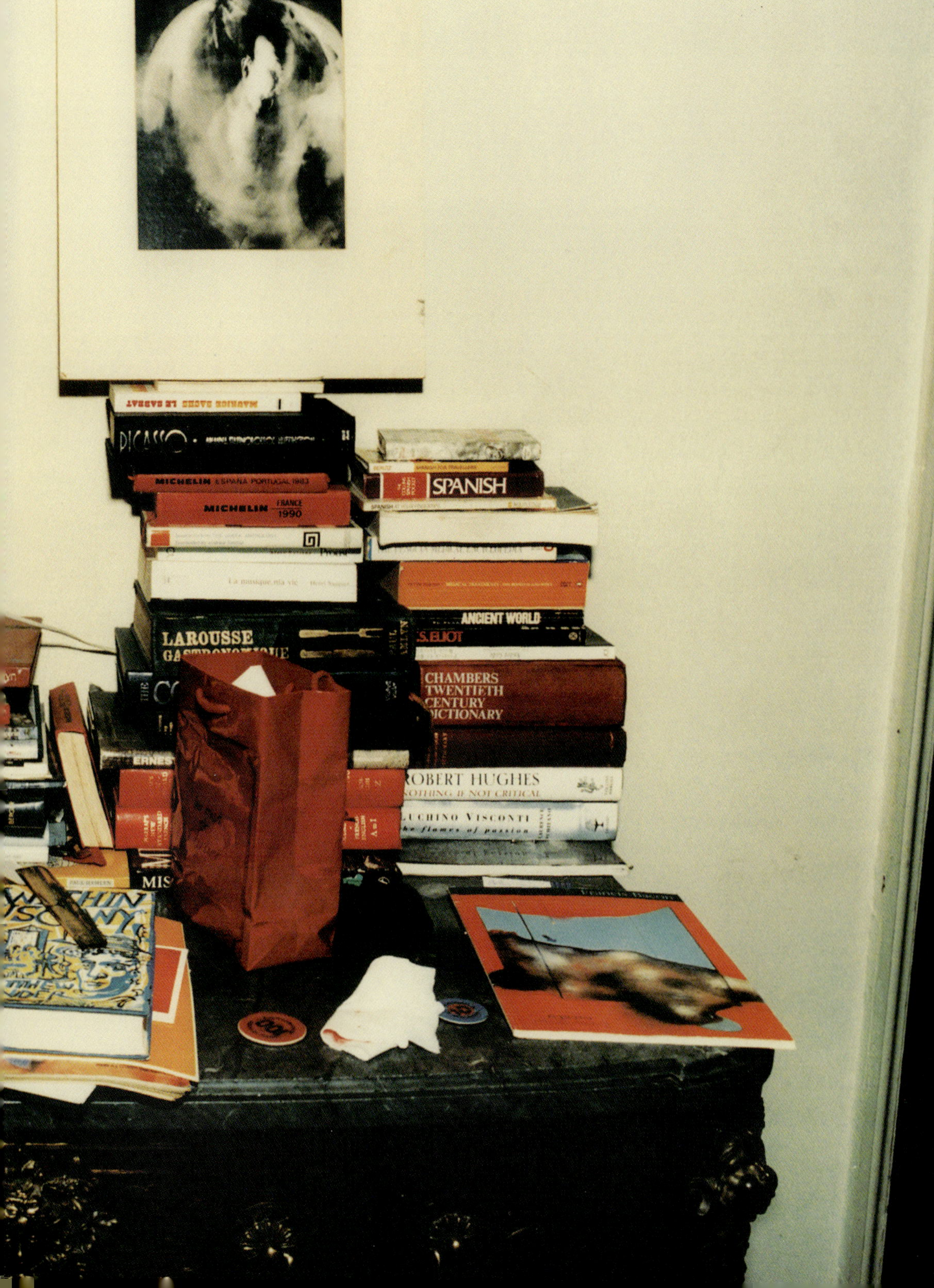

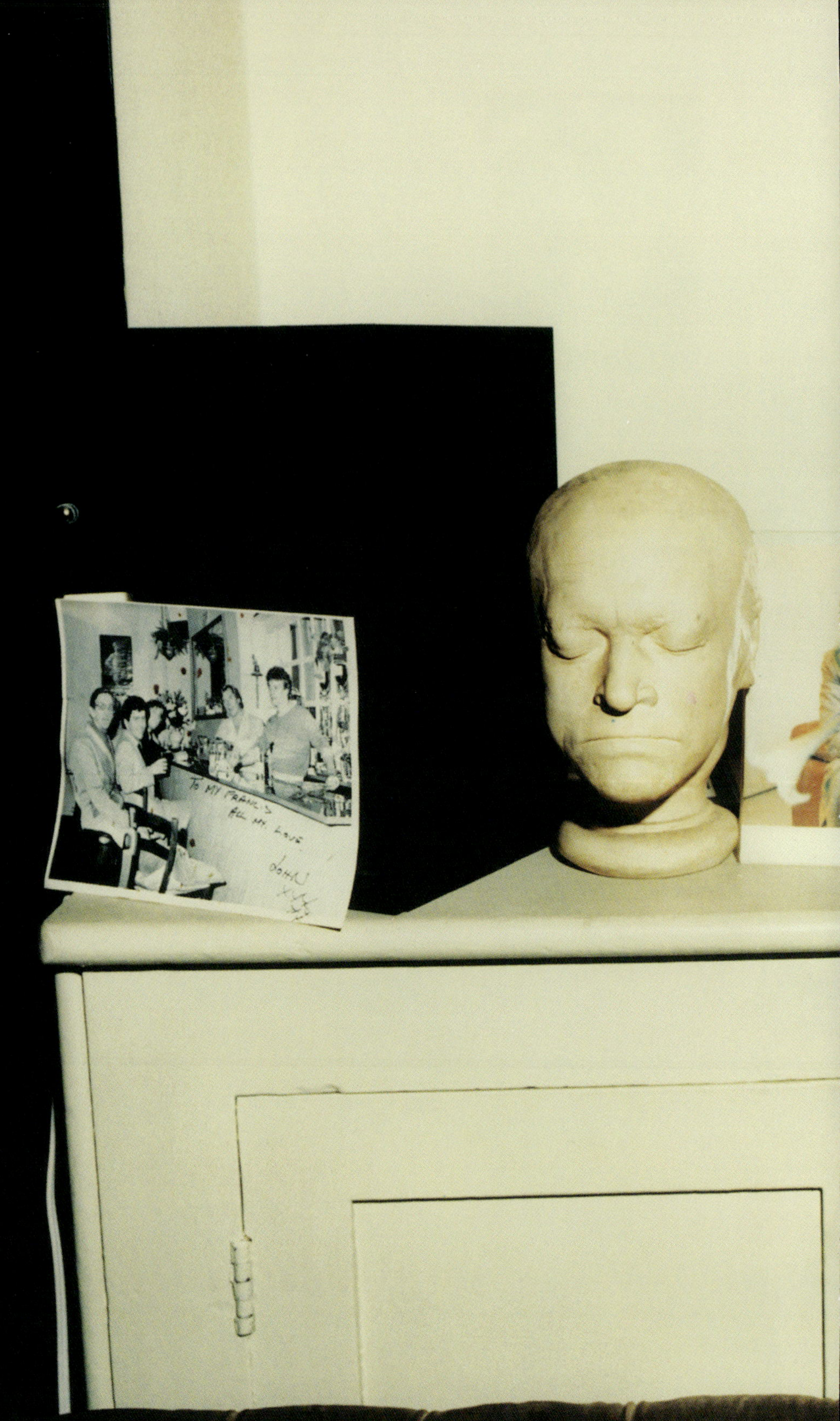
To my Francis
All my love,
John
xxx

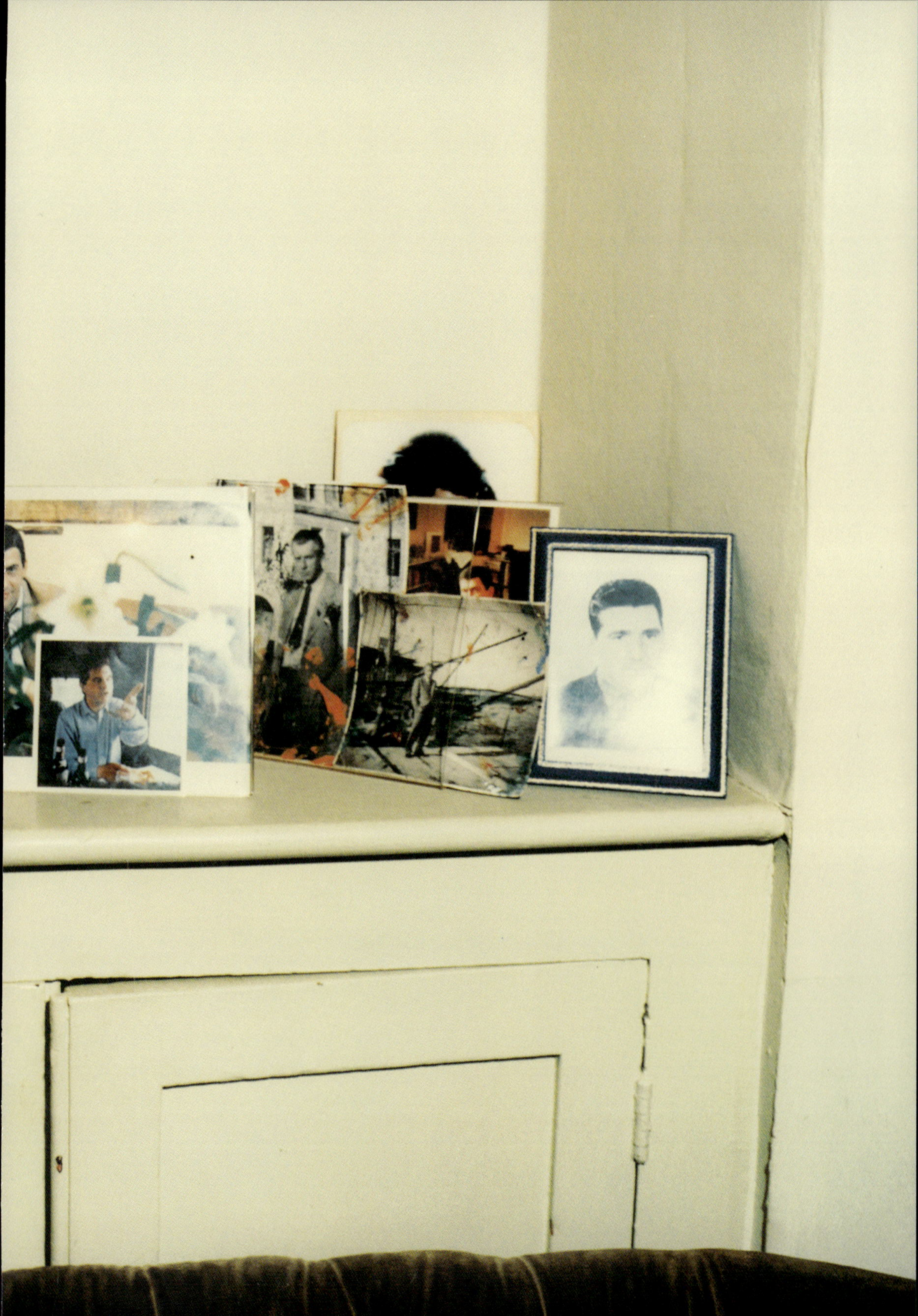

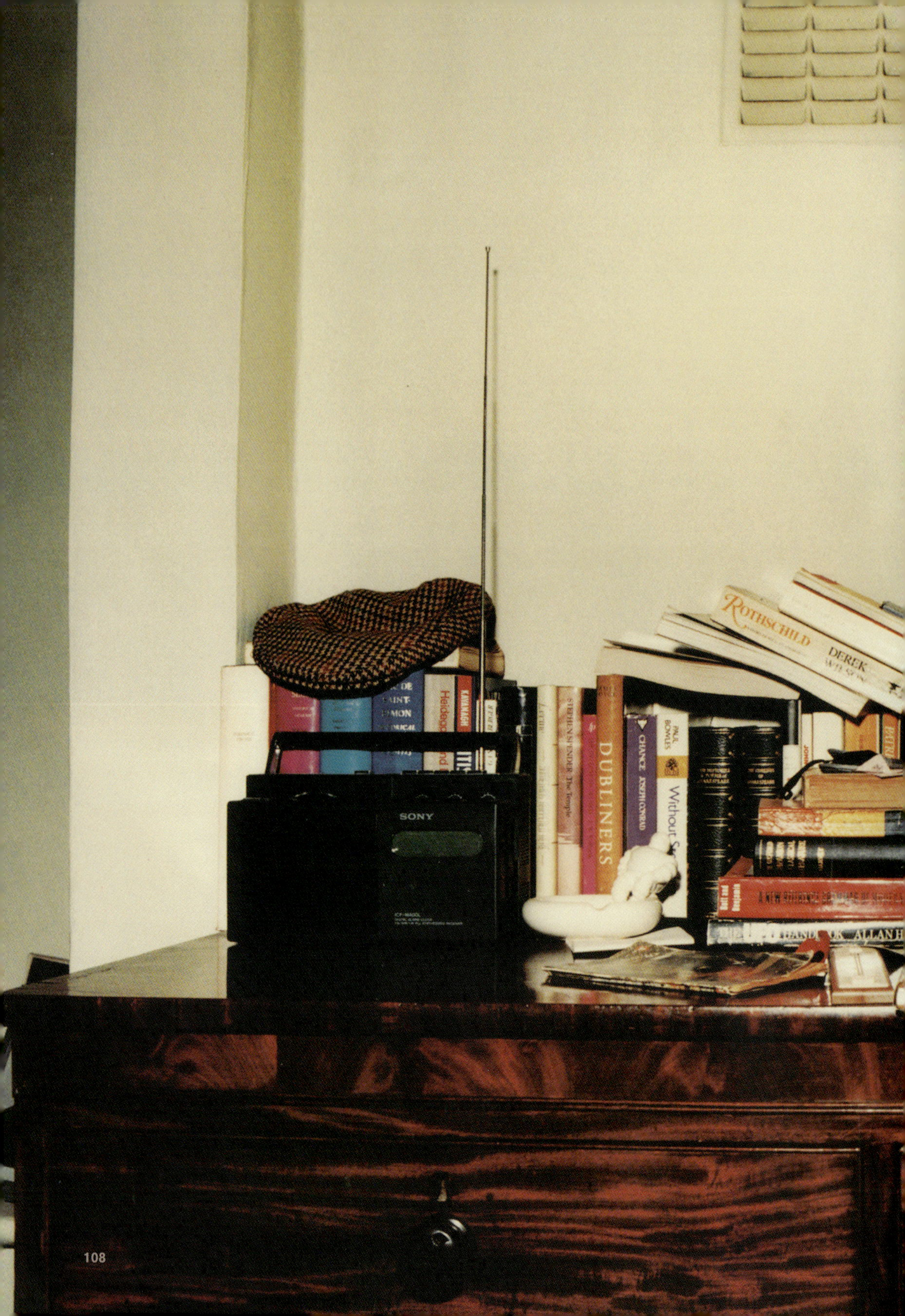

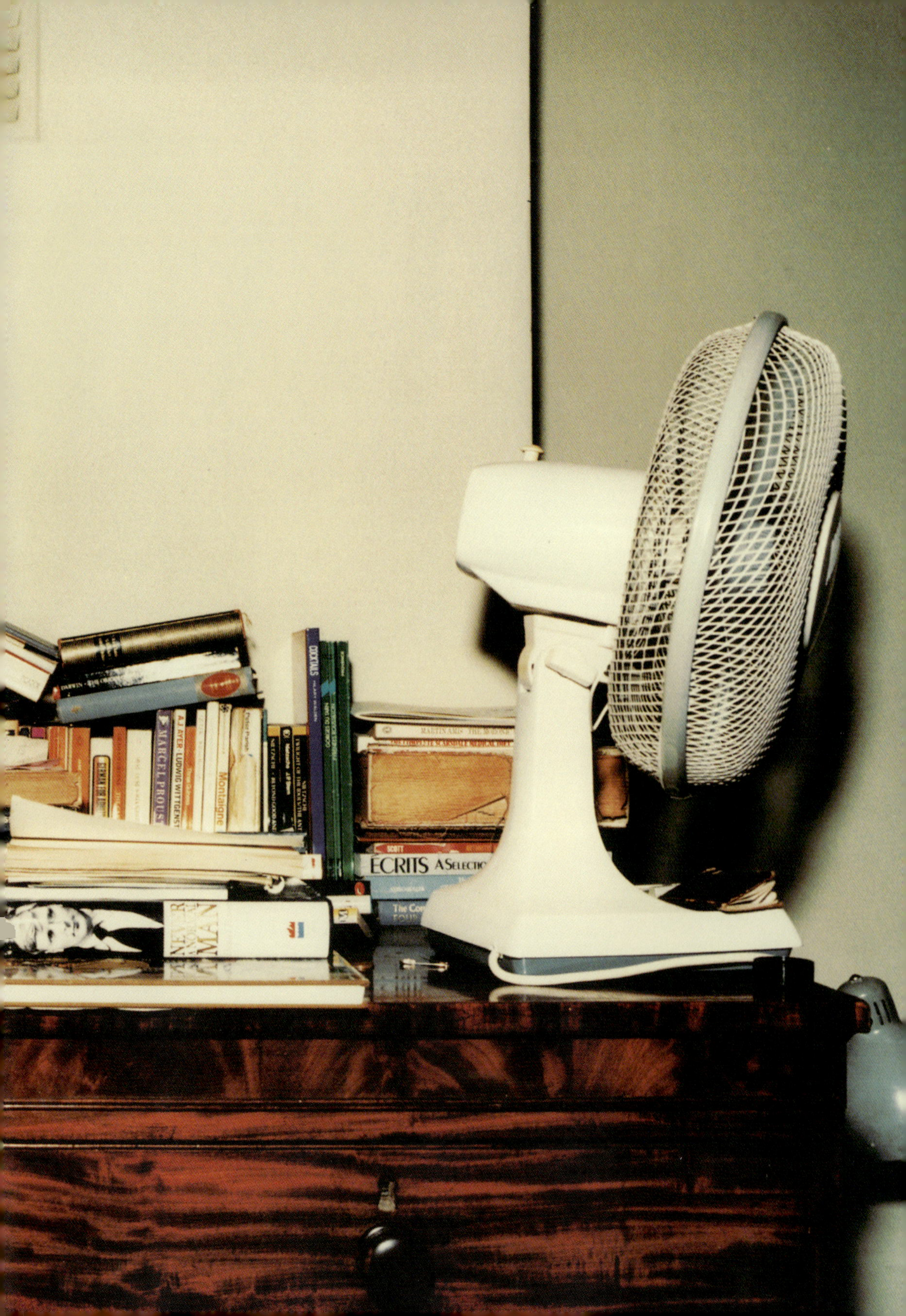
MARCEL PROUST
A.J. AYER LUDWIG WITTGENSTEIN
Montaigne
COCKTAILS
MARTIN AMIS
ÉCRITS A Selection
SCOTT
NEVER A NORMAL MAN

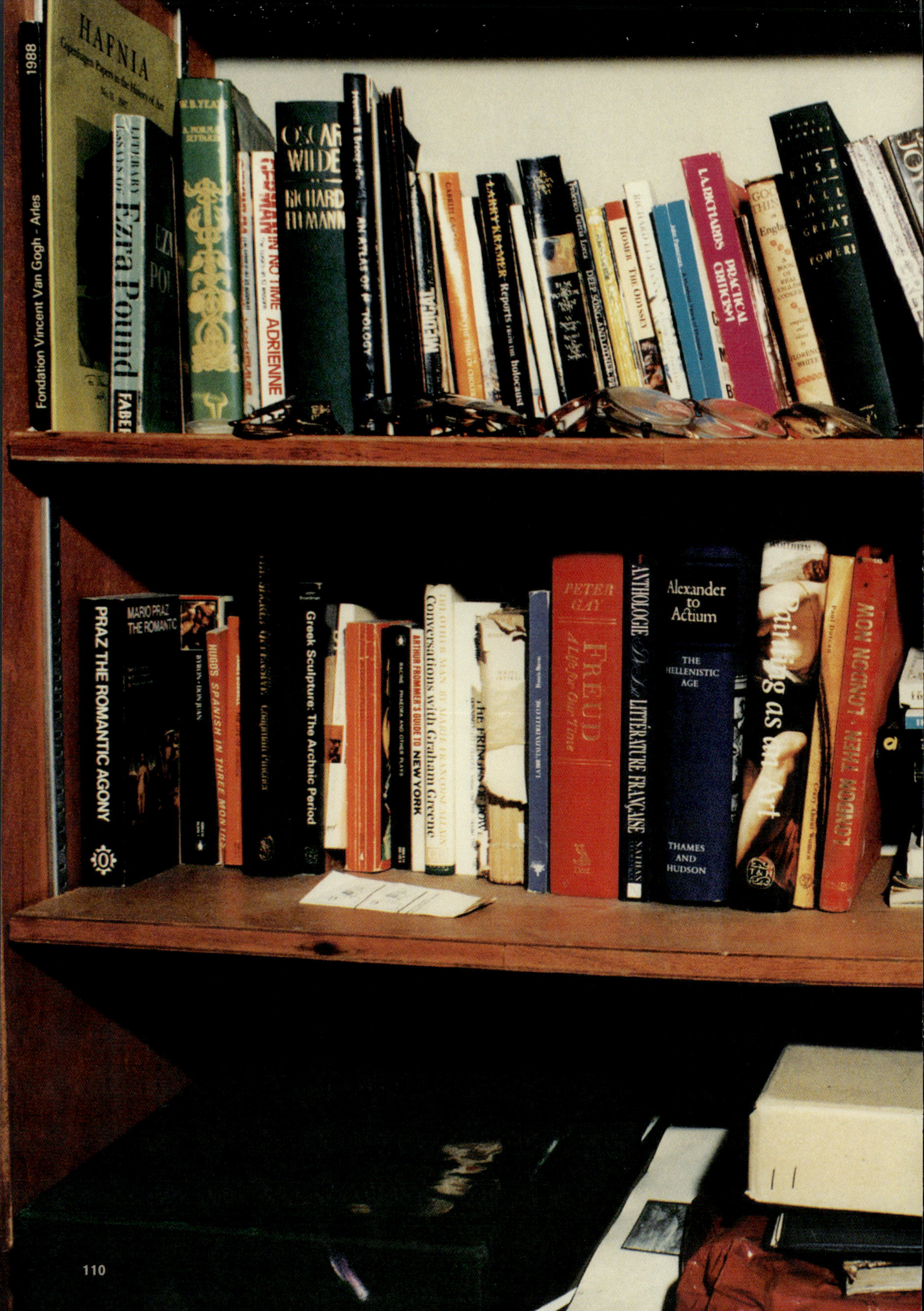

1988
HAFNIA
Copenhagen Papers in the History of Art
Fondation Vincent Van Gogh - Arles
Ezra Pound
FABER
W.B. YEATS
OSCAR WILDE
RICHARD ELLMANN
IN NO TIME
ADRIENNE
AN ATLAS OF ANATOLOGY
LARRY KRAMER Reports from the holocaust
DEEP SONG AND OTHER
HOMER THE ODYSSEY
I.A. RICHARDS
PRACTICAL CRITICISM
THE RISE AND FALL OF THE GREAT POWERS
PRAZ THE ROMANTIC AGONY
MARIO PRAZ THE ROMANTIC
BYRON · DON JUAN
SPANISH IN THREE MONTHS
Greek Sculpture: The Archaic Period
ARTHUR FROMMER'S GUIDE TO NEW YORK
Conversations with Graham Greene
PETER GAY
FREUD A Life for Our Time
Alexander to Actium
ANTHOLOGIE DE LA LITTÉRATURE FRANÇAISE
THE HELLENISTIC AGE
THAMES AND HUDSON
Painting as an Art
LONDON THEN LONDON NOW

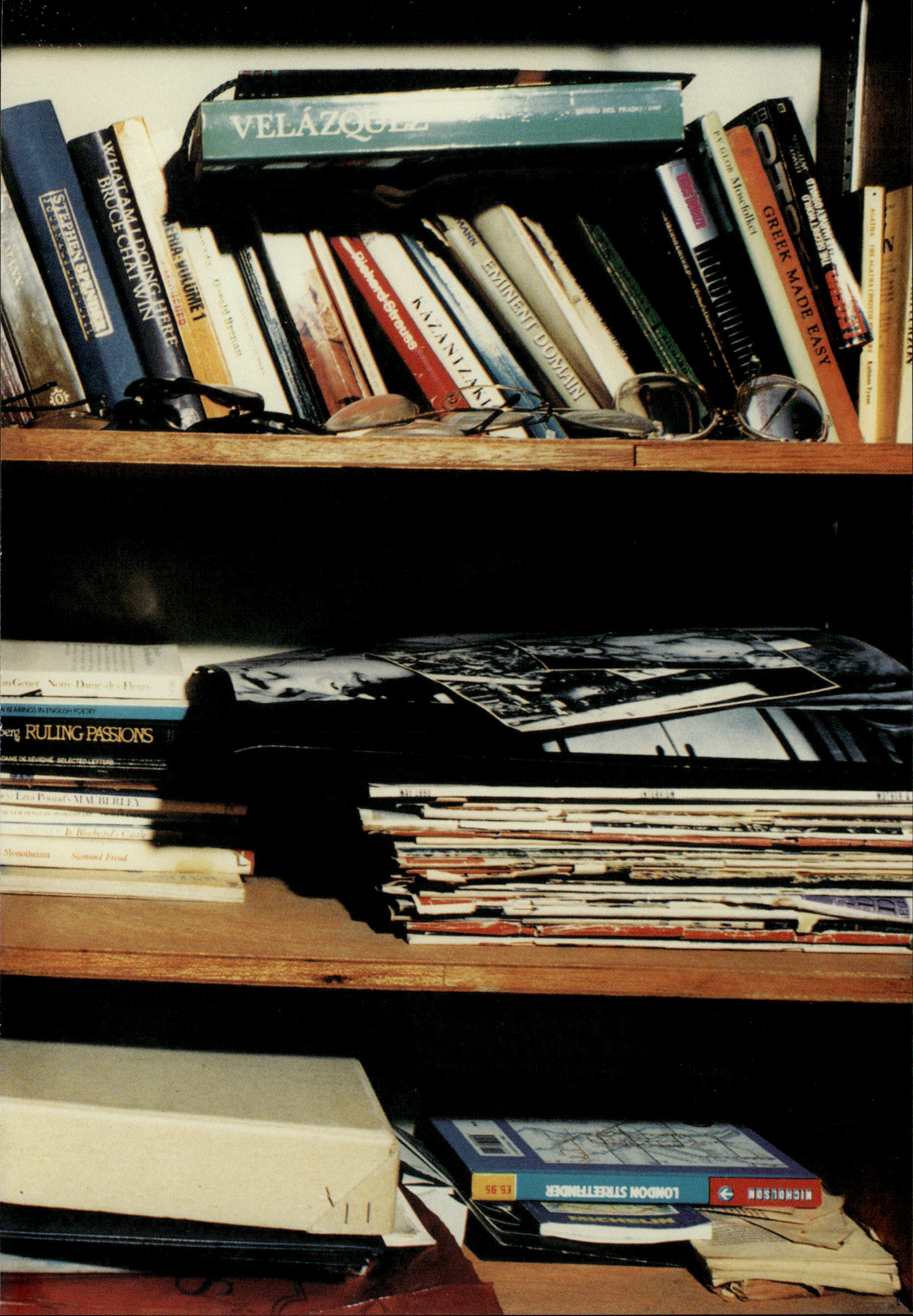

'For some reason the moment I saw this place
I knew that I could work here. I am very influenced
by places – by the atmosphere of a room, you
know. And I just knew from the very moment that
I came here that I would be able to work here.'

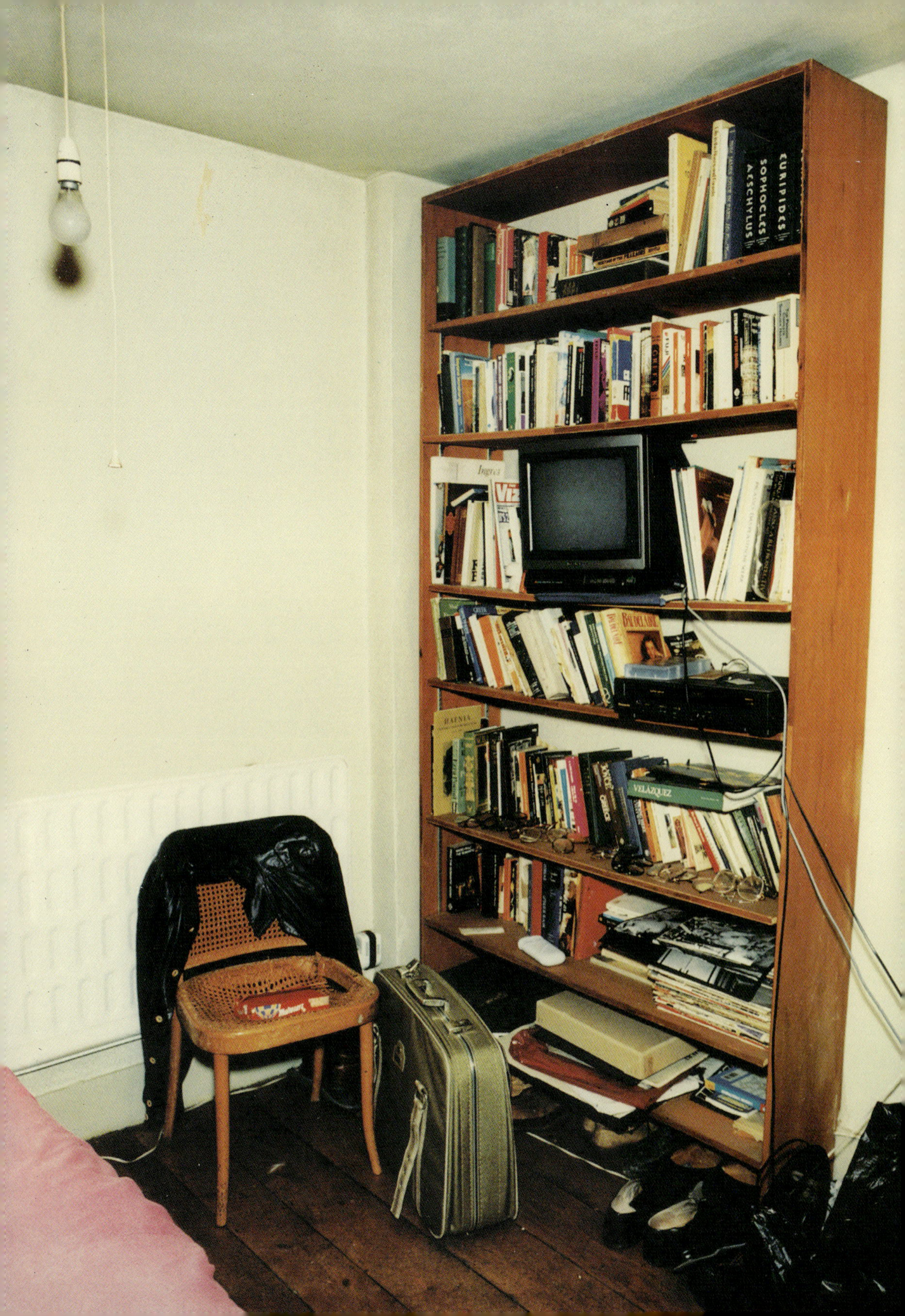

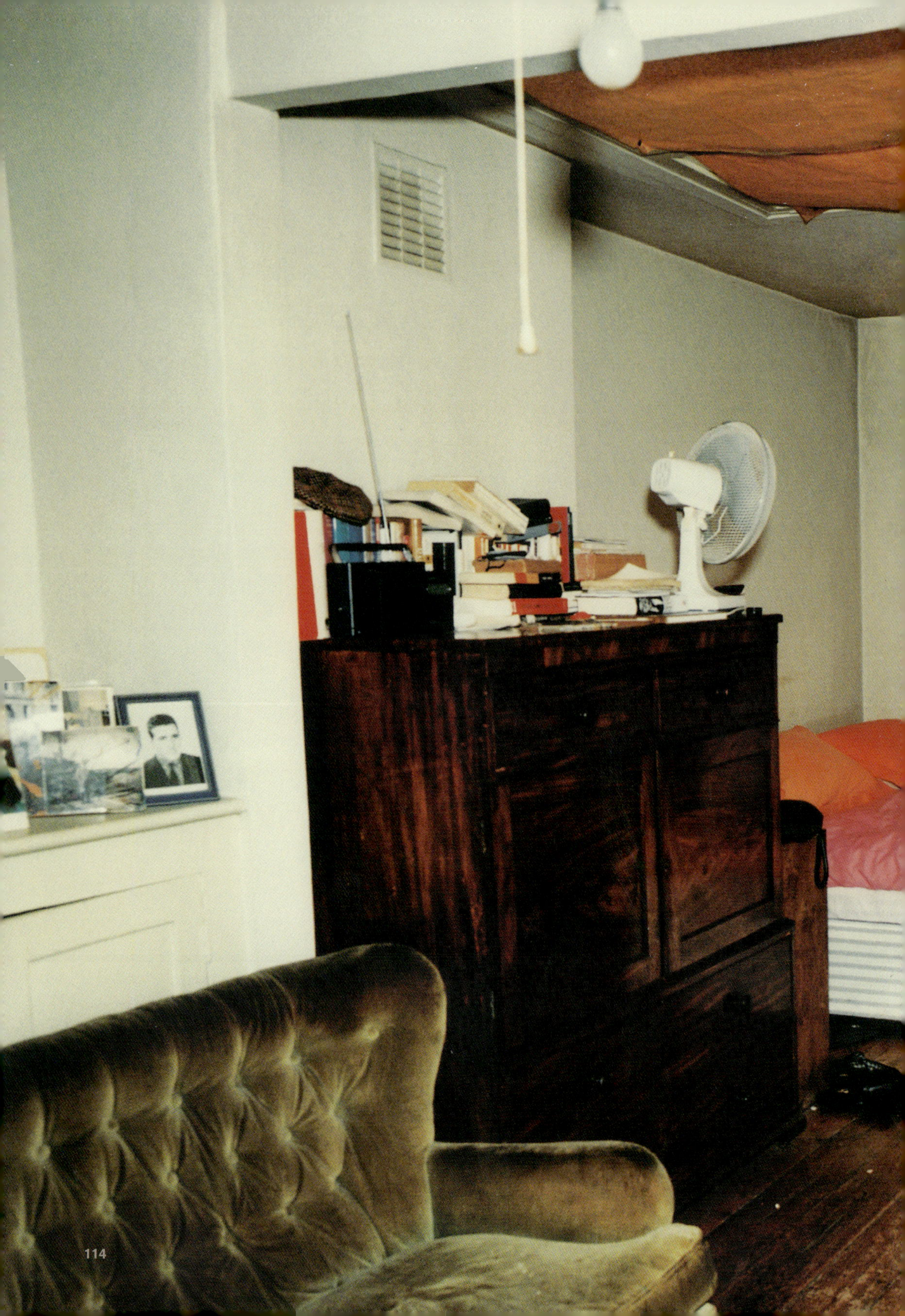

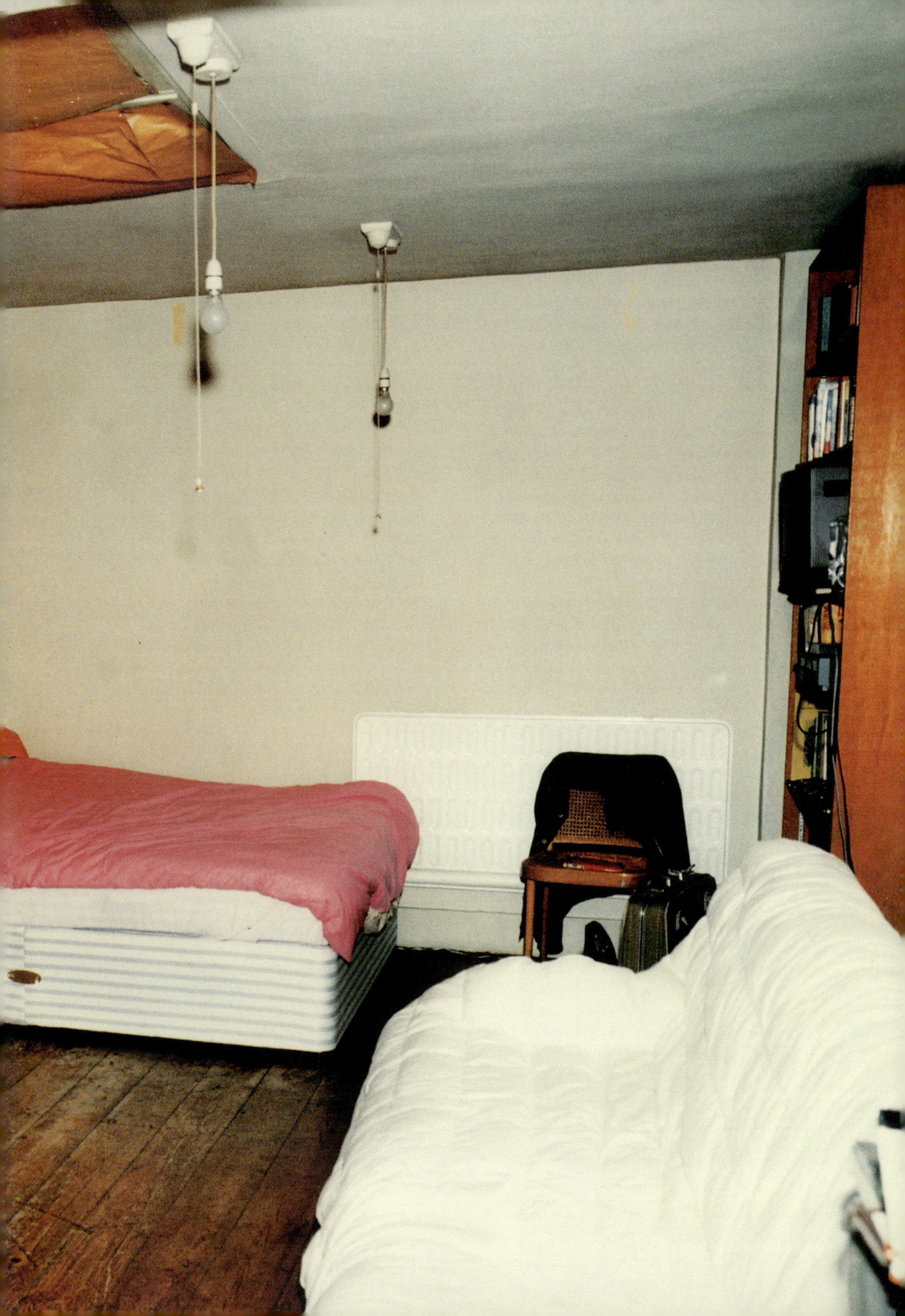

Notes to the Illustrations

Pages 14–15

This view from the door shows a large circular mirror on the end wall. It is likely that Bacon designed the mirror in the 1930s, when he was making his name as a furniture designer.

Pages 16–17

Pinned to the wall is a poster or book proof featuring two large triptychs that Bacon painted in the 1970s. The top half shows *Triptych 1974/77*, in its original state, before Bacon revised it in 1977 by painting out the figure on a bar in the foreground of the central panel. The lower half shows *Triptych August 1972*. The fragment of canvas in front of the shelves was cut from *Study for Man with Microphones*, 1946.

Pages 18–19

The black-and-white photograph on the left is an enlargement of American photographer and writer Peter Beard's passport photo. A large amount of material relating to Beard has been found in the studio. Bacon first met him at the Clermont Club in London in 1965 at the launch of Beard's book *The End of the Game*. His photographs of wildlife in Africa impressed Bacon and they became friends.

Pages 20–1

This unfinished canvas was on the easel when Bacon died and is now in the collection of The Hugh Lane Gallery, Dublin. Although it was initially thought to have been the beginnings of a self-portrait, the head of the figure bears a close resemblance to George Dyer, Bacon's lover for a time in the 1960s. Bacon's relationship with Dyer, whom he met in late 1963, was stormy and ultimately proved tragic. Two days before the opening of Bacon's retrospective at the Grand Palais in Paris in 1971, Dyer was found dead from a drink and drugs overdose in the bathroom of a Parisian hotel. Bacon painted portraits of Dyer obsessively, both before and after Dyer's death.

Page 26

This paint-splattered photograph of George Dyer in profile was taken by photographer John Deakin around 1964. Deakin was part of the Soho crowd and was a friend of Bacon's. Over 120 of his photographs were found in the studio, and while most of them are tattered and torn, their visual impact is still enormous. Many of Bacon's portraits were based on photographs he commissioned from Deakin, including those of George Dyer, Lucian Freud, Isabel Rawsthorne, Muriel Belcher and Henrietta Moraes. The central panel of *Three Studies for Portrait of George Dyer*, 1964, relates closely to this photograph.

Page 27

A photograph of Bacon in the kitchen at 7 Reece Mews, one of several taken by Peter Stark in the early 1970s. Bacon appears to have used these photographs as a source of inspiration for *Self-portrait*, 1973.

Pages 30–1

Among the numerous items seen here are photographs of Bacon's friend and fellow painter Lucian Freud, George Dyer, Bacon's sister Ianthe Knott, and a contact sheet of photographs of African wildlife taken by Peter Beard.

Page 36

Bacon had a keen interest in forensic pathology, skin disorders, surgery and other medical matters. This book on skin diseases is one of the many medical textbooks found in the studio. Imagery such as this clearly appealed to Bacon's artistic imagination, and some of his paintings from the 1980s feature gaping wounds based on the illustrations.

Page 37

A fragment of a photographic contact sheet with photos of two male wrestlers by an unknown photographer. It has been suggested that Bacon himself directed this photography, which probably dates from the 1970s. This series of photographs relates closely to works such as *Painting*, 1978.

Pages 46–7

An open drawer of the main table in the studio, showing clockwise from far left: a colour photograph of John Edwards, Bacon's companion for the last eighteen years of his life; a colour photograph of the right-hand panel of Bacon's painting *Three Studies for a Portrait of John Edwards*, 1984; a colour photograph of Swiss sculptor and painter Alberto Giacometti; and a leaf torn from pioneering photographer Eadweard Muybridge's book *The Human Figure in Motion* attached with sellotape to a piece of card.

Pages 48–9

The tools of Bacon's trade. He used not only conventional artists' brushes but also household rollers, old socks, bits of towel, rag and corduroy, and even cotton wool to apply his paint. For his palette, he used the walls of the studio or the backs of canvases.

Pages 54–5

One of Bacon's most frequently recurring motifs, especially from the 1970s on, was a bare lightbulb hanging from above, just like those seen dangling from the ceiling of his studio.

Page 60

A photograph of Lucian Freud, taken by John Deakin in the early 1960s. Freud was the subject of a number of Bacon's portraits.

Page 61

A photograph of George Dyer posing in the studio, taken by John Deakin around 1964.

Pages 62–3

The seventeenth-century Spanish painter Diego Velázquez was a constant influence on Bacon's work. The celebrated series of 'Popes' from the 1950s and early 1960s were based on Velázquez's portrait of Pope Innocent X in the Doria Pamphili, Rome. Bacon told critic David Sylvester, 'I've always thought that this was one of the greatest paintings in the world and I've had a crush on it.'

Page 73

Georges Seurat's cool and precise pointillist style may seem a world away from Bacon's explosive, often violent imagery, but the French neo-impressionist was in fact one of his favourite artists. When Bacon was asked to choose some paintings from the collection of the National Gallery in London for an exhibition, one of the works he selected was Seurat's *Bathers*.

He preferred Seurat's oil sketches, however: 'I think he was much more profound in his sketches – profound is the wrong word to use – I think he was more mysterious in his sketches than he was in his big finished pictures, although I love the big finished pictures for their grandeur.'

Pages 80–1

Among the newspapers and empty cases of vintage wine lie several small portraits that Bacon evidently thought unsuccessful. Bacon destroyed or asked other people to destroy a considerable number of his works.

Pages 88–9

This painting was first exhibited in 1946 as *Study for Man with Microphones*. Although it was thought that Bacon reworked this painting about 1947–8, this was not the case. Two large sections of the canvas have been cut out, and the lower section was also found in the studio.

Pages 104–5

A photograph by Arnold Newman, a gift to Bacon from the photographer.

Pages 106–7

From left to right: a photograph of John Edwards and friends in Jonathan's Bar, just off Leicester Square, inscribed 'To my Francis all my love John XXX'; a version of a plaster-cast life mask of the artist and poet William Blake made by the English sculptor and phrenologist J. S. Deville in 1823. In the 1950s, the Dutch composer Gerard Schurmann set some of Blake's poems to music and asked Bacon to design an image for the cover of the song cycle. Bacon painted a series of paintings based on the life mask during the mid-1950s; a photograph of John Edwards seated on a sofa; a small colour photograph of Bacon on the Orient Express train, taken by John Deakin in 1965; two black-and-white photographs of Bacon's lover Peter Lacy, who died in 1962; a framed black-and-white photograph of George Dyer.

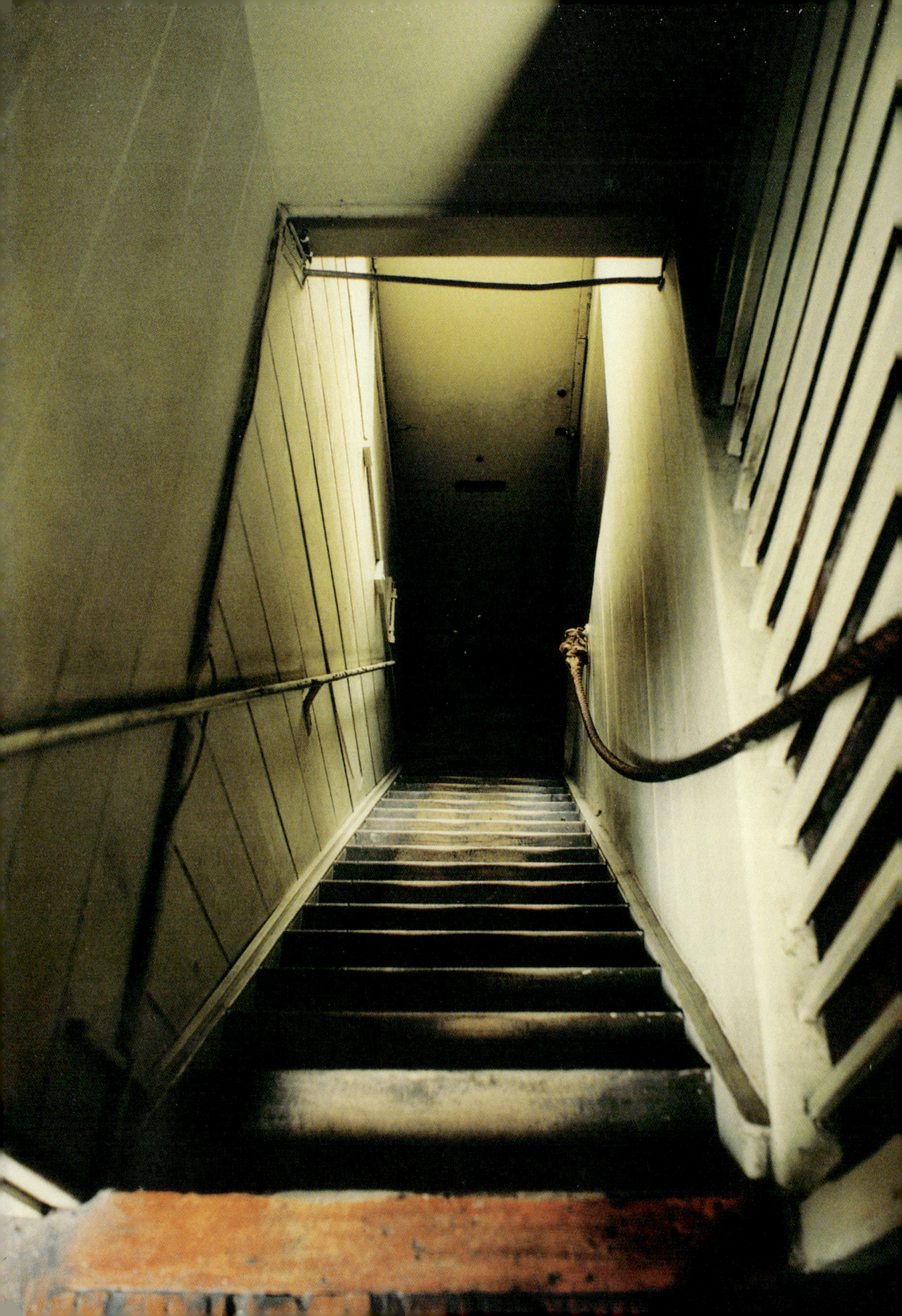

Francis Bacon lived and worked at 7 Reece Mews
from 1961 until his death in 1992. In 1998 John Edwards
donated the studio and its contents to the Hugh Lane
Municipal Gallery of Modern Art in Dublin. Perry Ogden
was invited to take the final photographs of that private
space before its removal from London.

First published in the United Kingdom in 2001 by Thames & Hudson Ltd,
181A High Holborn, London WC1V 7QX

Reprinted 2022

Captions by Dr Margarita Cappock,
The Hugh Lane Municipal Gallery of Modern Art, Dublin

Designed by Ciarán Ó Gaora, Designworks, Dublin

British Library Cataloguing-in-Publication Data
A catalogue record for this book is available from the British Library

ISBN 978-0-500-51034-6

Printed by GPS in Bosnia and Herzegovina

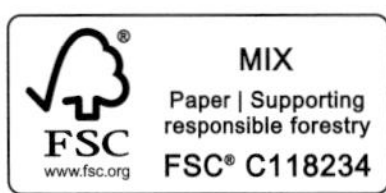